Happy
Birthday -
Merry Christmas

Eleanor & Harry

Thirty-Five Years in the Frying Pan

Books by BILL HOSOKAWA

Thirty-Five Years in the Frying Pan
Thunder in the Rockies
The Two Worlds of Jim Yoshida
Nisei
The Uranium Age

Thirty-Five Years in the Frying Pan

Bill Hosokawa

McGRAW-HILL BOOK COMPANY 1978

New York St. Louis San Francisco Mexico Toronto Dusseldorf

Book design by Anita Walker Scott.

1 2 3 4 5 6 7 8 9 B P B P 7 8 3 2 1 0 9 8

Library of Congress Cataloging in Publication Data

Hosokawa, Bill.
Thirty-five years in the frying pan.
1. Japanese Americans—Social conditions.
2. Japanese Americans—Evacuation and relocation,
1942–1945. 3. Hosokawa, Bill. 4. Pacific citizen.
I. Title.
E184.J3H623   301.45′19′56073   78–9534
ISBN 0–07–030435–1
Published in association with
SAN FRANCISCO BOOK COMPANY

To memories,
fickle and elusive companions of life,
which reward us best with gentle prodding.

MEMORANDUM FOR THE SECRETARY OF WAR

The Japanese race is an enemy race and while many second and third generation Japanese born on United States soil, possessed of United States citizenship, have become "Americanized," the racial strains are undiluted. . . . That Japan is allied with Germany and Italy in this struggle is no ground for assuming that any Japanese, barred from assimilation by convention as he is, though born and raised in the United States, will not turn against this nation when the final test of loyalty comes. It, therefore, follows that along the vital Pacific Coast over 112,000 potential enemies, of Japanese extraction, are at large today. There are indications that these are organized and ready for concerted action at a favorable opportunity. The very fact that no sabotage has taken place to date is a disturbing and confirming indication that such action will be taken. . . . As the term is used herein, the word "Japanese" includes alien Japanese and American citizens of Japanese ancestry. . . .

I now recommend the following: That the Secretary of War procure from the President direction and authority to designate military areas . . . from which, in his discretion, he may exclude all Japanese, all alien enemies, and all other persons suspected for any reason by the administering military authorities of being actual or potential saboteurs, espionage agents, or fifth columnists. . . .

J. L. DeWitt, Lieutenant General, U.S. Army
February 14, 1942

EXECUTIVE ORDER NO. 9066

Whereas, the successful prosecution of the war requires every possible protection against espionage and against sabotage of national-defense material. . . . Now, therefore, by virtue of the authority vested in me as President of the United States, and Commander in Chief of the Army and Navy, I hereby authorize and direct the Secretary of War, and the Military Commanders whom he may from time to time designate . . . to prescribe military areas in such places and of such extent as he or the appropriate Military Commander may determine, from which any or all persons may be excluded, and with respect to which, the right of any person to enter, remain in, or leave shall be subject to whatever restriction the Secretary of War or the appropriate Military Commander may impose in his discretion. . . .

Franklin D. Roosevelt
February 19, 1942

A PROCLAMATION

February 19th is the anniversary of a sad day in American history. It was on that date in 1942, in the midst of the response to the hostilities that began on December 7, 1941, that Executive Order No. 9066 was issued . . . resulting in the uprooting of loyal Americans. Over one hundred thousand persons of Japanese ancestry were removed from their homes, detained in special camps, and eventually relocated. . . . We now know what we should have known then —not only was the evacuation wrong, but Japanese Americans were and are loyal Americans. On the battlefield and at home, Japanese American [names] have been and continue to be written into our history for the sacrifices and the contributions they have made to the well-being and security of this, our common Nation.

The Executive Order that was issued on February 19, 1942, was for the sole purpose of prosecuting the war with the Axis Powers, and ceased to be effective with the end of those hostilities. Because there was no formal statement of its termination, however, there is concern among many Japanese Americans that there may yet be some life in that obsolete document. I think it appropriate, in this our Bicentennial Year, to remove all doubt on that matter, and to make clear our commitment in the future.

Now, therefore, I, Gerald R. Ford, President of the United States of America, do hereby proclaim that all the authority conferred by Executive Order No. 9066 terminated upon the issuance of Proclamation No. 2714, which formally proclaimed the cessation of the hostilities of World War II on Dec. 31, 1946.

I call upon the American people to affirm with me this American Promise—that we have learned from the tragedy of that long-ago experience forever to treasure liberty and justice for each individual American, and resolve that this kind of action shall never again be repeated.

Gerald R. Ford
February 19, 1976

Contents

Preface

Late in the 19th Century, when Europeans were migrating to the United States by the tens of thousands annually, a tiny trickle of Japanese started to these shores. By 1910 there were fewer than 75,000 Japanese immigrants here.

Most of them had come with no intention of staying permanently. They hoped to set aside enough from a few years of labor on farms and railroads to go home with a nestegg. Some succeeded. Many others found it impossible to save up enough money to realize their dreams.

As the years slipped by these immigrants found they liked living in America despite the harshness of their lot. They were the targets of a virulent anti-Orientalism. They were denied the right to become naturalized citizens. Anti-alien land laws prevented them from buying property. Still they persisted.

These were the *Issei,* a Japanese word meaning "first

generation." These were the immigrants, unschooled in American ways, yet driven by a desire to improve their lot here. "No immigrant group encountered higher walls of prejudice and discrimination," Harvard's Edwin O. Reischauer has written.

In 1924 the United States passed a law prohibiting further immigration from Japan. By then a new generation was on its way—the American-born offspring of the Japanese immigrants. In appearance these youngsters were Japanese. But they were United States citizens by right of birth. They were educated in the public schools. Although influenced to a degree by their ancestral culture, in the same way as children of European immigrants, their outlook was American.

These were the *Nisei,* the "second generation."

Unfortunately, America wasn't quite ready to accept them. The *Issei* and *Nisei,* totaling less than 127,000 in 1940, were largely confined to farms and Oriental ghettoes on the West Coast. Many *Nisei* were college graduates but their degrees opened few doors of professional, economic, or social opportunity.

This was the situation when World War II came to the Pacific.

The whole world of the Nisei was destroyed on Pearl Harbor Day. Suddenly they were equated with the enemy. The fact of Japanese blood was considered proof of their disloyalty. A syndicated newspaper columnist helped whip up the hysteria with words like these: "Herd 'em up, pack 'em off and give them the inside room of the badlands. Let 'em be pinched, hurt, hungry and dead up against it." A Congressman speaking in the House declared: "I'm for catching every Japanese in America, Alaska and Hawaii now and putting them in concentration camps. Damn them! Get rid of them now!"

The nation's response was to round up everyone of

Japanese descent—aliens and citizens, men and women, the senile aged and tiny youngsters—in all of California and the western portions of Oregon and Washington. More than 110,000 of them were forced to leave their homes and farms and were herded into ten sprawling inland concentration camps. These people were never charged with anything except having Japanese forebears. Not one was convicted of espionage, sabotage or disloyalty.

My wife and I, who are *Nisei,* and our *Sansei* (third generation) son, were evacuated to the camp at Heart Mountain, Wyoming. It was during this evacuation period that I began to write a weekly column for *Pacific Citizen,* the publication of the Japanese American Citizens League.

Late in 1943 my family and I were permitted to leave Heart Mountain and I took a job on the Des Moines (Iowa) *Register.* In 1946 we moved to Denver where we have lived ever since.

Now there are five *Yonsei* (fourth generation) grandchildren in the family. Fortunately the outlook for them is substantially more promising than mine was at their age.

BILL HOSOKAWA

Denver, Colorado
March 1978

1

A Small Contribution

Unlike most other Nisei, Larry Tajiri lost his job on Pearl Harbor day. The majority enjoyed a reprieve from unemployment while hysteria was building up to the proper pitch. Tajiri's problem was that he worked in the New York news bureau of the Asahi newspapers of Japan and it is understandable that FBI agents hurriedly padlocked the premises.

Asahi's bureau chief, who was interned preparatory to being sent home to Japan, somehow managed to transfer Larry title to his middle-aged Studebaker sedan in lieu of severance pay. That dark winter of 1941–42, Tajiri and his wife, Guyo, drove the Studebaker back to their old haunts on the West Coast.

One early spring day Larry happened to visit the Japanese American Citizens League's national headquarters in San Francisco, located in President Saburo Kido's modest law office. The place was frantic with activity. The U.S. Army recently had ordered Japanese Americans evacuated from the West Coast and the volunteer JACL staff was almost overwhelmed by the problems it faced. Directing the activity was Mike Masaoka, the twenty-six-year-old executive secretary and the only paid employee.

That day Tajiri overheard one side of a curt telephone conversation that changed the course of his life. He heard Masaoka say something like this: "No, sorry. Just haven't got time to talk to you now. Good-bye."

"That was the Associated Press," Masaoka explained. "They wanted a statement from JACL." Then he returned to the work that even then was piling up on his desk.

Tajiri as a professional newspaperman was aghast that JACL was so short-handed it couldn't even maintain a proper public relations program. There and then he made up his mind to throw in his lot with JACL.

A few weeks later the Tajiris headed for Salt Lake City, outside the evacuation zone, where wartime JACL headquarters were to be established. His assignment was to convert JACL's sporadically published monthly news organ, Pacific Citizen, *into a viable weekly newspaper.*

Until then Pacific Citizen *had been a sad excuse for a newspaper. In an effort to keep it going, Jimmie Sakamoto in the mid-Thirties volunteered to publish it in Seattle with the staff of his* Japanese American Courier. *Tooru Kanazawa, Jack Maki, and I worked on it at various times. We considered* Pacific Citizen, *even then called simply PC, an unpleasant but necessary chore. Our system was to thumb through a monthly accumulation of Seattle, San Francisco, and Los Angeles Japanese American dailies and rewrite items relating to JACL chapters. Thus, outside of a top policy story or two, the monthly was made up of double-rehashed items about chapter activities, basket socials, and names of newly elected officers.*

2

The first issue of the new **PC** *under Tajiri's editorship was published on June 4, 1942. By then all other West Coast newspapers serving Japanese American communities had closed up shop. The Evacuation from the western portions of California, Oregon, and Washington into fifteen crude detention centers was all but completed. Evacuation of Military Area 2, the eastern half of California, was about to begin. The* **PC** *carried the news under a headline across the top of page one:* ARMY TO ORDER EVACUATION OF MILITARY AREA 2. *A second headline read:* JACL TO CONTEST ATTACK ON CIVIL RIGHTS. *It appeared over a story reporting that the Native Sons of the Golden West, the American Legion, and the California Joint Immigration Committee had filed suit in federal court to deprive Nisei of their right to vote.*

Tajiri's first editorial was titled "U.S. Nisei; 1942" and it said in part:

Born of America, we are citizens of America. Our rights, as those of every other American, are guaranteed us by the Constitution and implemented by the Bill of Rights. The citizenship we possess is our badge of honor. We will not abuse it. The records prove that we have been good citizens. We have accepted every civic responsibility and we have exercised the right of franchise, not as persons of a single race but as citizen Americans in a democratic community. Living among free men, we have lived and acted as free men. We believe in freedom of thought, of speech and of action. . . .

Today we learn that there are men and organized interests in America who would deny those privileges to our children yet unborn. These men claim that we are racially inassimilable. These men besmirch the Constitution which would grant equality to all persons of all races. They would establish Nazi-like "Nuremburg Laws" against us in their

3

hysterical attempts to foster an American version of Hitler's pogroms. Should they succeed their actions menace all Americans. . . . We hold that it is our sacred duty to fight.

In a second editorial, titled "Loyalty Demonstrated," Tajiri wrote:

When military authorities announced that West Coast Japanese, regardless of citizenship, would be uprooted from their homes and placed in government supervised settlements for the duration of the war, the citizen Japanese announced that he was willing to cheerfully cooperate with the dictates of military necessity. Although realizing that he could have protested and fought evacuation and subsequent orders from the standpoint that his rights as an American are no different from the rights of Americans unaffected by the evacuation, the majority of U.S.-born Japanese took the position that no personal hardship should be too great if it contributed to the final American victory. . . . The first thought of all Americans must be for the war and the winning of the war.

The attitude of the American citizen Japanese during evacuation has demonstrated that they are willing to sacrifice everything for the war.

In the best traditions of pioneer journalism (and Nisei journalism was in that stage) the PC's *editorial columns were boldly outspoken. Tajiri's editorials became the rallying cry of Nisei morale during the darkest days of the Evacuation.*

At the time I was in the detention camp hurriedly constructed on the fairgrounds at Puyallup, Washington, a place of disagreeable memory. The new PC's *arrival was awaited impatiently each week. One day a Nisei came up to me with anxiety written on his face and a* PC *in his hands.*

4

"Don't you think," he said, "that this is a little too outspoken?"

I was about to lecture him regarding First Amendment rights when he added: "I'm afraid the Army will clamp down on the Pacific Citizen, and then we'd be left without any newspaper."

Fortunately no one tried to crack down on Tajiri and PC and it went on to become, as Mary Oyama once observed in remarkable understatement, a newspaper "of which the Nisei need not be apologetic or ashamed."

Immediately after the June 4 issue of PC reached Puyallup, I wrote to Tajiri, an old friend, suggesting I would like to contribute to it. He replied warmly, and the first "From the Frying Pan" column appeared June 18, 1942. It was of no great moment and does not deserve quotation here, but the column's name needs explanation.

I had gone to the Far East late in 1938, working first in Singapore and later in Shanghai. In the summer of 1941 it took no prophet to see that war between the United States and Japan was close. Late in July I left Shanghai for Japan, intending to catch a ship and sail home to Seattle. That ship never left. On July 26 President Roosevelt abrogated the treaty of trade and friendship and shipping between Japan and the West Coast came to a standstill. I flew back to Shanghai, and finally in October I was able to find passage aboard a U.S. liner, the President Cleveland. We docked in San Francisco late that month. Six weeks later Japan attacked Pearl Harbor. I was lucky to have leapt from the fire of the Pacific war into the frying pan of evacuation, so that's what I called the column.

The first Frying Pan of any consequence appeared July 2, 1942, and even though it was written from within a concentration camp it was properly patriotic in view of Independence Day:

5

A hundred thousand Americans of Japanese blood and their parents are living unobtrusively behind barbed wire today as their part toward American victory in a fight to the finish against the Axis. Several thousand others, sons, brothers, husbands of those confined to camps, are bearing arms for the United States; some of them already overseas.

A still smaller handful is behind the lines in highly specialized war work—teaching the Japanese language to intelligence officers, studying and analyzing Japanese propaganda, making use of specialized training and aptitude so that the United Nations may emerge victorious.

At the same time there is a persistent voice being heard from within this nation, representing but a small portion of its citizens and calling upon hatred, discrimination, and prejudice because of race.

This is the voice of people who would disenfranchise the Nisei, who would deport everyone of Japanese descent, who would deny the right of citizenship to those not of Caucasian blood, who would rescind the civil rights of American citizens as a gesture of American patriotism.

These people are un-American. They would negate the spirit of the Constitution and disavow the efforts of great men who strove to defend it. They would deny the validity of the principles upon which President Roosevelt outlined the Atlantic Charter.

They would also disrupt the war effort of the United Nations. The issue of race arouses the anxiety of the millions of loyal American Negroes, one-tenth of the total manpower of the United States. They would slap the faces of the courageous Filipino and Chinese allies of America, and of the fearless Indian troops of Britain's armies.

Their voice is the voice of Hitler and the Axis who speak of chosen people and divine mandate to dominate lesser peoples. Theirs is the voice of distrust and dissension.

The Nisei are doing all in their limited power to prove

6

that their Americanism is no sham. Their conduct during the Evacuation and in the first months of reception center life have shown all who have come in contact with them that they are cooperating with America's total war effort.

The Nisei might be able to play a greater and more important part if they had their freedom. This privilege has been denied them.

But they must realize that much of what their position will be after the war will depend on their conduct during the conflict. The battle for recognition has only started. The real battle for the Nisei may well take place in internal conflict after an armistice has been declared along the worldwide battlefronts.

For this we must be prepared. The JACL chose well when it adopted the slogan, "Security Through Unity." The JACL as spokesman for the Nisei has undertaken a task which no other group could hope to accept.

There must be no relaxation of vigilance by this organization, nor must its members cease to support their chosen leaders. Otherwise our fate will be that of a people without a country.

There were other such earnest and ringing columns, but fortunately not many. At first, angry and indignant essays were inevitable, and were welcomed by PC readers who needed someone to express their frustrations and bitterness.

But in time the war ended. The War Relocation Authority camps were closed. In the Frying Pan of January 12, 1946, I wrote:

For almost four years now we have sizzled in the Frying Pan at stupidity and unfairness, reminisced, applauded, cajoled, cast judgment and otherwise inflicted our opinions on the public from this column.

The time has come for reconversion.

7

It is difficult to wax indignant week after week, or to hand down pontifical judgment on the follies of men when times have changed so since the bleak days of the home front war against the West Coast's selective prejudices.

There are signs of the new times:

John Lechner is orating on the Red menace in the California teacup and lorgnette league; Art Ritchie, who was convincing enough to get otherwise solid citizens to pay him a $10 initiation fee for the privilege of hating fellow Americans, is sponsoring appearances of a Filipino guerrilla; Floyd Bowers, who won an acquittal for a dynamiting suspect with the argument that this is a white man's country, is now representing a Japanese American family in a California escheat case; Martin Dies, John Costello and company have gone the way of all political demagogues; Senator E. V. Robertson of Wyoming is back to being the watchdog for the cattle interests; the trained typewriter-punching seals of Hearst, the Denver *Post* and a few other journals long since have found other menaces to pummel.

And so, the editor willing, we plan to reconvert to a column of random comment, trivia, whimsy, useless information and perhaps a little alleged humor.

For old time's sake we may sizzle on an occasion when we feel the world isn't going right. But we hope that will be infrequent.

So Frying Pan became just that, reporting on my thoughts and observations; the antics and problems of our children as they lost baby teeth, went on to school and eventually grew up and left home; the activities and accomplishments of various Nisei; the small pleasures of life like good food and football games and growing tomatoes; the vagaries and uniqueness of Nisei life and reminiscences of an earlier and less complicated time.

Tajiri continued to use the column until he resigned the

8

editorship in 1952. His successor, Harry Honda, didn't ask me to continue. He simply assumed I would, because after ten years Frying Pan had become something of an institution. In the early 1960s, however, Honda made a change. He alternated Frying Pan every other week with a column by Tajiri called "Vagaries." The problem was budget. Honda couldn't afford to pay both Larry and me each week.

After Larry's death in 1965, Frying Pan returned to its weekly schedule. The column has been running now for thirty-five years. That makes it the oldest continuous Nisei feature by far. In that time approximately 1,750 columns were published, and they provide an unusual insight into Japanese American life and thought of this span of years.

Now, largely at the urging of some long-time readers, some of the more interesting columns have been assembled in this book with suitable commentary. In them you will see the Japanese American community maturing, as well as my family. After the early stridency in the writing, there was time for humor, and I hope you will enjoy that, too.

PC's fiscal problems, mentioned above, need a bit of explanation. At first, as I recall, Larry Tajiri paid me fifty cents a column. I had expected no pay when I approached him with the idea, but Tajiri recognized that writing was my profession and insisted I should be compensated if only in token. He was apologetic about the rate, of course, but both of us knew that was all his budget could afford. Eventually Larry raised payment to one dollar per column, then to two dollars, and ultimately to ten dollars which is still the going rate.

No matter. Frying Pan was never written for money, but for fun and as a small contribution to the fabric of Nisei life.

9

2

Indignant Times

We had cooperated in our own incarceration because we had been convinced it was our patriotic duty to do so. But one of the deeper frustrations of the Evacuation stemmed from the fact that politicians continued to snipe at us, and few of the officials who had urged us to cooperate had the courage to stand up for us in opposing the tide of hate.

Among the more vicious measures was a suit (later thrown out) filed in Federal court by U.S. Webb, former Attorney General of California. Its objective was to strip Japanese Americans of their U.S. citizenship. Webb was acting on behalf of the Native Sons of the Golden West, a California organization. About the same time Senator Tom Stewart, Democrat of Tennessee, introduced a bill to confine all Japanese Americans in full-fledged concentration camps.

That sort of harassment led to this Frying Pan column on July 16, 1942:

". . . they are not of an assimilable race and they are strangers to our customs, our way of life, and it is utter folly to expect the Japanese viewpoint to become American. . . . The people of the United States generally cannot realize the harm that has already resulted from the presence of Japanese on the Pacific Coast and if they are permitted to live at large among us the possibility of disaster cannot be reckoned."

These words report the opinion, not of a chuckleheaded crackpot, but of a supposedly responsible attorney general of one of the Western states where Japanese residents have established an admirable record for citizenship, industry, and public spirit for more than a quarter of a century.

The words are quoted from a Congressional report presented by Senator Stewart regarding a bill authorizing the Secretary of War to take into custody all persons of Japanese race.

The editor of the *Pacific Citizen* has assailed the bill vigorously and well. Americans could take no stand other than to protest such an action.

But the point that intrigues those of us who were born and grew up as Americans, who were taught to live the American way of life, is how Americans in public life can betray so shamelessly the principles they are pledged to defend and for which they are supposed to stand.

". . . if they (the Japanese) are permitted to live at large among us the possibility for disaster cannot be reckoned."

What sort of alarmist talk is this, and how villainous that 1-1000th portion of the population of the United States made up of Japanese has become in the last few months.

The Japanese have lived "at large" in almost every state in the Union for almost a generation now without dire results. In fact, they contributed mightily to the development and wealth of great sections of the West and played a role no less proportionate than any other racial group in creating the America of today.

Within the past decade anti-alien land legislation came up in the state whose attorney general now makes these unfounded charges regarding the Japanese. At that time legislator after legislator got up to denounce the Filipino element against whom the legislation was directed, and not a word was said publicly against the Japanese. That is in the record.

Thus has it been with the Chinese, the Jews, the Negroes, the Catholics and other minority groups. Each in their turn have been attacked. Right now the particular victim is the Japanese.

Surely it is un-American to kick a man when he is down, but that is exactly what is taking place. Yet it is still more un-American to give up when the going seems tough.

Thinking Americans cannot stand by and watch their fascist-minded politicians victimize a minority group, for America's majority is made up of many minorities. The persecution of one group easily can become the persecution of others.

We paraphrase scripture: What availeth it a nation to win democratic principles for the world when it loseth them at home?

One afternoon several weeks after this column appeared, I was summoned to the office of J. J. McGovern, director of the Puyallup camp. He told me the Army had ordered that I, together with my wife Alice and infant son Mike, was to be sent that very day to the Heart Mountain War Relocation (WRA) camp in Wyoming.

It had been announced previously that the people in the temporary Puyallup camp, where I had been locked up with other Seattleites, would soon be moving to the semipermanent WRA camp at Minidoka, Idaho.

"Why is the Army separating me from my friends?" I asked McGovern.

He said he didn't know, he was simply following orders. But the answer was obvious. The Army considered me a potential trouble-maker. The Army was sending me out among strangers with whom I was likely to have a minimum of influence.

I was given four hours to pack. That was no problem. We had been able to bring only what we could carry into camp. At dusk, with Mike in my arms, Alice and I were escorted out the main gate. A large crowd gathered behind the barbed wire to bid us goodbye. I didn't have the courage to look back. We had no idea when we would see our friends again.

A guard accompanied us aboard a train and took a seat across from ours. Sleep was hard to come by that dreary night. Next morning the train stopped in Spokane. It was as far east as I had been in the United States. Late that second night we got off at Billings, Montana, and were taken to a small hotel. In the morning we climbed on another train for Deaver, Wyoming, a little whistle stop where a WRA official accepted our custody.

For some reason I still don't understand now, I mentioned none of this in Frying Pan. Perhaps, at that stage, I did not want to personalize the column. Perhaps I felt that the experiences of adjusting to the frontier conditions at Heart Mountain were too familiar, too commonplace to make good reading matter for other Nisei. At any rate, the column continued to yammer at the native fascists much of the time with little personal mention.

In November 1942, JACL called an emergency meeting in Salt Lake City and was given WRA permission to summon two representatives from each of the camps. I was surprised to be asked to attend, and even more surprised that

I was allowed to go. The long bus ride across the length and breadth of Wyoming from Heart Mountain to Salt Lake, the first freedom I had enjoyed in six months, produced this column on November 19:

He was a young red-headed soldier who talked with the drawl of Dixieland, and he had kept the whole bus entertained most of the evening with his quick humor. Somehow the talk turned to Negroes, and the redhead went to town.

"I'll put 'em in their place," he was saying. He didn't like the way some Negro sat down beside him at the last bus stop.

"I tol' 'im, 'nigger get out of here an' don' you never sit down by a white man.' "

"That's right," the fat woman from St. Louis said. "Back in St. Louis we put them in their place, and they ride their own buses and stay in their own districts."

Now it was the Georgia woman's turn. She talked with a drawl, too, and she said Jews were "just niggers turned inside out. They can make money on a popcorn stand and they stink."

The red-headed soldier was talking again. "One night I had a gal out in Seattle who said a nigger was just as good as any other man. I says, 'Honey chile, I guess you want to go home right now,' and so I took her home and I ain't went back since."

The others in the bus had kept their peace, but now a slim, quiet girl with corn-colored hair said suddenly: "I wouldn't be judging others by yourself." The others stopped to listen. "I think any man is just as good as any other man and I wouldn't hate a man on account of his race."

The redhead flared up: "If you want to go live with a nigger, go ahead."

"I don't want to live with a colored man," the girl retorted, "but that doesn't stop me from respecting him."

14

The soldier shut up. The fat woman from St. Louis and the woman from Georgia kept quiet. The bus rolled on.

This was in the washroom at Cheyenne. Three soldiers were standing around drinking out of a pint whiskey bottle when they saw me come in.

"Betcha he's Chinese," one of them said.

"Naw, he's Japanese," another said.

The third said: "Let's ask him," and they did.

"I'm an American," I said.

The three suddenly stood up a little straighter and one of them came forward with his right hand extended and said, "Put 'er there, fellow, we're all Americans." The one with the bottle offered me a drink.

The third said: "Sure, we're all Americans. But tell me, what's your descent? Japanese or Chinese?"

I told him.

"Hell," he said, "I'm of German descent. What the hell, we're all Americans." We shook hands all around.

America is a great, grand country whose horizons are almost endless. On her broad plains grow the wheat and the corn that will help feed the post-war world. In the foothills and on the prairies graze the cattle and sheep which will help to meet the needs of the world for meat and wool and hides.

It's a great, rich and glorious country, and the only things mean and petty about it are the prejudices of some of her people. Jew, Gentile or "Jap," white, colored, or yellow, they're all Americans.

We often wonder about what that red-headed soldier believes in, and what he thinks he's fighting for with the millions of other fine Americans in uniform.

Some of the most persistent foes of the evacuees were the newspapers—the Hearst press, the Los Angeles Times *and*

15

the Denver Post, *among others. The* Post, *because it was widely circulated in Wyoming as well as Colorado, took frequent potshots at Heart Mountain, and Frying Pan fired back. This next column appeared April 1, 1943:*

Just when we thought we had the "coddling" and "pampering" issue regarding operation of WRA centers pretty well straightened out, the Denver *Post* came out late in March with a vicious cartoon calculated to do the evacuee's position no good. The *Post,* renown in journalistic history for its utter lack of inhibitions, still doesn't bother to pull its punches, and it certainly wasn't thinking about the welfare of the evacuees when it published this cartoon.

Technically, the WRA's treatment of evacuees wasn't attacked at all because part of the cartoon is a sign on the wall which labels the scene as a Japanese alien enemy concentration camp. But the loose manner in which concentration camp and relocation center have been used interchangeably by the popular press makes it inevitable that the public—never much at trying to keep such technicalities straight—will think of WRA centers. . . .

The cartoon depicts a toothy and repulsive-looking Japanese family sitting about a dinner table while a tall, smiling Uncle Sam looms nearby, standing like a waiter at attention with a great trayful of things labeled "meat" and "luxuries."

A buck-toothed little "Jap" is saying: "Home was never like this," and everyone is grinning happily while an American couple with a child, all three looking thin and wan, are outside gazing hungrily through the window. . . .

The issue of whether or not we are being pampered and allowed to get fat has been pretty well settled in some convincing statements by investigators who should be in position to know. In fact the statements of some congressional investigators, who pointedly acknowledge the fact that the evacuees were being treated to no frills, were published with some prominence in the *Post* itself.

Now comes the cartoon. It has taken much time and effort to try to convince timid evacuees that the world is not full of super-patriots just waiting to slit their throats should they ever set foot outside the centers' barbed wire confines. It has also taken much time and effort to educate some of the general American public about the evacuees, and the part that these people can play in the nation's war effort. . . .

We are against government regulation or restriction of newspapers because we believe in journalistic responsibility. But surely the manner of presentation and circumstances surrounding the publication of this cartoon indicate an utter lack of a sense of responsibility. Its publication can be termed only as malicious, and we have no place for that sort of journalism in this country, especially when we are striving for national unity. . . .

That cartoon could not have done a single thing to promote the national war effort. The damage it did is immeasurable.

A little more than three years later, after the Post *came under new management, I went to work for it and met Paul Gregg, the man who had drawn the cartoon. He was a kind, gentle person, quite unaware of the damage his drawing pen could do. We became friends.*

Frying Pan continued to joust with the hate-mongers, but it was a feeble and ineffective voice in terms of winning public sympathy. But sometimes there were more encouraging columns, such as this one dated May 13, 1943:

The barrage of anti-evacuee activity set off by the Denver *Post*, and echoed by politicians who know of no better way to get newspaper space, emphasizes more than ever the need for a comprehensive public relations program.

On the government front, the church front, the liberal organizations front, and in a number of other places we have made considerable progress in getting recognition of the special problems of the evacuees. But there is much to be done with the general public.

A government official (not WRA) of Jewish descent dropped in the other day, and although he had come in to talk business he got sidetracked on evacuee problems and spent more than an hour giving his views. In retrospect, his most important contribution to the issue was a reminder of the power within a postage stamp.

His thesis was that the American people are fundamentally good. A public figure popping off about the evacuees does not necessarily mean that he is unalterably opposed to Americans of Japanese descent, he contended. In his opinion it was much more likely that the individual is honestly misinformed, and is willing to hear the other side.

With some, of course, this is not true. Senators Tom Stewart and Bob Reynolds and Congressman John Rankin have proven beyond a doubt that their bigoted views of race superiority cannot be made compatible with a fair-minded outlook on the evacuee issue. With others, like Senator E. V. Robertson and Congressman Frank Barrett of Wyoming, there has been no effort to ascertain the facts. In the fashion of the worst politicians they have picked up a piece of bad newspaper reporting, paraphrased it, and issued it under their names as something approaching gospel truth. Perhaps there is not much hope of ever converting these individuals.

But vast sections of the American public have shown that they are willing to be shown. We have had countless reports of individual evacuees telling their stories in face-to-face contacts, in written applications for jobs, in casual meetings, and getting sympathetic, understanding reception.

Busy businessmen have taken time to hear the stories that evacuees have to tell of their problems. "No," one of them said, pounding his desk when he heard of indiscriminate mass evacuation, "they can't do that to you in America." But it was true, and he hadn't heard about evacuation, much less realized its implication, a whole year after it had taken place.

Another girl, whose family name is Tojo, suggested to a prospective employer that she might change her name. He was aghast. That wasn't the American way and she was going to be judged on her individual merits, regardless of her name. Now she's working in the office of a defense plant.

There is much truth and good advice in what this American of Jewish descent says. "Keep your problems before the public. Every bit of newspaper publicity counts. Write articles telling your side of the story. They may be rejected, but at least someone will read them and some day someone important may become interested. Write letters, send out circulars, keep your problems public. Don't let them forget you or you will become a lost people. . . ."

We agree with his final analysis that while the government and the public can help, the solution to evacuee problems is in the hands of evacuees alone. They must save themselves, because no one else can save them.

But appearing more frequently were angry columns, like this which was published the following week, May 20, 1943:

What a bunch of bloody, villainous cut-throats we have suddenly become since Pearl Harbor!

Our native fascists, professional race-baiters, politicians who can find no better way to get into the papers than to lash at the defenseless evacuees, super-patriotic sadists whose motto is "kick 'em while they're down," and countless others of peanut-size brain capacity are having a field day. Unable to find factual information with which to persecute us, they are spreading such monstrous opium dreams as the following under the heading of gospel truth:

That there was no sabotage in Hawaii because it was Tokyo's objective to stun, and not capture, the Hawaiian Islands at the time of Pearl Harbor.

That there was no sabotage on the Pacific Coast because the FBI had rounded up all dangerous Japanese.

That all Japanese are deceitful and tricky and no one can tell a loyal one from a dangerous one.

That the riot was staged at Manzanar to fool the American public into thinking that some of the evacuees are loyal.

That it is undesirable to permit evacuees to return to the Pacific Coast because all the Chinese and Filipinos there would butcher them.

The dreary, sickening parade of viciously calculated half-truths, falsehoods, and figments of a warped and depraved imagination could be continued for columns. They will make bitter reading for historians in years to come, for a cloud has come over the reasoning and sense of equilibrium of a goodly portion of sunny Southern California.

The lies are spawned and perpetuated by organizations which have become notorious for their misguided Americanism. There are old and familiar foes like the California chapters of the American Legion, the Native Sons and Native Daughters, the West Coast congressional bloc and their cohorts of similar venom like the Stewarts, the Rankins, the Reynolds and the Robertsons.

Most of these individuals and organizations contend, when they speak publicly, that the fact of a man's race and blood is conclusive of certain undesirable traits. They subscribe, without admitting it, to the race theories of Tojo and Hitler and the rest of the bigoted rabble-rousers who have sold their people a phoney bill of goods based on scientific balderdash.

Consequently a whole race is condemned without trial or hearing, and nothing is so un-American as assumption of guilt without the accused being given due hearing.

What our persecutors refuse to understand is that the Nisei, as well as a large proportion of the non-citizen group, are as alien to present-day Japan as the Joneses and Smiths and O'Briens and Slavinskys that make up America today.

There never has been a definite race line in this war. Americans named Fritz Grabner and Antonio Santucci have fought against Germans and Italians with similar names on the battlefields of North Africa. Rufus Tojo and Fred Yamamoto will soon be on the front lines of American forces pledged to decimate the armies and navies of Gen. Hideki Tojo and Adm. Isoroku Yamamoto. . . .

Because a good deal of the harassment of Japanese Americans originated in California, Frying Pan carried on a sporadic sniping match with Californians. Portions of two of these columns follow. The first was dated June 3, 1943:

That peculiar phenomenon known as the California mind deserves the attention of psychologists. Someone—it might have been Westbrook Pegler—once called Los Angeles the great, slobbering idiot of American cities. That's one man's opinion, but a hundred-thousand exiles will concur in the conclusion that something as bitter and unreasoning, and more dangerous than the deep South's Jim Crowism, has developed in certain quarters in California.

In appalling contrast to the fair play committees, the

church groups, and even the majority of the common men on the street who are interested in winning the war of democracy at home as well as abroad, there are vociferous groups of native fascists to whom reason, common sense and fairness are as alien as they are to Hitler's storm troopers or Tojo's "ronin" masquerading in the mustard brown uniforms of the Kempeitai.

The individuals and organizations who are preaching and practicing fascism's vicious racial tenets against Americans with Japanese faces would bridle with indignation if anyone accused them of un-Americanism. To the contrary they are, either sincerely in a misguided way, or in the interests of their own purses and those of their keepers, operating on the delusion that they are doing a patriotic duty.

We term this strange quirk of mentality the California mind, with due apologies to the many true democrats in that sunkist land who have kept their emotional equilibrium, some of whom, in fact, have been our staunchest friends. But because of the rabid few, inevitably the whole state becomes associated with rabble-rousing, race-hating demagogues who make their bread and butter by persecuting a minority group of their fellow citizens. . . .

The pious rascals are not satisfied with banishing native-born Americans from their state. They carry the persecution further, trying to influence Americans in other sections of the country who refused to be contaminated.

One California newspaper turned renegade to the tradition of tolerance in the country publication field, and came out with an open letter directed at a Midwest publisher who hired a Nisei. The letter was headed "Japs is Japs" and "Breed Like Guinea Pigs."

A month later, July 24, 1943, Frying Pan once more took after the "California mind" of some extremists:

The California mind, which in some aspects of reasoning power compares favorably with the cranial capacity of Neanderthal man, is busily at work again rationalizing the treatment of all persons tainted by Japanese blood.

The sickening self-hypnosis practiced by the leaders of the "Japs Out Forever" movement makes one wonder if the objective is worth the price of playing the perfect idiot bereft of all reason, logic or understanding.

Take for instance the testimony of one Grover Tholcke, appearing before a California state legislature sub-committee investigating, to put it euphemistically, the return of Japanese Americans to the Pacific Coast.

Speaking from thirty years of experience, Tholcke declared he had employed as many as ninety-eight Japanese prior to Pearl Harbor but, he said, "out of all the alien and American-born Japs, I have known not one who is loyal."

We can almost see him, seated comfortably in the witness chair and punctuating the remark with either a sage nod of the head or an indignant arm gesture. And we can see the committee also nodding sagely in assent, much, yes very much pleased with such conclusive, damning and valuable testimony.

Only, of course, one might ask about the meaning of loyalty, a word bandied around so frivolously. What is your criteria of loyalty? What makes one law-abiding citizen loyal and another one disloyal? The color of a man's skin and the shape of his nose?

The California mind would be the first to deny that its judgment is thus colored by prejudice. But their words betray them.

This furtive scratching up of old ghosts, this painful effort to read subversiveness, unreliability, deceit and all things hateful into actions of decades ago as a means of justifying discriminatory persecution of a national scapegoat unable to answer back is a repulsive spectacle of American fascism.

One wonders how a man can say with a straight face—and be accepted at face value—that in forty-five years of association with Japanese they proved in numerous instances "their disloyalty to this country and their allegiance to Japan."

A Sunday school teacher who taught Bible lessons to young Nisei children before the war gives that fact as his qualification for the statement that all "Japs" in the Salinas Valley are loyal "only to Japan." Another makes the worn-out claim that many Salinas Valley Japanese knew the exact date of the Pearl Harbor attack but would not notify the authorities.

Only the California mind is capable of such inconsistency as that advocated by this same Sunday school teacher who advocates training and sending these treacherous Japanese to Japan after the war to supervise reconstruction instead of training Caucasians.

In any court of public opinion or law out of the zone of madness, these witnesses would be laughed off the stand and told that burning of witches through perjury or even honest delusion went out of fashion centuries ago.

But to the California mind all this makes wonderfully fine, enlightened sense.

The California mind has a knack for distorting anything that it does not want to believe. For instance it was pointed out that thirty Nisei girls had spent some time rolling Red Cross bandages. But oh no, that wasn't a demonstration of loyalty at all—even when those bandages might have helped to save the life of a soldier brother or husband of one of the girls—because they were instructed to do so by "local Shinto priests, later identified as dangerous."

In our travels we witnessed the rites of penitence in which the Tamils, the little black people of India, whip themselves

24

into a frenzy while mutilating their bodies. A priest inserts steel skewers through their cheeks, hangs bells suspended from hooks into the flesh of their chests and backs, and then the penitent starts a pilgrimage through the streets.

His physical self cries in pain from the ordeal. But mentally he is in ecstasy, for he believes he is doing penance and insuring entry into heaven. He has the power to deny the obvious, to delude himself into thinking that something which isn't so is actually a fact.

When we first saw the sight we marveled at the self-hypnosis of these people. But now we realize that an even more amazing feat of self-hypnosis with regard to truth is being practiced every day by possessors of the California mind.

We saw those little Tamils again, rolling their eyes and frothing at the mouth and building themselves up to an ecstatic frenzy, when we read about the Californian who advocated immediate organized action against the evacuees because "we are apt to lapse into a state of indifference when the war is over if such an organization is not forthcoming."

3

Relocation

Relocation—from the desert camps into the great unknown Outside—was in full swing by the fall of 1943. WRA was anxious to move as many evacuees as possible back into the mainstream of American life before the camps deteriorated into a squalid new kind of reservation bereft of hope, pride and ambition.

Most of those leaving were young, ambitious, adventurous, with marketable skills. That left the old and very young.

Dillon S. Myer, director of The War Relocation Authority, was anxious to see me relocated. On more than one occasion he said getting Bill Hosokawa out became his private relocation project.

The first consideration in relocating an evacuee was to find him a job. In my case that was not excessively difficult. Myer talked to Gardner (Mike) Cowles of the family that owned Look magazine and newspapers in Minneapolis and Des Moines. Cowles talked to his editor in Des Moines and

eventually I got a letter asking me to outline my qualifica-
tions. Bless the Des Moines Register. *They were willing to*
take a chance on hiring a new hand they'd never seen,
straight out of a concentration camp.

The second consideration was to get security clearance,
which meant making sure there was nothing derogatory in
FBI and military intelligence files about the individual. Usu-
ally this was routine, but they must have had something
suspicious about me. Clearance was delayed week after
week. Whatever the problem, it must have been connected
with the matter that led to my being shipped hurriedly out
of Puyallup. Perhaps it was that I had spent so much time
in Asia. Perhaps they just figured I was a natural-born
trouble-maker.

But clearance finally came in October, 1943, and we set
out for Des Moines—a job and a new life in a town I had
never seen and a newspaper I had never read. In the Frying
Pan for October 30 I wrote about my impressions:

DES MOINES, IA.—If trains are to continue as the most
widely used mode of transportation, city designers of the
future have a responsibility to dress up the sections that line
the tracks leading into American cities. Des Moines is no
exception to the almost universal practice of cities exposing
their most undesirable facets to the incoming rail traveler.
And with this first impression, we approached this city with
a sinking feeling.

A second look was more pleasant. For instance, all street
cars and buses have painted on them, "Welcome to Des
Moines." Although the necessity for this sort of publicity
is hard to justify because of the town's relatively stable
population, one gets a warm sort of feeling when he reads
the signs for the first time.

Des Moines is a place where there was just one Japanese
American family before the war. It is a place where in the

last few months Nisei have gotten jobs clerking in grocery stores, keeping books in dry cleaning plants, and where some half a hundred evacuees go to college.

It is a place where a Nisei medical student assigned to a public clinic has delivered babies whose fathers are in uniform overseas. It is in the heart of one of the world's richest agricultural areas where there may be untold possibilities for evacuee farmers.

We are speaking in generalities now because we haven't been here long enough to make specific observations, but one of the surprising things is the willingness of employers to take on Nisei for positions in which they make direct contact with the public. In fact, no one seems to question a person's national extraction.

A prospective landlady said to me: "I judge people on their personal approaches, as individuals. I don't care who your father was, if you look all right, that's fine with me."

Another Nisei, working part-time while he goes to school, tells of being stopped occasionally by patrons. "What are you?" they demand. When he tells them, they say: "Well, I'm German. Think nothing of it," or "You're a damned good American."

The question seems to be the result of simple curiosity, and not suspicion or maliciousness.

The greatest mistake an evacuee can make is to form preconceived ideas regarding lack of acceptance, which might be the result of the period of confinement in the centers.

One finds an amazing lack of knowledge about the WRA camps. Many persons are not even aware that there was an evacuation.

We went down to the U.S. Employment Service office to get a statement of availability, and had to tell the interviewer all about the centers before he began to realize that technically I had been unemployed for the last eighteen months. Then he had to ask five or six people before he learned there was a WRA office in town which could certify me as available for employment.

On another occasion we had to explain the leave procedure to a woman who had a house to rent, simply because she was curious. When she asked if we could provide references, she caught herself and said, "Oh, but the fact that you were permitted to leave the camp after investigation is the best reference you could give me."

We soon settled into the routine of Midwestern life, winning quick acceptance at the Register, *finding new neighbors friendly and helpful. Still, an Oriental face was enough to attract curious stares, and that was the subject of a column on June 3, 1944:*

There was a Nisei girl among the hundreds that crowded the bridge to watch the flood-swollen torrent of the Des Moines River. She noticed a little boy's eye on her, and as she looked, he smiled.

"Hello," he said.

By now she was used to having strangers say hello to her, and so she smiled right back and said hello, too.

Then, as the boy melted back into the crowd, she heard him say to his companion: "See, I wasn't afraid of her."

If she could have heard more she might have heard a youthful and serious discussion about not all "Japs" being like the "Japs you see in the movies."

The other day we were invited to speak to a small group of young married women. When we first saw the audience we were surprised that they should interest themselves in the problem of Japanese Americans. The group appeared as if it would be more interested in bridge parties, in their children, and the trivialities of upper and middle class social life.

But they listened with more than ordinary interest to the story of the Japanese Americans, and their questions in the discussion period were pointed and intelligent.

Many of these young women had had their own lives disrupted by the war. Many of their husbands were in the services, others had had to make adjustments in their living because of the war's effect on their husbands' businesses.

But they could listen to a talk on the Evacuation and relocation with understanding and sympathy.

And when it was over, one of them, speaking for the group, asked, "What can we, as an organization, do to help the Japanese Americans?"

To employ a word trite by careless usage, it is understanding that is needed in the problem of Japanese Americans.

As one of the women put it: "I think I understand the situation now. I wasn't hostile toward the Japanese Americans, nor did I ever go out of my way to think about them. But now their story has been personalized by hearing it told first-hand by one of them, and I can understand their fears and hopes and aspirations."

And so it was with the boy on the bridge. His natural little-boy friendliness toward all around made him want to say hello to someone who was a stranger and yet, because he could not understand, he was apprehensive about what the reaction would be.

His solution was easier than that of an adult. For him, a person is either friendly or hostile, and there are few intermediate shadings and no explanations are sought as to why an individual should smile back or ignore him.

An adult's world is more complicated, but basically the issue again is that of understanding. Experience has shown that this understanding is reached best by face-to-face contacts. A personable Japanese American can do more toward understanding within his own sphere than all pronouncements of high government officials.

On any number of occasions I have had individuals say to me: "Do you happen to know, mmm, ah, well I can't recall his name, but he went to college in Jonesburg. He was a young Nisei—is that the way you pronounce it?—and there wasn't a smarter or more popular fellow on the campus."

Now that question is being modified and it sounds like this: "Do you happen to know George? I can't remember his last name but he came out of one of those camps and he's doing a crackerjack job at the such and such plant." Or farm, or restaurant, or shop.

Every evacuee who leaves the camps for life on the outside is helping to develop understanding for himself, and also for others of his kind. For, inevitably, Japanese Americans are members of a special American minority as well as individuals, and they are likely to be considered as part of a group as often as individuals.

And despite all the War Relocation Authority, other government agencies, and all our splendid friends are doing for us, the ultimate determination of whether we will be re-accepted into the American lifestream depends to the greatest extent on each of us.

The months sped by, and there were times when it appeared the Evacuation and camp were experiences of another lifetime. But there were other occasions when the memories returned sharply, and they were distant enough that I could write of them, as I did on November 25, 1944:

One of the fellows at the office is a member of the Unitarian church. He came up to me the other day and said:

"I'm going to put the touch on you for about a quarter. (Ed. Note: We were working for about $40 a week.) The national Unitarian church has a project this year of collecting 1,000 Christmas gifts for the kids at Poston, and I thought you'd like to contribute. You have a little boy, haven't you? Well, you can put his name and age on a card with a gift, and we'll do the rest."

So it's Christmas again.

Christmas, 1941, was a pretty bleak affair. War and blackouts and a continual stream of bad news from the Far East where we were taking the licking of our lives. Fear, anxiety and gloom that scarcely was penetrated by the tinsel and colored lights of the Yuletide.

In many ways Christmas, 1942, was even worse. Out of the barracks window there was only gray sand, scudding gray clouds, gray sagebrush that stretched to the gray horizon. Gray wallboard on four walls and ceiling of our cubicle, a floor gray with the desert dust ground into it until it turned only more gray with each scrubbing.

It was Christmas and we tried to make it gay with little gifts and trinkets purchased through mail order houses, even a little artificial tree fashioned of odds and ends and draped with cotton snow.

And yet the grayness permeated the air, for we were lonely in the midst of the 10,000. It wasn't a longing for any particular friend or group of friends; it was the hollow, numbing feeling of being outcast, unwanted and forgotten. Outcast from the communities where we belonged, unwanted by our nation in a war emergency, forgotten by our fellow citizens.

The gray skies turned darker, and with the suddenness of mountain blizzards, the wind whipped snow across the camp. At least it would be a white Christmas.

It will be difficult to forget what happened that night. The mess hall was crowded with wide-eyed children and their parents trying to be gay, and leaders struggling almost frantically to whip up a Christmas cheeriness. Slowly the crowd warmed up, and even the cynical youngsters who wore their hair long and brushed back, their Levi's rolled high over their boots as marks of distinction, joined in singing the carols they had learned as children in a happier day.

Then came Santa Claus, riding from mess hall to mess hall in an olive drab WRA truck. Clad in an ill-fitting red suit, his whiskers awry, he stomped into the mess hall, full of loud cheer.

The younger children gaped in pop-eyed amazement. Many of them were too young to remember their last Christmases, and here was a real, live Santa Claus with a great bulging sack on his back.

The gifts were passed out, and there was enough for everyone from the youngest tot to the oldest grandmother. There were books and toys and games, pictures to hang in the barracks, wash cloths and toilet soaps, trinkets and useful gadgets, all of them poured into the desert camps by the great, generous heart of Americans.

There were cards with the gifts. They came from the Joneses, the Smiths and the Browns, **and** common folks whose names indicated they'd come to America with later waves of immigration. The gifts came from Billings, Montana, and Boston, Massachusetts; from a mountain colony in New Mexico and an orphange where the children had saved pennies to buy gifts for little evacuee children who had no homes either.

The grayness left the camp that night, and never really returned. It wasn't the gifts alone. It was the realization that we no longer were forgotten nor unwanted. They—the American people—remembered us, and had let us know with this outpouring of little gifts from cities and hamlets the country over.

"Sure," I said, "count me in. I'm very proud to be asked to take a part in this project."

33

*While the relocatees were making an encouraging adjust-
ment to their new homes in places like Des Moines, Chicago,
Cleveland, and elsewhere, the super-patriots on the West
Coast continued an almost psychopathic drumfire against
the Japanese Americans. Many of the most rabid were public figures.*

*One California official who did not cover himself with
glory during the evacuation period was Earl Warren, attorney general at the time of Pearl Harbor, and later governor.
He was a vigorous advocate of evacuation, and for a long
time he opposed the return of Japanese Americans to his
state. However, when he was named Chief Justice of the
United States Supreme Court he seemed to become aware
of the grievous injustice he had helped perpetuate. Some
students of the Warren court feel that the landmark civil
rights decisions it wrote were influenced in considerable
part by the knowledge of his errors. "The Japanese Americans," one observer has suggested, "paid the ransom that
liberated the Blacks."*

*Be that as it may, in the summer of 1944 Governor
Warren made the keynote address at the Republican National Convention in Chicago, waving the flag of Americanism and mouthing time-worn but time-tested shibboleths.
Frying Pan on July 1, 1944, was moved to comment in this
manner:*

It is likely that when Governor Warren wrote his 4,000-
word speech, California's political exiles, the Americans of
Japanese descent, were far from his thoughts. They would
have had to be, or else Earl Warren would have been guilty
of the worst kind of cynicism.

For the ideals that Governor Warren expounded before
the Republican national convention were in an astonishing
number of instances the very same ideals which had been

34

denied in practice to California's citizens of Japanese origin. Let us take a few quotations from Governor Warren's address, and see how they are applicable to a minority of Warren's own state.

"This is our job: To open the doors for all Americans—to open it, not just to jobs, but to opportunity," Warren told the GOP gathering.

In desert relocation camps in various parts of the country, Japanese American evacuees are looking for that kind of opportunity, but they cannot return to California to find it, even if the military permitted, for they have been promised violence by highly vocal members of Governor Warren's constituency.

"It is the purpose of this convention," Warren continued, "to put the public welfare above private self-interest; to put the nation above the party; to put the progress of the whole American community above special privilege for any part; to put indispensable principles once and for all above indispensable men."

Of course Warren was attacking President Roosevelt and The New Deal, but the same words are applicable to selfish private interests like the California Grange, certain farm interests, and other organizations which find it profitable to keep the Japanese Americans outside their sunkist borders.

"In those states where the people have returned to the Republican party," Warren thundered, "government is not only for the people, but of and by the people. That means not some of the people, but all of the people. Their kind of representative government reaches from ocean to ocean and border to border."

Warren was charging, without saying it in so many words, that in the deep South the white supremacists of the Democratic party keep the Negroes in virtual serfdom. But he forgot, or carefully ignored the fact, that some of his most

35

faithful supporters have tried to disenfranchise citizens of California because their ancestors happened to have come from Japan.

"But this war cannot be fought and won as Republicans and Democrats," Warren asserted. "This is an all-American war. There is a place for every American in it. There is no place of honor for any American who is not in it."

Sure, sure, the old call for unity, a protestation that Republican opposition to the administration is not to be construed as disloyalty. But Governor Warren, why do you stand by giving tacit approval by your silence to California campaigns to keep Japanese Americans out of the state where, by all laws of reason, they could play their most effective war role?

"To that we dedicate ourselves as our first objective; to keep the war out of politics and politics out of war, to strengthen, among us, that spirit of single-mindedness, of unity, of self-forgetfulness that will hearten our military leaders."

Our military leaders have asked for justice toward loyal Japanese Americans. They have pleaded that prejudice not be permitted to color American justice, for loyalty is a matter of heart and mind, and not a thing of race, ancestry, or complexion. Where is that spirit of unity in California?

But here is Governor Warren's crowning piece: "It (the Republican party) will devote itself fervently to the problems of the people. In everything it does the Constitution of the United States of America will be its guiding star. It will function through established law and not through the caprice of bureaucratic regulation. There shall be one law for all men."

Some in California would be guided by the Constitution, but only if the Constitution suits their particular fancy. If it doesn't, change it, it's outdated, and improper interpretations have been placed against it in the past, they cry. That's

36

the argument of the Native Sons, who actually went to court in an effort to disenfranchise Japanese Americans and Chinese Americans, too. . . .

It is possible that Earl Warren himself is little interested in or concerned about the problems of Japanese Americans. But as chief executive of the state of California, he has permitted to go on, under his very nose, the vicious racist campaigns that are giving American democracy a black eye among the watching, hopeful peoples of the Orient.

Neither by word nor action has Earl Warren ever indicated that he opposed the racism of California's lunatic fringe, nor has he ever given support or encouragement to the hundreds of splendid, courageous Californians who have fought tirelessly against the racists.

Whether in the Republican party or among the Democrats, we condemn the irresponsible, selfish, and expedient policy like that taken by Earl Warren toward the Japanese American issue. If he, or anyone else can be so callous about one small, unpopular point of principle, it is logical enough to assume that he would choose the expedient out in larger issues. . . .

On October 11 and 12, 1944, the U.S. Supreme Court heard the Korematsu and Endo cases. Fred Korematsu, a native of Oakland, California, had refused to be evacuated and he had been convicted of remaining in a military area from which persons of Japanese ancestry had been excluded. Mitsuye Endo, through her attorney James Purcell, had sued the United States government, charging she had been deprived unlawfully of her rights as an American citizen by being confined in a War Relocation Center. Korematsu's appeal tested the right of the military to order the evacuation of Japanese Americans. The Frying Pan for October 21 read:

37

At this stage of the evacuation and relocation program there seems little to be gained, other than the all-important matter of principle, in seeking a final ruling on the legality of the evacuation of Japanese Americans from the West Coast.

Some 110,000 men, women and children have been removed bodily from their homes, and that disruption long has been completed. The financial loss resulting from that disruption is irretrievably gone.

The aching hearts and bitter memories have become less poignant with time; the sharp edge of nostalgia has been dulled by the years and their events, and the bewilderment, frustration and humiliation of being singled out are only slightly less vivid.

Accepting on face value the government's assurance that the evacuees will be restored their rights "as soon as the military situation permits," the only objective in testing the legality of the exclusion orders is to determine the validity of deep-rooted American principles, principles so fundamental that the American way of life is based on them.

Among the questions posed by the Evacuation are these:

Can an American civilian be deprived of his liberty at the direction of a military commander who has acted without proclamation of martial law?

Is it compatible with the American way to direct a discriminatory order, such as the evacuation order, against a group of citizens solely on a basis of ancestry? Persons who spoke no word of Japanese, who never had been to Japan, who had no contact with other persons of Japanese descent, were forced to leave the Pacific Coast under the military's ban because a fractional part of their ancestry happened to be Japanese.

If these questions can be answered affirmatively, as apparently they can when applied to Lieutenant General John L. DeWitt's exclusion orders, then there are grave portents indeed for the future of the American way. What is there to prevent some future use of these precedents against some other minority group when the compelling causes are less urgent than that of war against a treacherous foe?

If anything is to be salvaged out of the tears, the cost, both monetary and to American prestige; the endangering of American principles, then there must be once and for all an unambiguous ruling by the courts which will answer the questions raised by the Evacuation.

Thus the argument of Solicitor General Charles Fahy that the legality of the Evacuation must be considered in the light of sacrifices made by millions of other citizens so far in the war has a hollow ring.

Mr. Fahy is quoted in press reports as having said: "Many persons have been required to endure dislocation. Hundreds of thousands already have been casualties. Those who have been injured, temporarily, in relocation efforts should be asked to view their cases along with the great hardships millions of our people have already endured in this war."

That, it seems, is beside the point. The privations and loss of evacuation are not the points of contention. The evacuees themselves would be the first to agree that millions of others have been subjected to hardships by the war. The evacuees have shared with them the inconveniences of rationing, and at the other extreme of wartime sacrifice, the loss of sons who will not be coming back. These are things to be accepted as a consequence of war.

It is another thing for American citizens to be herded from their homes and placed within barbed wire barricades, under the eyes of armed guards in watch towers equipped with floodlights and machine guns, and for no reason other than that the citizens' forebears were Japanese.

This experience is more than an ordinary sacrifice.

Despite whatever resentment the evacuees may have felt

over this treatment, it is now largely a thing of the past. What matters now is that we must use this tragic episode in the lives of a small fraction of the American population to make sure that similar abridgment of rights cannot take place.

The high court ruled on the Korematsu and Endo cases on December 18, 1944, three years and eleven days after the outbreak of war. Korematsu's guilt was upheld, in effect endorsing the military's right to exclude certain classes of citizens from specific military areas. Mitsuye Endo was ordered released from WRA custody. The court's rulings meant that while evacuation was considered legal, a loyal citizen could not be kept confined once that loyalty was confirmed. As a result the Army revoked its exclusion orders and told the evacuees they were free to go home after January 2, 1945. The War Relocation Authority also announced all its camps would be closed before the end of 1945, no matter what happened in the war.

But regardless of what black-robed jurists ruled, there were still people like Andy Hale, whose treatment of a GI named Private Raymond Matsuda made him the subject of a Frying Pan column on November 18, 1944:

A barber named Andy Hale didn't like the Japs, so when a wounded Nisei soldier in uniform, his tunic ablaze with service ribbons, hobbled into Hale's shop with the aid of a crutch, Hale did what he thought was the American thing to do. He gave the damned "Jap" the bum's rush.

The first impulse is to get boiling mad about the bigotry and blind prejudice of the Andy Hales, in Arizona where this incident took place, and elsewhere in this world. But the Andy Hales aren't going to read this, and it wouldn't help matters a great deal even if they did.

Reading a column isn't going to change the benighted

40

views of the Andy Hales who believe that the rights and privileges of America are the God-given gift of Anglo-Saxons alone, and damned be any foreigner—Negro, Mexican, Italian, Jap or American Indian—who thinks he's as good as a "white" man.

It is deplorable that we have our Andy Hales in America. It is also deplorable that we have persons who pick the pockets of blind newspaper peddlers, who poison their mothers and abandon their children, who bribe tricycles away from kids with a candy bar, who ransack the homes of servicemen's widows and try to pawn medals which some Yank paid for with his life.

These are incidents that in the overall picture of American life do not amount to a great deal. In newspapers they are scarcely more than one-day stories, read today and forgotten tomorrow.

But each little incident is an outrage to the American sense of human decency, and Andy Hale added to the foul record when he let his emotions overcome logic and reason.

Andy Hale joins the same class of super-patriots as the unidentified man on a New York subway car who berated a Nisei soldier for daring to have Japanese ancestors, and for having the impudence to be in the U.S. Army, only to discover, as did others in the car, that the Nisei Yank was blind.

We hope Andy Hale is proud of himself for the way he treated the wounded Nisei. It would not do for Andy Hale to be remorseful, for that is not in keeping with the spirit of his sense of patriotism. Besides, nothing would have been gained for the glorious cause of democracy—for which we presume Andy Hale believes he struck a mighty blow—if there were remorse attached to such an act of courage.

Besides, it's possible you know, that the wounded veteran might have struck back with his crutch, and so maybe it was an act of self-defense after all.

And we rather fancy Andy Hale's motto which he has emblazoned on his barber shop, like a coat of arms: "Japs Keep Out, You Rat."

Somehow, we feel that we are taking this incident much more seriously than the Nisei veteran himself. It is altogether likely that out of the thunder and misery and sudden death of the battlefield, the agony of field hospitals, the tedium of long months of recuperation, he has built up a tolerant, understanding philosophy about the outlook of the Andy Hales.

The wounded Nisei probably feels that it was an inevitable insult—inevitable so long as men are human and therefore often stupid and not always rational animals. It is probable that he feels the American Army uniform was left out of it when he was affronted on the basis of his facial characteristics.

But others of us who have not had our philosophies tempered in the heat of battle cannot be so charitable. We feel that an American soldier honorably wounded in battle and wearing the decorations of meritorious service was subjected to an unnecessary and humiliating affront solely because of his racial origin.

We do not know what Andy Hale's three sons in service are fighting for if they back their father's actions. But we do know that millions of GIs will condemn an insult to one of their number as unforgivable and inexcusable.

4

Exiles' Return

The Army's revocation of evacuation orders created a new set of problems for Japanese Americans, particularly those who had re-established themselves in inland communities. Those still in the camps knew they would be moved out in due time; their decision was made for them as surely as when they were herded behind barbed wire. But those who had relocated had a choice. They could stay where they were, enjoying new jobs, new homes, new friends, a new way of life. Or they could return to prewar homes on the West Coast.

But if they did return, what would they find? First indications were that they would encounter more hostility than welcome. Would the socially comfortable Little Tokyos be restored? Could businesses be revived? No one could say for sure. On December 30, 1944, Frying Pan wrote:

The three-year exile of Japanese Americans from their homes is about to end. It has been a period of toil and tears,

43

of fear and gnawing uncertainty, of doubts that shook men's faith in democracy. It has been a period of raw emotions when bigots stood unashamed to trumpet their bigotry, and others made light of the Constitution in efforts to promote their economic self-interest.

It is too early, even now, to assess accurately the full, long-term significance of the Evacuation. It would seem a dangerous precedent has been set in the exile, solely on a racial basis, of an American minority. . . .

But two tangible, constructive results of the Evacuation already are evident. The first is the effect on the Nisei themselves; the second the effect the Evacuation has had on the people of the United States.

The Evacuation has opened new vistas of opportunity for the Nisei. It has accomplished in a sudden, revolutionary and oftentimes cruel manner something that would have come to pass in a generation or two. And the Nisei and their offspring will profit when the pain of being wrenched from their homes is forgotten.

The story of the prewar Japanese communities is too well known to need much repetition. There the talents of eager young Nisei were stifled for lack of opportunity. There were not jobs enough to go around, and prejudice kept the Nisei from finding opportunities in the cities which surrounded these colonies.

The bonds of family and habit kept all but a few of the Nisei from leaving the West Coast in search of a livelihood elsewhere.

The prewar plight of the Nisei well could be epitomized in the youth who wore a Phi Beta Kappa key on his watch chain and stacked oranges in a fruit stand for a living.

Now, thanks to the Evacuation, the Nisei are scattered in forty-seven of the forty-eight states. They have found, on a large scale, job opportunities undreamed of before the war. In spite of occasional local prejudices they have found the chance to compete for jobs and advancement on the basis of merit. And they are making good.

The Nisei have lost their narrow provincial outlook. California no longer is the limit of their interests. They speak more casually of traveling 2,000 miles across the country than they did before the war about making a trip from Los Angeles to San Francisco.

The Nisei have discovered the real America. They have seen for the first time its towering mountains and its broad plains, its wheatfields and cornfields and the forests of industrial smokestacks. They have found the heart of America, and they know now that they no longer need be a group of marginal citizens of questioned loyalty.

And perhaps unconsciously, America is the stronger for having undergone the difficulties of the Evacuation. Thinking Americans have had it brought home as never before that this is a war of ideals and not of races. They are more cognizant of America's racial minority problems. They understand better the meaning of democracy.

In the once-upon-a-time of prewar days the so-called "Jap" problem was thought to be solely California's concern. Outside of the Pacific Coast the Japanese American had his prototype in the grinning gardener and truck farmer, or the domestic who spoke in Hashimura Togo English.

Now the Nisei are a curiosity no longer. The American public has found through the dispersal of the Nisei that they are thoroughly American with valuable skills to be contributed to the war effort. Americans have discovered that Nisei make good neighbors and are of credit to the communities in which they have resettled.

Nisei soldiers have brought home dramatically the lesson that the color of one's skin and the shape of one's facial features do not preclude loyalty or disloyalty. . . .

And finally, the super-patriots have been unmasked. Their argument that American citizens should be punished

45

because their forefathers were Japanese always had a phony ring. Now, by their own actions they have revealed themselves as of the lunatic fringe, not hesitant about denying Constitutional rights or inciting to riot and violence in order to satisfy their pettish prejudices or to fatten their pocketbooks.

Because the facts were little known, it was not difficult at one time for many Americans to believe the charges that West Coast hate-mongers leveled against the Nisei. So skillfully were the lies and half-truths interwoven with the truth by paid propagandists that it was well nigh impossible for anyone to distinguish the facts for certain.

Thanks to national publicity in newspapers, magazines and the radio, the truth has come out. When organizations continue to beat the drums of hatred, to warn of violence against returning Japanese Americans and then go out of their way to arouse unrest, it is obvious that there is more than patriotism behind their efforts. It is only too obvious that covetous eyes are being cast on the verdant fields—most of them developed out of wasteland by Japanese Americans—which evacuation forced their tenants to leave behind. Americans will not be fooled so easily hereafter by cries of wolf on this or other issues.

The Evacuation has been a tragic experience both for those who were affected directly and the nation as a whole. It is the duty of evacuees as Americans to see that an evacuation is never repeated on a racial or any other basis. . . .

The Evacuation in 1942 was carried out with military dispatch. Overnight, exclusion order placards appeared on buildings and utility poles. Armed soldiers supervised the actual movement of civilians into barbed wire enclosures. The speed and impersonal efficiency were such that even the crackpots were awed and stood by silently. No one could fail to be impressed by the thousands of men, women, and

46

children being moved out bag and baggage, leaving their home towns in train after train, bus convoy after bus convoy. It was a spectacular and tragic process.

But it was not a process that could be thrown into reverse like movie film run backward. And perhaps that was why the crackpots who stood silent when the trainloads pulled out found their tongues and unleashed a cacophony of hate and misrepresentation when the Army told the evacuees they could return home. The evacuees were hesitant at first about going back. They returned home singly, as though they were sending out advance scouts, and in twos and threes. And some of them met violence. On May 26, 1945, Frying Pan wrote:

It was a hesitant, sometimes frightened homecoming, just undetermined enough to encourage the American racists, the dollar patriots, the barroom bullies, to pipe up. It seems certain most of this element would have kept its own counsel had the return been in force with the same quick determination and efficiency of the Evacuation.

Let us suppose that it had been possible logistically and practical sociologically and economically to undertake the return on the same mass basis as the Evacuation. Let us suppose that busloads and trainloads of persons from the WRA centers were poured back into their prewar communities with military escort. That placards were posted warning all persons that the return would take place within a specified time, that guards were stationed to see that there was no violence nor undue confusion in their dispersal. That penalties were provided for anyone hindering the progress of the program.

There are valid and logical reasons why this sort of program could not have been undertaken. But from the standpoint of justice pure and simple—outside of practical considerations—such a program would not be entirely unjustified. And certainly the justice of the case would have been more emphatic to the same crackpot fringe. A little show of force goes a long way with this class of individual.

It is encouraging to see that increasing numbers of evacuees are returning to their prewar homes and businesses in California, Oregon and Washington.

They are demonstrating that they are not intimidated, that they are returning to their homes to reclaim what rightfully is theirs. The Evacuation would have been all the more tragic if persons with the reason and the right to return to the Pacific Coast failed to do so in fear of social discrimination, economic boycott and possible physical violence....

As for myself, there was nothing to go back to in Seattle. For the time being I was happy to remain in Des Moines. But one day there was a letter from the Minidoka camp in Idaho that made return to the Coast a personal thing. My parents were going home. My father's decision inspired this next column, which was published June 2, 1945:

The peasant boy, not yet sixteen years old, said farewell to his father and mother and two younger sisters and set out for the unfamiliar city. There he purchased a third-class railroad ticket and rode to the capital, which he never before had seen.

From a nearby port he embarked on an ancient, smelly steamer for a three-week voyage. His quarters were deep in the hold where the odor was so nauseating that he and the many companions like him spent as much of their time as possible on the after deck, their only alternative.

On an early summer day in 1899 this boy reached the end of his journey. At last he was in the promised land.

To this point the peasant lad's story is no different from the story of millions of other peasant boys who left the crowded, tradition-bound, oppressive, hunger-haunted countries of Europe in search of opportunity, freedom and wealth in the United States.

But in this story the port of entry was Tacoma, Washington, and not New York. He was an immigrant from Japan, and he sailed eastward across the ocean in search of the things he never could hope to gain in his native land.

His lot was not easy. First he was sent by a labor contractor into the towering passes of Montana where he laid the steel tracks and kept up the roadbeds for the great trains which connected the East coast with the growing West.

He spent time as a migrant laborer in the vineyards of Fresno and the Sacramento deltaland. While a schoolboy he worked for $1 a month and the privilege of a room, three scanty meals and the opportunity to practice his newly-learned English on the household.

He was in San Francisco in 1906 and survived the earthquake. He shipped as a messboy aboard an American Army transport on the Philippines run and he made eight or ten round-trips before he decided to forsake the sea.

In time he married, fathered children, acquired his own business, prospered in a modest way and grew to love the land which had been so good to him. His parents had died, he had lost track of his sisters, and the thin bonds of sentiment which tied him to his native land grew more tenuous daily.

Last week, from a war relocation center, he wrote a letter to his two sons who with their own families had resettled in the Midwest. This is what he said:

"Your mother and I have decided to go back to the Pacific Coast, for that is our home. I do not know how we will fare, but I am not worried. I have been through more difficult times.

"Thank you for your invitation to us to come and live

with you. I do not expect to retire until I am seventy. After that perhaps I shall accept your hospitality. Meanwhile, if I should die, I know you will take care of your mother.

"But now, I am going back, for that is where I belong. I helped to pioneer the American West. I have another opportunity to pioneer, for there are many people in the camp who are afraid to return to the Coast. Since it became known that we are going back, twelve other families decided to go back, too, and in this way we are helping the American government to solve a problem.

"We have spent three years in camp and have nothing to show for it. At my age three years means a great deal. I have much to do to make up for those wasted years.

"We are going home now, and we are happy."

Almost from the day the Nisei first felt himself to be neither fish nor fowl in America, and especially since Pearl Harbor, Japanese Americans have had reason to believe their ancestry a detriment.

But in those moments of bitterness or despondency, or when they upbraid their parents for their set ways and overcautiousness, the Nisei forget that their immediate forebears have a long and honorable record as residents of the United States. Many of them are to be numbered among the venerable pioneers who arrived in this country when the West was young and who helped in the development of a frontier.

The perfidy of a Pearl Harbor has not marred that record, nor the record of their American-born sons and daughters. True, a segment of the nation—and for a while the nation itself—lost track of the fact that the law-abiding resident Japanese and the Americans of Japanese extraction had nothing to do with the savage militarism of Japan itself.

But now that the fear and urgency of war have been dissipated by the power of Allied arms, there is time for reason and understanding. And if any further proof of the basic loyalty of these people were needed—over and beyond the record of peaceful evacuation, the heroic feats of the Nisei soldier, the Japanese American's contributions on the home front production line—there is the return of these elderly people to their homes, uncomplaining and hopeful.

5

The Nisei GIs

In October 1940, when the Selective Service Act went into effect. Nisei men between the ages of twenty-one and thirty-six registered just like other Americans. Nearly 3,500 Nisei were drafted for the compulsory one-year military training period and no one thought anything of it.

It all changed drastically after Pearl Harbor. That frantic December hundreds of Nisei already in uniform were transferred into what was called the enlisted reserve "for the convenience of the government." That was another way of saying they were kicked out because their ancestors were Japanese.

Those who remained in service were almost invariably re-assigned from combat outfits into menial housekeeping jobs. Nisei civilians were re-classified 4-C, which was a curious action because that was the category for aliens not subject to military service.

Most Nisei resented this discrimination bitterly. Some volunteered for service and were quickly turned down. But as they went through the evacuation experience, the patriotic fervor cooled as frustration and resentment set in.

On January 28, 1943, the War Department announced it would seek volunteers among the Nisei for a special segregated combat unit. By then these Nisei had been in the camps eight to ten months. Some opposed the idea of an all-Nisei unit; the prospect of further segregation was anathema. Controversy raged in the camps. In some families one son volunteered for service, another vowed not to serve even if drafted.

Eventually more than a thousand Nisei stepped out of the camps to volunteer, leaving families and dependents behind barbed wire. They joined the Nisei already in uniform—and an overwhelming turnout of volunteers from Hawaii where there was no mass incarceration—to form the 442nd Regimental Combat Team.

The 442nd went on to serve with great distinction in seven European campaigns, suffering 9,486 casualties, including 600 dead. The casualties amounted to 300 per cent of the 442nd's original strength. The men of the unit won more than 18,000 individual decorations and sixty-five unit citations.

More than 6,000 other Nisei were trained as interpreters and translators in the Pacific, and 3,700 of them served in combat areas before the Japanese surrender. Selective Service figures show that in all some 33,300 Japanese Americans were in military service during World War II. The sacrifices of these men, and a number of women, were responsible in large part for the dramatic change in public attitude toward Japanese Americans.

Nisei servicemen were the subject of a number of Frying Pan columns. The following was published October 16, 1943:

"Four months ago," the Nisei soldier was saying, "I could look out my window in the WRA camp and see the barbed wire and the watch tower where the floodlights would go on at night.

"Just a couple of weeks ago, there I was, in U.S. Army uniform with a loaded rifle in my hands, standing guard over German prisoners of war in an Alabama peanut field.

"I don't know what to make of it. It's confusing."

The speaker is a Nisei who was among the first to volunteer when formation of the Japanese American combat team was announced early this year. He went through basic training, underwent a period of guarding prisoners of war, and received a furlough to visit his family in camp.

This soldier says he learned much about men and their ways in the last few years. He experienced life as the unwanted ugly duckling of America, uprooted from home, torn from possessions, and herded into camps behind barbed wire fences like a dangerous enemy.

Then suddenly he was the jailer. He was being entrusted with prisoners of war, captured at the expense of American lives, and he was responsible for their conduct during a critical labor shortage.

Life in the WRA camps under guard seemed to have given the Nisei soldiers poise. They watch their charges vigilantly but coolly, and their impersonal manner was appreciated by the prisoners. With other outfits, the Germans said, there was "over-guarding" because the men were too anxious about their responsibility. . . .

This Nisei fighting man's deepest impressions were in the treatment that the general populace accorded him.

"At first the people were curious about us, as they naturally should be," he says. "Then, as they realize we are part of Uncle Sam's army, and that we're out there to help them by guarding these prisoners temporarily, they make us completely at home.

"We were invited to homes and parties around the place during hours off, and I've never picked up more rides into town from the camp than I did there."

This soldier's experience is but one indication of a great many being manifested in increasing volume that there is a place for Americans of Japanese descent in this country, and the people in general are willing to accept them on a basis of complete equality. . . .

The 442nd completed its training and disappeared behind military security. The Japanese American public figured it had been sent to Italy to join forces with the 100th Infantry Battalion, the crack Hawaiian Nisei outfit that had gone into action while the 442nd was still being whipped into shape. On July 15, 1944, I wrote:

The first indication that the "Go For Broke" boys of the 442nd were in action was a sentence or two in an Associated Press dispatch from Rome.

The 442nd Infantry Regiment Combat Team attached to the 34th Division, the dispatch said, had been in heavy fighting a few miles south of the key city of Livorno (Leghorn) as German resistance stiffened all along the Italian front.

And the war was suddenly closer to thousands of homes here on the mainland and in the Hawaiian Islands.

The 442nd is but one regiment among thousands of regiments, attached to one division among hundreds, assigned to one army of scores fighting under the United Nations colors.

But because they are "our" boys—fellows we grew up with, the sons and husbands and fathers of persons we know—our hearts go out to them a little more personally than to other fighting men of the Allied forces.

This war has been the particular concern of every Japanese American from the moment that Pearl Harbor was bombed. It is not their fault that up to now they could not play more active, more spectacular roles in its prosecution. . . .

Instead, many loyal Nisei already in army uniform and aching for vengeance against Pearl Harbor's perfidy were demobilized into an enlisted reserve. Other eligible Nisei were classified 4-C. . . . And all Japanese Americans on the Pacific Coast were told in effect that their wartime role was peaceful and cooperative evacuation from their homes to the isolation of inland camps. That they played this ignoble role well is a matter of record. . . .

It has taken something spectacular and dramatic like a whole fighting force of Japanese Americans to capture the public's attention. First it was the 100th Infantry Battalion, and now the 442nd Regiment—which will have far to go to equal the record of the 100th—that personalized the realization that this is our war.

The knowledge that our own boys are in the fighting gives special meaning to the home front role that we civilians must play. . . . The men at the fronts suffer the privations, face the dangers, and eke out what little glory there is in war. . . .

Most, we hope, will return sound of body and mind and unembittered by what they have seen and experienced. But the men in uniform realize better than we do that many will not come back, and that others will have left a part of themselves on the battlefields. . . .

For us, war is no longer a distant thing.

Soon the casualties lists began to appear in the pages of Pacific Citizen. *We scanned them for fellows we knew. There seemed to be an extraordinary number of Seattleites. In one terrible interlude there appeared the names of four young men I knew and liked and admired who had volun-*

56

teered from Heart Mountain—Lt. Moe Yonemura, Lt. Kei Tanahashi, Fred Yamamoto, Ted Fujioka, all guys with great promise, all dead.

But realization of the cost of war hit most sharply the day a government telegram came to my brother Rube, announcing the death of Technician Third Grade Ken Omura. He had died of drowning in New Guinea, apparently the first Nisei graduate of the Military Intelligence and Language School to be lost in the Southwest Pacific. Ken was a Kibei. He was also my cousin. He had listed my brother as next of kin. When his mother died, Ken and his sister were sent to Japan to be brought up by relatives. They came back to the States when he was about fourteen.

The draft took him before Pearl Harbor and he thought it great fun when he was assigned to an artillery company. After Pearl Harbor he went through the futile anger, then the heartache of being held suspect, of being refused a chance, an experience so familiar to all Nisei soldiers. They took him out of the artillery and lined him up with a half-hundred other Nisei. They counted off, one-two, one-two.

The evens got hospital detail. The odds were yardbirds, policing the grounds, digging drainage ditches, landscaping Army posts. He volunteered for special service, and that was his chance because the Japanese language was still familiar. The day Ken's things came back, I wrote the column which appeared January 6, 1945:

The last, pitiful possessions of a Nisei GI Joe have come home. He died almost a year ago. And now through the slow, inevitable unraveling of government red tape, the little things that were dear to him and gave him individuality in the regimentation and anonymity of the Army have been returned to the next of kin.

There were a few snapshots, meaningful and full of memories to the Yank who had treasured them. There was an overseas cap, worn jauntily in one of the photos. And ribbons: Good Conduct, pre-Pearl Harbor, Asiatic Theatre, a couple of battle stars.

There was one other item, a wrist watch rusted with sea water, and with a few grains of sand ground into the worn leather of the strap. That was all.

A few days before these personal effects arrived, the army had ruled that loyal Japanese Americans were free to return to their prewar homes in the evacuated areas. One part of the army's proclamation reads:

"The outstanding record which these men (the Nisei) have made fighting for the United States in Italy, in France, and in the Pacific has shown conclusively that it is possible to make sound judgments as to their loyalty."

In considering the various factors that prompted the Army to rescind the evacuation orders, we wonder if the Japanese American public realizes fully the part its men in service had in this restoration of the rights of all Nisei.

It is not necessary to review the meaning to the Nisei of the evacuation order's end. Every loyal Nisei knows—and he needs no one to tell him—that a dark, depressing cloud has been dispersed after its shadow had hung over every act of his life in every minute of almost three years.

Now the cloud is gone, and the Nisei is no longer a restricted citizen. He can walk erect and unflinching in every part of his country. . . .

The methods of proving loyalty have varied. But the most spectacular, dramatic and costly way was through service in the armed forces. The Nisei who bear arms have kindled the public's imagination, and they have paid the price.

Gold stars hang in many a Japanese American household's window, and now the little packages of faded and wrinkled pictures and brave bright ribbons are coming back.

The Nisei who wore them are the ones who made the supreme sacrifice.

But they and each of their buddies, maimed and unscathed alike, went into combat with a double responsibility. In addition to carrying out unflinchingly the duties expected of every American soldier, these Nisei fought with the knowledge that the lot of all Japanese Americans would be influenced in large measure by the valor in battle of a chosen few.

Many Nisei GI Joes will never see the victory for which they are giving so much. Many have given their all already, and many others will fall before the Axis is crushed.

But if there is comfort to be had, they deserve it richly in the knowledge that they have had a great part in the restoration of rights to their fellow Nisei. Nisei soldiers have proven gallantly their right to be called Americans, and we civilians have been caught up in the reflection of their glory.

We civilians owe an everlasting debt of gratitude to our fighting men.

For a long time, because the Nisei translators in the Pacific were a "secret weapon," all the publicity about Japanese American fighting men was concentrated on the 442nd in Europe. That led to a strange and unfair distortion of the truth, which was the subject of a column October 27, 1945:

"People were killed in Italy, too," said Staff Sergeant Dave Hirahara. "I was there. We went where the Army told us to go."

Sergeant Hirahara made the statement with a puzzled expression, for he had run into people who asked why he hadn't been in the Pacific if he wanted to fight.

59

If these people had been a bit more observant, they would have noticed that Sergeant Hirahara holds his head a little differently. That's because a German bullet caught him in the head, took the sight of one eye. But Sergeant Hirahara considers himself lucky. There were a lot of his buddies on that particular mission who didn't come back.

Sergeant Hirahara wanted to fight. That's why he left his pretty young wife and infant daughter in a relocation camp and volunteered to go wherever Uncle Sam saw fit. The War Department sent him to Italy with the Nisei 442nd Regimental Combat team, and from there the unit went to France and back to Italy again. That unit suffered thousands of casualties, including 569 dead.

And they want to know why he hadn't been to the Pacific if he wanted to fight.

They got their answer last week, straight from MacArthur's headquarters. The Nisei were in the Pacific Theatre by the hundreds, assigned to intelligence work so secret that the existence of their units was not revealed for six weeks after the formal end of the war.

These units were of the Allied Translator and Interpreter Section (ATIS) made up principally of Japanese Americans. They operated so skillfully on Pacific battlefields, according to the Associated Press, that they often knew the telephone numbers of Japanese billets.

Among the Nisei were some taken off Corregidor before the Philippines fortress fell early in 1942.

The commander of the section, Colonel Sidney F. Mashbir, says: "No group in the war had as much to lose. Capture would have meant indescribable horror to them and their relatives in Japan."

Other sources have revealed that every division in the Pacific had at least ten Nisei translators and interpreters attached to it. These Nisei specialists took part in virtually every Japanese surrender at the termination of the fighting.

They proved themselves so valuable in combat that they were on loan to the U.S. Navy and Marine Corps, and to British and Australian forces fighting in Burma and Borneo.

The men who were assigned this hazardous duty are all volunteers who mastered the Japanese language at the grueling pace demanded by pressing military necessity.

It is welcome news that at long last their record in the Pacific Theatre has been made known. The need for security silence blacked out the story of this American secret weapon while unsung Nisei heroes were carrying out one of the war's most thrilling episodes.

Unwittingly, the government decision to organize the segregated 442nd for action in Europe gave the unreconstructed racists the chance to say the Army didn't "trust" the Nisei to fight in the Pacific. It gave at least one Navy officer speaking from California lecture platforms the opportunity to declare the 442nd had set its brilliant record only because the Nisei "were killing white men."

Now the lie has been given to this racist talk. The Nisei of ATIS have been responsible for the saving of countless American lives, and for the death and capture of even greater numbers of Japanese. When the whole story of ATIS and its individual members is known, there will be many tales of personal heroism, initiative and sacrifice.

The Nisei of the 442nd who suffered from trenchfoot and frostbite in the war against the Nazis have worthy comrades in arms in the Nisei of ATIS, who had to contend with malaria and jungle rot in addition to the Japanese.

While virtually all Nisei servicemen went into the 442nd or military intelligence, there were a number of notable exceptions. The best-known was Sergeant Ben Kuroki, the Nebraska farm boy who was accepted by the Air Corps. Kuroki flew thirty missions, five more than required, as a gunner on Liberator bombers against targets in North Africa and Europe. After that he asked for duty in the Pacific and flew twenty-eight more combat missions in B-29 bombers, many of them over Tokyo. But there were others who somehow slipped through the Army's red tape. The July 24, 1953 column told about two of them:

It just goes to show that rules are made to be broken. Take the case of Junie Kawamura of Minneapolis. Junie volunteered for the Nisei 442nd Regimental Combat Team a decade ago and wound up as a paratrooper.

You may recall that the Army, Navy, and Marine Corps were being terribly choosy back in those days. For a long time after Pearl Harbor they didn't want to induct anybody with a Japanese face and name. Then the Army lifted the lid to the extent of taking a small corps of volunteers for training in military intelligence. After that the 442nd was authorized and scores of Nisei who'd been in service before the big freeze were "volunteered" in the segregated unit. They made up the cadre of the fightin'est outfit in the whole bloomin' war.

At any rate, Junie and a Caucasian pal of his went down to the draft board in Minneapolis one day all prepared to get into uniform. Of course Junie expected to join the 442nd. But when a recruiting sergeant asked for paratroop volunteers, Junie's pal said: "Well, what the heck. If we're going to die, we might as well live like kings until we get it. I hear they eat good in the paratroops. Let's volunteer." So they stepped two places forward and promptly found themselves accepted.

Until he actually landed in Europe, Junie kept expecting to get booted out of the paratroops and sent over to the 442nd. But the red tape experts never did catch up with him and pretty soon Junie found himself making a combat jump into southern France. The only thing that spoiled the fun was getting ripped up after running afoul of a minefield.

Once Junie was called on to interrogate an Asiatic prisoner of war. Junie tackled him in Japanese, Nisei version, but drew only a blank. He wonders to this day whether the prisoner was a Mongol, or whether he was a Japanese baffled by Junie's Nisei accent.

Junie Kawamura's experience in the Army is reminiscent of the situation Harry Yanagimachi found himself in. Harry, like Junie, is an ex-Seattleite. He volunteered for the 442nd from Minidoka WRA center, reported for training and found himself picked for officer candidate school. That could have been expected because Harry is all man—big enough and tough enough to quarterback the University of Washington freshman football team back in the mid-Thirties.

While Harry was learning to become an officer and gentleman, the 442nd took off across the Atlantic. Harry expected to join them in time but after he got his lieutenant's bars he found himself headed out across the Pacific.

When Lieutenant Yanagimachi reported for duty the CO looked at his name and at his face and asked: "Are you an interpreter?"

"Hell no, sir," Yanagimachi replied. "I can hardly speak the blankety-blank language, sir."

"But you can't go into combat."

"Why the hell not, sir? That's what the hell I came out here for, sir, and that's what I intend to do."

Overwhelmed either by Yanagimachi's profanity or his determination, the CO gave Harry a platoon. Harry led it into combat in some of the jungle fighting around Manila and managed very well not to get shot at by his own men.

Odd world, isn't it?

Some years after war's end, a movie was made about the 442nd. It was called, "Go for Broke," which was that outfit's motto. Perhaps you've seen the film on the late, late,

late show. It was probably the first full-length feature in which Nisei were cast in roles other than the butler or the houseboy and it played two- and three-week engagements in the larger cities around the country. On June 2, 1951, the following column appeared:

I have just seen "Go for Broke." It's a great movie, one that all Nisei and Issei ought to see, and one that I hope millions on millions of Americans will see.

If that's advertising, Metro-Goldwyn-Mayer deserves to get rich for having the courage, professional foresight, and ability to put such a picture on the screen.

The story of "Go for Broke" is too familiar to need retelling here. But it is a picture that made me laugh, chuckle, squirm, sweat, yes even weep a little, so well has it caught and portrayed the Nisei of the 442nd.

I talked to a couple of veterans of the 442nd immediately after the showing. "It brought tears to my eyes," said one. "That's just the way it was," said another. Its realism, and its studied understatement are the film's strongest points.

Of course the film is far from perfect, and one of "Go for Broke's" shortcomings from the Nisei viewpoint is the lack of emphasis on the relocation camps. You get the captain talking about evacuation, and letters from home telling about camp life. But you never see a camp.

It would seem that the millions of Americans to whom the Evacuation is still nothing but a vague rumor would miss the point. A quick shot, perhaps of some volunteers leaving the wire-ribbed gates of a WRA camp on their way to Camp Shelby, would have clarified that part.

Nisei and Issei should see the picture because this is the first time the sacrifices made by their sons, brothers and friends have been presented in the motion picture's graphic form. The Army's shorts on the 442nd's training did not

64

tell the whole story, simply because they were not designed for that job.

We've all seen war movies. And we've heard vets talk about some war incidents. But mostly they don't talk about the more grim experiences and words can never be quite so graphic as a movie. Now we're seeing our own kind right smack in the middle of situations which, until now, may have been something vaguely terrible. You may find yourself in a rough situation, but sometimes you don't realize the real horror of it until afterward. And that's where "Go for Broke" has its greatest impact on the Nisei.

"Go for Broke" should help to win for the 442nd a firmer niche in the history of American military valor. But more important, it is a record of how Nisei soldiers secured the future of their parents, their kin, their friends, their children, and themselves. It is a record of how they "won a big chunk of America with their blood."

Perhaps the message of "Go for Broke" hit this observer closer than it did others. Let it be said that the preaching is usually unobtrusive, that the picture is excellent entertainment. And that's the best way to get an idea over.

"Go for Broke" is a worthy tribute to all Nisei servicemen, and a memorial as well to a good many Joe Nisei who didn't come back.

It made a fellow proud of the Nisei, proud to be one.

Over the years I've met a surprising number of people who had some association with Nisei servicemen and wanted to talk about those experiences. Some of them made interesting Frying Pan items. This first one was published August 12, 1955:

Gerald Quiat is a young and prominent Denver attorney who recently was named commander of the Leyden-Chiles-

Wickersham Post of the American Legion. With something like 10,000 members, the post is either the largest or second largest in the country. I met Quiat for the first time the other day.

"Did you know," he asked, "that my life was saved by a Nisei from the 442nd Combat Team?" Then he went on to unfold a fascinating story. Quiat was a lieutenant, a platoon leader of a rifle company. He picked up a stomach wound in battle, was captured by an advancing party of Germans. He was thrown into a prison camp, his wound left to bleed and fester.

"One of my fellow prisoners was a Nisei," Quiat told me. "He took care of me like a mother. I lost weight—about seventy pounds—and I grew so weak that I couldn't take care of my personal needs. But this Nisei buddy brought me food, kept me clean, washed my clothes. He even found some sulfa tablets—I don't know where—that stopped the infection. Without him I would never have lived through the ordeal.

"The Nisei boy's name was Masa Uchimura. Do you by any chance happen to know him?"

Know him? The Uchimuras and the Hosokawas were neighbors a long time ago in Seattle. Masa and his sister, Lily, had been sent to Japan to live with their grandparents when they were just toddlers. I remember when they came back to Seattle, and how he used to struggle with the English language. One year, I think it was 1929, we went to work in the Alaska salmon canneries in the same crew. After a while we moved out of the neighborhood, and we sort of lost track of the Uchimuras.

And now, after all these years, we heard about Masa again. It was nice, remembering.

The other column was dated June 15, 1956:

66

The blood-drenched Italian hills of Cassino are distant in terms of both time and geography, but Len Smith had occasion to remember them a few days ago. Len was a correspondent for *Stars and Stripes,* or perhaps it was *Yank.* It doesn't matter which for purposes of this story.

Today he's a crack public relations counsel in Denver. It was at Cassino that he first encountered and learned to admire the original 100th Battalion, the tough, brilliant, combat-wise Hawaiian National Guard outfit made up almost entirely of Nisei.

The battle for Cassino was not going well for the Allies. The Nazis were firmly entrenched on high ground and repeatedly they would push back Allied assaults with heavy casualties. The 100th Battalion was being thrown into the line wherever the going was heaviest. During the day, when activity let up, the Nisei troops would be pulled back to rest. But at night, when attacks and counter-attacks could be expected, back they would go into combat.

The way Len tells it, some Nisei trooper with a devilish sense of humor, or perhaps it was pure inspiration, came up with an idea for harassing the Krauts. Back in the rear area during the day, this Nisei collected a few empty C-ration cans and polished them to a mirror finish. That night, when he went back into combat, he waited until the moon came out, weighted the C-ration cans with rocks, and threw them in the general direction of the German lines. Moonlight reflecting off the flying cans quickly caught many eyes. The cans landed with a reassuring thump. A few minutes later the Nisei GI lobbed several grenades after the cans. The grenades were black and therefore invisible. They exploded with a fearful noise. In the German lines rumors spread swiftly that the Yanks were employing a mysterious new secret weapon.

Soon, almost all the enlisted men in the 100th were

spending their free time collecting and polishing C-ration cans. Some punched holes in the cans so they gave out a disconcerting whistle when they were thrown. At night, all along the line, these cans would arc through the moonlight toward the enemy, gleaming mysteriously. Invariably, invisible grenades followed them. And equally invariably these weird missiles would explode with devastating results, sometimes seconds after they landed, sometimes many minutes later.

The secret weapon preyed on the nerves of the Germans holding the line night after night. German intelligence tried to discover the nature of the weapon so countermeasures could be devised. German propaganda broadcasts beamed at the Americans at first warned the Yanks to cease and desist, later shouted in almost hysterical tones that vengeance would be wreaked on "the Japanese traitors who are fighting for the Allied forces."

But apparently the Germans never did catch on to the secret of the polished tin cans. In the sector defended by the 100th Battalion, the nerve-wracked Germans began to pull back. As Smith recalls it, they retreated a good two miles and thus gave the Americans a toehold which finally led to victory.

"Of course I wrote the story for my paper," Smith told me. "But censors wouldn't let it get through. I tried several times after that to get the story published, but someone always thought it would be a breach of security to reveal the story of the tin can weapons. It's still one of my favorite war yarns."

Smith never was able to learn who first dreamed up the idea. Possibly, in view of the heavy casualties suffered by the 100th, the man is dead. Or again, he or his buddies may see this column and recall this small episode in a large war.

Len Smith is dead now, and we never did learn the identity of the Nisei GI who invented what may have been World War II's cheapest secret weapon.

In 1968, a good quarter-century after the war, I had the privilege of attending a reunion of military intelligence veterans in Los Angeles and that led to this column of November 22:

The years fell away, and warm memories of a quarter-century ago came flooding back for the Veterans of Military Intelligence Service who held their second national reunion here last weekend. An odd and perhaps fortunate thing about human nature is that, if one is normal, the bitter memories fade while the fun and good times are remembered. Thus it was with the men who gathered here to talk fondly about training days at the Presidio in San Francisco, Camp Savage and Fort Snelling in Minnesota, or of Monterey, where the West Coast branch of the Defense Language Institute is now located.

Some shook hands with comrades they hadn't seen since the day they were graduated from the language school and sent off to far-flung fronts. "Gee, your face is familiar, but damned if I can remember your name." Or, "I didn't recognize you at first. You used to be such a skinny guy."

They remembered fondly the way they tackled the mysteries of the Japanese language, the gut-tightening tension of the exams, the strict discipline imposed on them by John Aiso who knew the men just had to make good, and the way the Nisei had to work over lessons that were laughably easy for the Kibei members of the class.

And for outsiders at the reunion they recounted the feats of men like Sergeant Hoichi Kubo who earned a Distinguished Service Cross for risking his life to persuade a group of dangerous Japanese holdouts on Saipan to surrender, of Sergeant Frank Hachiya, who was awarded the Silver Star posthumously in the Philippines, of Sergeant Kenny Yasui, who captured a band of enemy soldiers in Burma and also won the Silver Star. Yasui, who lives in Los Angeles and has been in ill health, showed up for the reunion. A mild, quiet, almost shy man, now he is reluctant to talk about his war experiences and looks and acts nothing like the popular conception of a war hero.

Late at night, when memories are most mellow, men like Ben Sugeta recalled uproariously funny and unprintable escapades that made the listener wonder how we ever managed to win the war. Sugeta remembered the fun and mischief, others had to tell how half dead of exhaustion and disease, he had to be flown out of interior China to save his life.

It is at events like the reunion that one becomes aware of the tremendously valuable part the Kibei played in World War II. They were the real language experts. Most Nisei were not nearly so well qualified. Some Kibei, like Kenny Yasui, had been in the Army before Pearl Harbor and were transferred to the enlisted reserve—a nice way of saying kicked out—in the hysteria following the outbreak of war. Yasui was bitter over this affront, but as the bitterness wore off he was stung by bigoted charges that all Kibei were not to be trusted. So he volunteered for intelligence work to demonstrate his loyalty and was decorated by a grateful nation.

In Burma Yasui learned the Japanese division in the area was from Kyushu, where he had spent his boyhood. Yasui knew the enemy was doomed, and he was convinced that his own brother was serving with them. He searched the prisoner compounds anxiously for that brother until one day he ran into a classmate from the village school he had attended as a child. The prisoner told Yasui that his brother

70

had been transferred to another division and was not in Burma at all.

Sugeta, another Kibei, tells of going back after the surrender to the home he had known as a boy in Japan, and meeting his brother who was a Japanese Air Force officer. It took days for the Japanese brother to thaw to the point where he would even speak to Ben.

Other than this, service in military intelligence welded a comradeship among diverse elements of the Nisei community—mainlanders, Hawaiian islanders, and Kibei—a comradeship that has survived the years and stood the test of time as was amply demonstrated in Los Angeles.

6

On the Move

The end of the war started the Nisei in motion again. Many of them were going back to the West Coast and a surprising number passed through Des Moines. Unexpectedly our home became a house by the side of the road where travelers stopped. On April 6, 1946, the Frying Pan column was about these travelers:

Often the visitor is someone heading back to what appears to be the greener pastures of the Pacific Coast. A few weeks ago it was LeRoy Takaichi who, with his brother Sam, was headed west to complete the San Jose-Santa Anita-Heart Mountain-Cody-Minneapolis-San Jose cycle.

Sometimes it's an old friend passing through on a business trip, like Jim Sugioka or Masao Satow.

Last week it was a soldier, Frank Muramatsu, on furlough en route to a California staging area from where he expects to be shipped overseas for a tour of duty with the occupation forces in Japan.

This week it was another soldier, Bob Yosh Kodama, proudly wearing his "ruptured duck" discharge button, hurrying leisurely to Los Angeles to rejoin his wife and son.

They are travelers all, and most of them drop in with no more warning than a telephone call fifteen minutes before they show up.

But they always are welcome, for we are glad to see old friends and happy to be able to provide them with shelter, a meal, or a hot bath.

We pull out the extra sheets and convert the studio couch into a bed; we set another place or two at the table. The hospitality is simple but sincere; we're glad to have them.

The talk waxes on deep into the night. We're catching up with the latest news and gossip. Bob's bought a house. May's expecting her second. Yukio, who used to stack oranges in a supermarket, has a responsible job with a leading firm of architects; Ed's got his mother and dad with him and is planning on going into business soon; Ted's out of service and looking for a job. And so it goes.

Our home is like an inn, and part of our return—like that of an innkeeper of old—is in the news that the wayfarers leave before they speed on.

Mostly, the news is good. It has to do with instances of assimilation, heartening economic and social readjustment, of the fruits that are being enjoyed as the result of courage, perseverence, ingenuity, and opportunity to employ skills and training. . . .

By this time our Mike was going on 5½ years old. He had been joined in Des Moines by his sister Susan in 1944. She had signaled her impending arrival one night while I was at work. Alice did not telephone me, first because we didn't have a phone in the house, and second because it

73

*wouldn't have done any good because we didn't have an
automobile. She simply asked a neighbor to call a cab and
went to the hospital, leaving Mike with Grandma.*

*I got off work at midnight and took the streetcar home.
Grandma was still up and told me Alice had gone. I hurried back to the carline; the streetcar had rattled off to the
end of the line and was returning to town when I caught
it. I reached the hospital about 2 A.M. and a nurse let me
in to see Alice. The baby hadn't arrived and there was no
telling when it would come. Alice told me to go home and
because I was pooped, I did, catching the 3 A.M. streetcar.*

*Next morning I hurried up to Eisentraut's drug store on
the corner and telephoned the hospital. They told me Susan
had been born and everything was fine. I walked back to the
house, gave Grandma and Mike the good news, had some
breakfast, and then caught the streetcar to visit Alice and
our daughter. That's the way it was during the war years.*

*As the children developed personalities, they began to
appear occasionally in Frying Pan. Other Nisei families
were having children, too, and my reports on the doings of
my youngsters struck a responsive chord. Columns about
Mike and Susan, and Pete and Christie who came along
some time later, turned out to be among the most popular.
On March 16, 1946, I wrote this little item about Mike:*

What made him ask the question we shall never know.
It was bedtime, and as he lay stretched and luxuriating in
the comfort of his bed he asked:

"Dad, if they blew up the world with atomic bombs,
would it make a big noise?"

What was that? A big noise? The first thought that occurred was that there would be no one left in this world
to determine if it were a "big" noise, or just an ordinary
noise. But we said: "Yep, it sure would."

Then he shouted as loudly as he could: "Bang!"

74

"Gosh," he said, "I bet an atomic bomb would make a noise louder than I can yell. How many bombs would it take to blow up the world? Two? Three?"

A moment later he was asleep, deep in the untroubled sleep of a five-year-old kindergartener exhausted by a day of glorious new discoveries, of learning, of play, of frustration and triumphs.

Later we heard a newscast and came away depressed. Nothing but alarums on the air—defiant words, charges and countercharges, forebodings.

The voice of the brave new world that trumpeted such hope on VE-Day and VJ-Day is a feeble piping now. The calls for understanding and common sense are strained, almost hysterical in their urgency.

There is a need now as never before for world statesmanship. But no man has come forth with a magic formula. Even the great warrior who rallied Britain in her darkest hour and who carried her to triumph had only a plan whose essence was that of the discredited old scheme of power politics.

In short, his solution was that of pitting one combination of nations against another, each threatening the other with destruction and forcing the maintenance of a precarious peace.

Perhaps there is no magic formula. Perhaps the answer to peace is to be found in the hearts of Dads whose little sons ask: "If they blew up the world with atomic bombs, would it make a big noise?"

Susan, at age two, would talk pretty well but her interests were on a somewhat different level, as reported in the column of May 4, 1946:

Our younger offspring is at the stage where she asks questions merely for the thrill of wrestling with words and

75

emerging triumphant. The information she draws out with her questions is incidental—she's usually asking another question before the first one is answered.

After a preliminary imperative phrase (like "Get up, sleepyhead!") the interrogatory sentences follow upon each other. Samples:

"Wha choo sleepin' for?"
"Wha choo takin' a bath for?"
"Wha choo dressin' up for?"
"Wha choo combin' your hair for?"
"Wha choo eatin' for?"
"Where you goin' now for?"
"Wha choo goin' to work for?"

So far we've been passive about answering, but we're toying with the idea of introducing a new routine soon, just to avoid the monotony.

Memories of wartime experiences receded, but every once in a while old matters would pop up, like this question articulated on June 1, 1946:

One of the still-unsolved evacuation-connected mysteries is the form letters which the Army sent out to a number of Japanese Americans in 1942.

These letters were printed, appeared over the name of Colonel Karl R. Bendetsen, and started:

"Certain Japanese persons are currently being considered for repatriation to Japan. You, and those members of your family listed above, are being so considered."

Strangely enough, these letters were addressed to many prominent Nisei whose loyalty was beyond question.

The common reaction was anger and deep indignation, for in effect American citizens were being "invited" to agree to deportation from their own to an alien land.

Many strongly worded letters were sent to the Army in

reply and apparently nothing much came of the "repatria-tion" movement.

Almost four years have passed now, and the war that brought about such a weird incident is ended. But there has been no explanation. Certainly one is overdue.

I had forgotten about these letters until I chanced across the item while preparing this book. So far as I am aware, the question raised in the column has never been answered. What was Bendetsen, identified by the Army's official historian as its "most industrious advocate of mass evacua-tion," trying to do?

(Bendetsen says the evaluation of his role is merely the opinion of the author, Stetson Conn. "I was not an advocate at all," Bendetsen has written, adding that he was merely a staff officer carrying out the orders of his superiors. Ironi-cally, Bendetsen is now a trustee of Freedom House, a dis-tinguished national organization dedicated to strengthening democratic institutions.)

Our Des Moines interlude came to an end that June. New opportunities beckoned, and this is how the move was explained in the Frying Pan for June 29, 1946.

And so once again it is time to pack up our things and move on. This is our last week in Des Moines. When we settle down after several weeks of traveling, our address will be Denver.

Moving no longer is a novelty. This is our tenth jump in nine years. A few of the moves were at the urgent request of Uncle Sam when it was popularly believed that ridding the Pacific Coast of Japanese Americans was essential to winning the war.

But the rest were the result of the search for greener pastures, and we have no regrets for making those decisions.

In many ways we are reluctant to leave Des Moines.

It has been home for more than two and a half years. It welcomed us at a time when many communities were openly hostile to the evacuees.

When we first arrived we were amazed at the friendliness of the people. And as time went on our amazement grew, and increasingly we realized that we were being accepted—without our making any extraordinary efforts—as part and parcel of the community's lifestream.

There is much that is solid and reassuring and basic about life in the Midwest. We have had a chance to sample it, and we feel we are better Americans for having had the opportunity.

All this is aside from the fine personal friends we have found. But making friends and leaving them is an inevitable part of moving about, and we are reconciled to the hope that in the coming bright new world transportation will be so easy that our paths will cross frequently. . . .

It's funny how values change. Among the more treasured items we are packing this time are a jar of shortening and a bottle of salad oil, still rationed, which the clerk at the chain store slipped to us from under the counter. They've been packed carefully, for we hear they're rare items anywhere.

Among the adjustments to be made in Denver will be finding a butcher and a grocer with whom we can become friendly, for in these times of food shortages such friendships are priceless.

We cultivated relationships with the butcher here so that if he had a package of bacon or a steak, we'd be sure of getting them if we wanted. It gave one a certain satisfying (and smug) feeling to be a favored customer, especially when transient shoppers were being turned away with a doleful "Sorry, we haven't got a thing."

Oh yes, we're going to work on the Denver *Post*.

The publishing plant is the same, and so are many of the employees, but the *Post* is not the same newspaper which gave Heart Mountain in particular and Japanese Americans in general such a rough time during the war.

We feel that in joining the *Post* we are not compromising one whit the principles we upheld in more vigorous days in *Pacific Citizen* and the Heart Mountain *Sentinel*.

Rather, it is the *Post* which has come around to the ways of fair play and decency, and we are proud that we will be associated with it.

And so we set sail for the West, planning a brief stop in Denver before going on to Seattle for a visit with the folks before backtracking to Colorado. The trip was made in a 1936 Hudson which we picked up in a used car lot as a desperation measure just four days before starting out. We had hoped to travel in style, in a brand-new Chevrolet. Each week after we placed the order the dealer kept assuring us a car would be available in time for our departure. D-Day came closer and closer, and still no car. Detroit's assembly lines, gearing up after the war, just couldn't supply the demand. Finally the dealer admitted he couldn't possibly get us a car. By then it was too late to get train reservations. The ten-year-old Hudson, which was the roomiest car on the lot, was the only way to get out of town.

The night before we were to start out the car developed a devastating shimmy at anything higher than thirty m.p.h. We got by cheap on that one—$4.25 to get the wheels balanced. Then in Arapahoe, Nebraska, the fuel pump went out and the mechanic discovered one of the radiator hose connections was shot. That was $5.50.

During the last few hundred miles into Denver we noticed a clinking and clunking in the drive shaft and differential region, and a mechanic agreed to fix that for $25. We did

79

get one break, though. The four retread tires, one of them with visible cracks in the casing, held up all the way.

On July 13, 1946, we wrote from Seattle:

We reach Seattle this week after a 2,500-mile Odyssey in a 1936 car. Miraculously we experienced no more mechanical mishaps than reported last week.

The old home town is an amazing place after an absence of more than four years. It has grown tremendously during the war. It is full of strange new bus lines. Familiar roads are now speedways to take care of the enlarged population.

But more apparent is the new tempo of the town—everyone seems to be racing along with his accelerator down to the floorboards. Everyone is in a terrific rush to get somewhere and do something.

Perhaps this is the normal tempo of a boom town, a city which grew from just another Pacific Coast seaport to a military and naval staging area and a producer of the sinews of war.

And then again, perhaps we have been too long in that easy-going overgrown Midwestern village, Des Moines.

Our car, naturally, bears an Iowa license. And as we plodded westward we often wondered what went on in the minds of those who passed us expecting to see a load of corn-fed, corn-growing Iowans.

A half-dozen persons—fellow wayfarers, service station attendants, an auto court proprietor who was born in Sioux City—asked us about Iowa. And we replied with the wisdom of one who has been a transplanted Iowan for thirty-two months.

Long hours of driving enabled us to get closer to five-year-old Mike than ever before. A sample conversation at forty-five miles per hour across the Wyoming wasteland:

"Dad, what's a dummy?"

"Well, a dummy is somebody that isn't very smart."

"Doesn't a dummy know what a tree is?"

"Nope."

"Doesn't a dummy know what a bird is, or a bus, or a diesel truck?"

"Nope."

"You mean a dummy is even dumber than you, Dad?"

In Denver, in Ogden, Portland, and Seattle, we ran into persons we haven't seen for years.

The gaunt ones were more gaunt. The thin ones leaner, the fat ones more rotund, the balding ones balder, the poor ones poorer and the rich ones richer.

The years, it seems, do little but accentuate the quirks and foibles that nature has foisted on us. As for our friends, we will let them guess about our description of them.

We soon found in Seattle that the conversation of Nisei is turning from baseball to babies.

Where once it was on Joe Nisei's prowess at the plate, now it's about his youngsters. And the Ann Niseis compare their children's growth, brag modestly about the number of teeth and exchange ideas on ways to overcome small-fry tantrums.

Verily, the one-time younger generation of Japanese Americans is well on the way to middle age.

The experience of seeing how childhood friends had matured must have made quite an impression, because on August 10, we wrote a remarkably prophetic column:

Of late we have been brooding more than ordinarily on the age of the Nisei, once referred to seriously as the younger generation. A Nisei in his fifties is no longer a rarity. The Nisei are growing families and pot-bellies, they

81

are becoming gray and bald and their wives are putting on weight where it flatters them least. How swiftly the years have been speeding lately.

In another fifty years, we ventured the other night, the Nisei and his offspring largely will have lost his identity as the so-called insoluble ingredient in the American melting pot. He will have scattered and inter-married and his communities will have dwindled into ghostly relics of what they once were.

This contention was challenged, but then we pointed out that the Issei will be no more in another decade or so, and at the progress the Nisei have made over their parents in the process described by the word Americanization.

Do you remember when the Nisei held their first public dance, and how many of their mothers were scandalized by the unladylike behavior of their daughters who dared indulge in such indecencies as embracing a man and jiggling in a foxtrot?

And when Mrs. S. learned that her daughter smoked cigarettes, why, she was fit to be tied.

There is bound to be another revolution soon. The offspring of the Nisei will rebel at the ideas of Pa and Ma, even as Pa and Ma once thumbed their collective noses at their parents and said: "But Mama, you're so old fashioned!"

Certainly the new lines of battle will not be so clearly marked as they were between Issei and Nisei. But conflict there will be, and progress there will be. Thus has it ever been.

In Denver we discovered that rental housing was virtually non-existent and the price of real estate was nearly double what it had been in Des Moines. We finally bought a big old house in a quiet residential area. It had two tiny apartments in the basement, and bedrooms on the second floor which could be rented. We counted on the rental income to help meet the mortgage payments. One reason we were anxious to get settled was that Mike was scheduled to enroll in first grade. The Frying Pan for September 28, 1946 was devoted to his first day:

"School," said our six-year-old, "wasn't hard at all."

Somewhere along the little boy grapevine he got the idea it was a terrifically big jump from kindergarten to being a first-grader. And he was relieved that it wasn't such a leap after all.

The six-year-old became a full-fledged schoolboy this week after a year as a despised kindergartener. There was a three-week delay due to the polio epidemic and some of the edge was taken off the business of starting school. But the big hurdle is over.

He isn't quite so excited about the prospect of school now as when he was a four-year-old waiting to turn five. But perhaps it is just as well because his four-year-old's ardor cooled somewhat after he started kindergarten.

First it was the rest periods he didn't like. They made everyone relax for ten or fifteen minutes during the morning. That meant suspending all activity and swallowing one's eagerness and excitement. That meant putting one's arms down on the table, and placing one's head on his arms and closing one's eyes.

No, he was too eager to be up and drinking in all the wonders of the kindergartener's world. There was too much to be done to waste one's time resting, so he didn't like school.

Then it was the physical examination he didn't like. That involved opening one's mouth and taking off one's shoes so the nurse could measure one's height. Opening the mouth was easy. But he didn't like the shoe business.

It was the beginning of a social and self consciousness.

Some of the other children could lace and tie their own shoes. He could lace his but hadn't mastered the mystery of a double bow knot. So he was ashamed and felt inferior and so he didn't want to go to school.

"What did you do on your first day in the first grade?" we asked him, trying to act fatherly.

"Well," he replied, "we drew pictures. But we mostly sat, and I didn't like that. We had recess."

"Is Teddy in your class?" Teddy is the tow-headed youngster who has been playing with ours.

"Teddy sits way on the other side of the room."

"Do you have your own desks?"

"We sit at tables. Two of us at each table."

"Who sits with you?"

"I don't know. I don't know anybody's name."

We sit here trying to recall our first day of school. It was so long, long ago that the events of the day itself have been forgotten. But fragmentary memories of the first year of school come back, like bits of a forgotten nightmare.

We spoke scarcely a half dozen words of English when we first entered school. We had been reared on the outskirts of a "Little Tokyo," and so we had no playmates other than little Japanese-speaking Nisei.

And our parents, who were acutely aware of the short-comings in their English pronunciation, had hesitated to try to teach us English for fear of corrupting our accents.

We have vague recollections of sitting blankly in class and reacting to instructions partly by intuition, partly by copying the reactions of the other pupils. We recall the misery of shyness until we became used to associating with other children and began to comprehend what was being said around us.

Any child, unless he is a brash, cocky youngster, is sure to feel shy when he is thrust suddenly among thirty or forty strange young children. This each child must contend with and meet in his own way. That is part of the process of growing up.

But at least our youngster has a working knowledge of his native tongue, and that, it seems, symbolizes the progress that Japanese Americans have made in the space of a single generation. May the world before him unfold with the opportunities correspondingly greater than those which were open to his Nisei father and his immigrant Issei grandfather.

We had been in our new home and the apartment-renting business for just a few months when a prospective tenant demonstrated to us that the war was indeed over. We wrote about it in the Frying Pan on November 30, 1946:

This is the story of Corporal Duane Wayman. He wears the shoulder patch of the Philippines Division, the head of a carabao or water buffalo on a red background. On his chest, among other ribbons, are a Purple Heart with two clusters, indicating three battle wounds; a Silver Star with one cluster, which means he was twice decorated for conspicuous bravery in combat; and a Presidential Unit Citation ribbon with three clusters, denoting that his outfit was cited four times.

Corporal Wayman appeared at the door one day.

"Mrs. Hosokawa?" he said. "The USO told me you had listed a room for rent. May I look at it?"

The room was satisfactory and he agreed to take it. She showed him the bathroom and said: "We have a big automatic water heater; you'll have plenty of hot water."

"There were times when I didn't get much of that," he replied.

"Oh? The Army?"

"I was a prisoner of war in Japan almost four years," he said quietly. "I'll be back tomorrow to take the room."

85

Corporal Wayman moved in the next day. He turned out to be a quiet, considerate tenant, and as the first strangeness wore off, we got to talking.

Duane Wayman was just out of high school when he enlisted in the spring of 1941. Pearl Harbor day found him in the Philippines. He was in an anti-aircraft unit, but before long he found himself on Bataan as an infrantryman. There were no more shells to be fired at the Zeroes.

After the surrender the Japanese marched the Americans five days and four nights with only two twenty-minute rest stops. That was the Bataan death march, although they didn't call it that then.

It was a long voyage to Japan, 5,000 men in the hold and only three of them allowed above decks at any one time to use the toilet facilities. Once they lay in a harbor in Formosa for nineteen days, kept in that stifling hold all that time except for the few moments when they were one of the fortunate three.

"None of use would have survived our years in Japan," Corporal Wayman declared, "if we hadn't been assigned to work around railroad yards and other places where we could steal food.

"Often we prisoners would go weeks without speaking to each other. We had talked ourselves out. We could only think food and talk food, and if anyone thought out loud, someone else would throw something to shut him up.

"Our captors would go out of their way to humiliate us. We would be subjected to savage beatings without cause. It was impossible to talk and try to reason with them as they had no sense of fairness.

"Our guards stole from Red Cross and relief parcels we received from home. My parents weren't notified I was a prisoner until two years after the capture. I was allowed to write one postcard home and it was delivered months after I got back.

86

"In all my time in Japan in the half dozen camps to which we were shifted, I met only two Japanese who went out of their way to treat us decently. And those two risked their own lives to be good to us.

"When the Japanese surrendered, ninety of us broke out of the stockade, climbed aboard a train and made our way to Tokyo. We were among the first to be repatriated."

How does Corporal Wayman feel now?

"I have no bitterness toward the people," he says, "only pity because they've never had a chance to learn differently. In some ways I respect them, for they gave everything to their nation until they were almost as poor as those of us in the prisoner-of-war camps.

"I hate some of the individuals who mistreated us so bitterly that if they came into this room this minute, I'd get my gun and shoot them down without hesitating. Almost every one of them has been executed as a war criminal or sentenced to long prison terms by Allied military courts."

And the Japanese Americans?

When Corporal Wayman got back, his hometown newspaper at Greeley, Colorado, published his picture and a story of his experiences. After that, Wayman noticed Nisei would cross the street to avoid meeting him.

These Nisei were afraid because they had been subjected to discrimination and hatred simply because they were of Japanese extraction. They feared that this returned soldier who had suffered so much in the hands of the Japanese would take it out on them.

But Corporal Wayman has another view. He says:

"I don't hate a man because of his race or who his ancestors were. A man must be judged as an individual—who he is and what he has done."

And that, it seems to us, is an eminently just and American viewpoint expressed by one who has gained wisdom through suffering.

7

The Growing Family

As the children grew older, reports of their activities showed up more frequently in Frying Pan. Over the years these accounts have drawn the most reader comment. Here are some favorite items:

Our six-year-old and the redheaded girl with whom he plays stumbled last week on a case of beer in an empty lot. Most of the bottles were empty, but four were still capped and intact. How the beer happened to be there, we haven't figured out. But unbothered by small fry compunctions the two promptly invoked the age-old principle of finders-keepers.

But beer was something different from Cokes and it couldn't be disposed of in the most obvious manner. So they got the idea of opening a beer store. The redhead recalled that bottled beverages are best cooled, so the two found a pan of water. Then they set up shop, shouting:

"Ten cents a bottle, beer for sale. Ten cents a bottle, beer for sale."

It wasn't long before the man next door popped his head out the window, wanting to know if it was real beer.

"Sure," said Mike, holding up a bottle and shaking it vigorously. The bottle foamed up and it hurt the man to see perfectly good brew being treated thus, so he cried:

"Stop, stop. Bring it here and I'll buy it."

So the redhead and the six-year-old were paid a quarter for two bottles without benefit of a bottled goods license.

As it turned out, the six-year-old kept the quarter and the redhead took the remaining two bottles home to her daddy. Don't ask why the spoils were divided in this manner. The ways of small fry are difficult to fathom.

(October 12, 1946)

We went to the ball game the other night—we being Mike, who is seven and a half, Susan who is four, and I who am old enough to be their father. We saw the Denver Bears play Pueblo in a Western League game. The Western is only Class A in the hierarchy of professional baseball, and they come up with some sour exhibitions, especially Denver which has a long-term lease on the cellar.

But that isn't what we started to write about, because it was the youngsters' first encounter with a real baseball game. They provided more fun for the people near us than the game itself.

We hadn't been seated very long when Susan started a conversation, in a loud voice, which went about like this:

"Daddy, are those men or are those boys playing base-ball?"

"Those are men."

"Well, how come they can run so fast? You're a man and you can't run fast."

Betraying her instincts as a future housewife, Susan was worried about the profligacy with which baseballs were being used. Every time a foul went out of the park or back against the netting the umpires would hand the catcher a new ball.

Susan, who has only one baseball and has been warned never to lose it, was amazed. "How many balls do they got?" she would ask. When assured they had plenty, she wanted to know where they were kept.

During one sequence the pitcher lost his control and walked the batter. Mike wanted to know why he was trotting down to first. "Because," we said without thinking of the consequences, "he got four balls."

"Four balls?" asked Susan who had come in on the end of the conversation. "Only four balls left? What are they going to do when they lose them, too?"

As in all good ball games there were a number of loud rhubarbs with a lot of yammering and angry gestures.

"What's the matter with the empire?" Susan would ask in that penetrating voice of hers. "What did the empire do? Why are they all mad at the empire?"

By that time we were attracting more attention than the ball game.

Along about the sixth inning the fascination began to pall and the youngsters looked with more interest on the peanut vendors than the athletes. So we bought a dime bag which contained all of a dozen peanuts, and for a while there was peace in the stands.

Let us pause a moment here to pass on a bit of advice to other parents. As a matter of practical strategy, never buy the youngsters peanuts, popcorn, crackerjack, soft drinks, or other aids to indigestion when you first arrive at the ball game, circus, or rodeo. It's advisable to ignore the vendors for at least half the show until the children's appetite is so whetted they'll appreciate your generosity.

Besides, if the kids start eating right off the bat, they'll get thirsty, sticky, and bored with the whole thing that much sooner. The parent, of course, wants to stay around and see the entire show and so it's to his advantage to delay the refreshments as long as he can.

However, by the seventh inning the peanuts were consumed and the kids were ready to go home. Their father wanted to see the rest of the game inasmuch as it looked like Denver was going to win one. We compromised by going home.

(July 19, 1948)

In our years of observing children we have tried to believe that they are innocent, guileless, sinless creatures who are plastic and pliable. Now, with regret, we must admit the error of our views.

Just this afternoon our Susan came into the house with woe on her face and tears in her voice and she said: "I want to play kick the can with the kids but they just make me hold their jackets."

It should be explained that Susan is only a few months past her fourth birthday and she tags behind children who are considerably older. Thus it is inevitable that she gets the short end of things, the dirty deals, the menial chores like watching jackets. Of course there are times when she is the pet and the center of everyone's attention, but these are in the relatively rare instances when the youngsters are feeling noble.

But when they are themselves—selfish, opportunistic, sometimes savage, willing and ready to exploit the smaller and the weaker—then little Susan is the scapegoat. It is amazing how much like their elders, in their petty cruelties, children can be. It is only after they acquire adult inhibitions that they begin to act more the popular concept of childish nobility.

(August 7, 1948)

Mike doesn't want to take piano lessons. He would much rather waste his time playing football, which is his current passion. The choice of football over piano is, no doubt, a natural reaction among eight-year-old boys and we haven't pressed the matter.

However, in the light of experience we do wish Mike would study piano. Many years ago we played football something like fourteen hours a day and refused to go near a keyboard. What did it get us? Well, now we're rapidly approaching the physical deterioration of middle age and no longer have a desire to play football for more than ninety seconds at a time. If we had put into piano practice the energy we expended on football, we might have developed something more than a trick knee that aches when it rains.

For a while we argued with Mike that piano players can amount to something. Take President Truman, we said, he plays the piano. Mike was not impressed. Apparently he is bent on growing up into a Republican.

Mike is usually too tired to carry the empty milk bottles out on the porch, but he always has enough energy to chase some long-legged playmate on the football field. The other day his newly-sprouted front teeth made contact with someone's heels in the course of a grab-tackle game. He spit out a little blood and kept on playing. Perhaps he has the makings.

Last Sunday we joined in a game of touch football with Mike and some of his friends, which was just about the right speed. And there occurred in one of our protracted and noisesome huddles an incident that seared the fact of advancing age into our consciousness.

A pert youngster named Bill Ingals was the quarterback

92

and Mike was playing center. Ingals' instructions were, to wit: "Mike, you hike the ball to your father. I'll run down to the right and, Mr. Hosokawa, you pass the ball to me. Think you can make it, mister?"

(October 9, 1948)

This is to introduce Pete, a fat and happy individual who came along five and a half months ago to join Mike and Susan in the Hosokawa menage. Pete is on the bald side and doesn't give much of a hoot about what's going on in the world provided his meals are served on time. If they're delayed he kicks up a royal rumpus.

At this writing Pete is a trifle distressed by dental difficulties. There's a tooth buried in his lower gum and the doggone thing just won't break through. It causes no end of irritation and discomfort, but there's nothing much we can do for Pete. Under the circumstances, Pete might as well reconcile himself to the fact that the human race is heir to various ills of the flesh, and that dental troubles are with us from infancy until death us do part.

We talked this matter over with Pete but he wasn't very philosophical about his discomfort. That, unfortunately, is the way of youth.

(November 13, 1948)

"Hey, Dad, I heard a new one at school today. What's the longest word in the dictionary?"

"I don't know."

"Give?"

"Yes, I give up."

"Eskimo."

"Eskimo? How come?"

"No, that's wrong. The right word is Alaska."

"Alaska? I still don't get it. Why is Alaska the longest word in the dictionary?"

93

"I dunno. But that's what the guy said."

"You mean 'elastic,' because it stretches?"

"Yah, that's it. That's the right word. What does elastic mean?"

(November 20, 1948)

Mike had been reminding me for two weeks that his school's annual Father-and-Son night was coming up, and at last the big day arrived. Mike dressed up in his best blue jeans and T-shirt, slicked down his bristle-like hair, picked up the cake Mom baked, and off we went. He doesn't get a chance very often to show off his school, or his school work for that matter, and he was tickled to the tips of his sunburned ears. Besides, he was one of the lucky six in his class who had drawn lots and won the right to put on a boxing exhibition.

The boxing matches are a big and traditional part of the Father-and-Son nights at Stevens school. The principal is a trim, clean-cut young man who was a college athlete and wrestling champ, and he believes in the virtues of physical contact sports.

He got up and gave a little speech about the fights which went about like this: "Youngsters in grade school aren't afraid to put on the gloves and mix it up, and they don't get hurt when they do. Unfortunately, by the time boys get to junior high school, a good many of them won't box, and if they tried they'd get hurt. I believe a boy ought to throw a little leather and grade school is the place for them to do it. I hope some of them get a good solid punch on the nose tonight. It'll do them good.

"I'm not trying to make fighters of your boys. But I'm trying to teach them to win and not be cocky, to lose and come up grinning. They'll have occasion to receive a good many punches in the nose in life. You Dads have had to take figurative nose-punchings yourselves, and you know

94

what it's like. We've been accused of coddling our youngsters and this is about the best way I know of to disprove that belief. I hope you Dads agree with me."

Before we had much time to ponder on the wisdom of the principal's words, the fights were on. They started with the little fellows hardly big enough to swing the over-stuffed gloves, but they put on a good show. They touched gloves in salute before the bout, and swung manfully if without skill. A round lasted about thirty seconds, and it ended sooner if someone were tagged with an especially jarring blow.

Sometimes a little fellow took a pretty hefty punch to the mush, and some of them back-tracked for a while. But when it was over they shook hands, scampered back to their seats, and cheered for the next pair of freckled gladiators.

Then it was Mike's turn and he bounced into the ring, grinning and thrilled and ready to mix it up. His opponent was a wiry little redhead about the same size and weight.

You know what they say about bleeding for a team. Well, I bled for Mike out there in the ring, swinging every blow with him, dodging every haymaker with him, taking every smack in the beezer with him. It left me limp, although Mike emerged from the encounter unscarred and still grinning.

Mike showed a thoroughly authoritative left. He kept jabbing it out into the redhead's face, jolting it back, jabbing, jabbing, jabbing. His right was wild, though, and once in a while he'd get pasted a good one when he threw that right and slipped out of position.

I suppose I'm prejudiced, but I think Mike won that fight by a comfortable margin. But that doesn't make much difference here, because they weren't out for a decision. What is important is that I learned Mike can take care of himself. He has learned to dish it out. He has also learned to get bashed in the face and not whimper about it. He was having a grand time punching another kid and getting punched back.

As we walked home, I thought back over those short, short years to the day when a cablegram reached me in Shanghai announcing Mike's birth in Portland, and of his first halting steps, of the nights of anguish when he lay wracked with fever, of his pranks and the spankings he got, and of the day he first went to school. And I wondered what tomorrow holds for our Mike.

(May 7, 1949)

The night of July 4th we piled into the car and drove out to Cheapskate Hill, which commands a good view of the sky above the stadium. Pretty soon the summer night bloomed with red, white, green, blue and yellow flowers —skyrocketing and exploding in a thrilling display of pyrotechnics. Even from our distance it was beautiful. And we had the added advantage of being away from the thunder and acrid smoke of the fireworks.

Out across the valley below us, rockets and Roman candles cut brief arcs before the night enveloped their incandescent trails. It was warm, a typical Fourth of July.

After the show was over we pulled out a few sparklers and a couple of Roman candles of our own. The children's eyes reflected the flash of the sparklers—they were happy as only kids can be when they are playing with forbidden fire.

The Roman candles were the finale, the dessert course. They had been treasured ever since we had bought them, and because they cost twenty cents apiece, the children received only one each. Susan offered to shoot hers off first. A match was touched to the fuse and for an instant there was the exciting sizzle that precedes the first outpouring of flame.

She clutched the candle tightly, tense and anticipating and half frightened by the novelty. She held it enraptured as one by one the balls of fire spewed forth and whistled out into the darkness. And when all too soon the tenth ball had glowed and died, a long, happy sigh escaped her.

Mike was next, and Susan stood by his side, envious and yet glad for him because it was his turn and he was having his fun. But it was all over quickly, and time to go home and to bed.

She cuddled up close as we started back and she said: "That was fun. Next year, Daddy, can we have TWO Roman candles? Please?"

(July 9, 1949)

Inevitably, our children discovered that they were some-what different in appearance from their Caucasian play-mates. We handled the subject of their discovery and coping in several columns, three of which follow:

We now live in one of Denver's newer residential areas where there is an abundance of children and, from all in-dications, most of the breadwinners are white-collar wage slaves beset with the same economic problems as you and I.

Our youngsters' introduction to the neighborhood was early, traditional, and thorough. About the second day, while Mike was playing catch with a girl from up the street, the ball got away and made a jagged hole through one of our windows. It so happened that the girl had thrown the ball with more power than control. It was just a stroke of fate that our Mike hadn't thrown the ball through someone else's window.

Mike's playmate hopped on her bike and pedaled home and presently she returned with her father. He introduced himself, apologized profusely and offered to foot the entire

97

bill. As it turned out, we agreed to split the cost, running to about a couple of dollars apiece, and we've been pretty friendly ever since. There's nothing like jumping feet first into the life of the neighborhood, even if a glass pane has to be shattered.

Mike, Susan, and Pete, being the only Oriental youngsters in a wide radius, naturally have attracted considerable attention. One of their new-found friends with the candor of childhood asked:

"Are you Chinese, Mike? Can you talk Chinese?"

"Naw," said Mike, "I'm not Chinese. I'm Japanese."

"Yeah? Is that right?" his friend asked. Then for confirmation she turned to an adult nearby and declared: "Mike says he's Japanese. Is that right, huh? Is that right?"

The adult, a total stranger to all concerned, settled the matter with rare wisdom. "No," he said gently, "Mike isn't Japanese. He's American, like the rest of us."

We would never have heard of this incident if Mike hadn't come home and talked about it. And we hope he will never forget the lesson that stranger taught him.

(August 20, 1949)

At the invitation of some good neighbors, our Susan is attending Sunday school again. Last Sunday she came home with the information that God loves all kinds of people—white, black, red, brown, yellow. "That's what our teacher said," she reported. Then her brow puckered up and she asked:

"Are there really yellow people, Daddy?" She was, of course, thinking of the sunshine yellow of her crayons, and she couldn't recall having seen anyone of that particular hue.

"Yes," I said the best I could. "I'm supposed to be yellow, and because you're our little girl, you're yellow, too."

98

"Well, why are we all yellow?" she wanted to know.

"Grandpa came from Japan, and so did Grandma. And people from Japan and China are called yellow people." We hoped the explanation would satisfy her.

"Well, what about Rosalind next door?"

"Rosalind is white."

"I don't think I'm any more yellow than Rosalind is. I'm just a little more tanned."

And with that she was off to play again, secure in the knowledge that God loved her just as much as Rosalind, and besides it didn't make any difference what color she was.

(August 27, 1949)

Susan, our kindergartener, has met and with a bit of outside assistance, overcome her first race problem. Since she and her brother are the only non-Caucasians in their school, it was inevitable that she should attract some attention. That was fine, too, until one day she came home and reported that "a girl named Nancy with white hair hit me and said she didn't like me because I'm a Mexican."

We watched for developments the next few days, hoping that Nancy would be more neighborly as soon as the novelty wore off. But Nancy continued to pester Susan with dirty digs and occasional wallops when the teacher wasn't watching, and Susan with great stoicism shrugged the insults off.

Finally, Susan reported that "Nancy told me to get out, because I don't belong in the school because I'm a dirty Mexican. I told her I was an American and I could go to school if I wanted."

Now it seemed that Nancy had been getting some parental coaching in prejudice, and the time had come for action. We called the principal, who was properly horrified.

Yesterday Susan came home and said: "Nancy was nice to me today and we holded hands while we was playing."

Somebody, it seems, has taken Nancy aside and taught her the facts of life as they pertain to schoolground democracy. And none too early at that.

(October 8, 1949)

Generally, though, this was a happy, tranquil period within a growing family and the columns reflect the mood which was being shared by many other Nisei families after the unhappy war years. We took delight in little episodes of innocence, like this pre-Thanksgiving story:

Our Susan still has difficulties getting the days of the week untangled. The other night, she said: "Tomorrow is Tuesday, and after that we get to eat turkey."

"No," corrected her brother. "Tomorrow is Tuesday and the day after that is Wednesday. You stuff the turkey on Wednesday. After that is Thursday, and that's the day you eat the turkey."

"Oh," said Susan. "You stuff the turkey on Wednesday, and then you stuff yourself on Thursday."

(November 26, 1949)

The crises we experienced were of little consequence, as witness this family discussion:

Our dinner table conversation has taken on a new, pedantic character these days since Mike has been promoted to 4A. There is talk now of long division, the lark bunting and the habits of alligators as well as small fry neighborhood gossip and who knocked out a home run during recess.

Spelling was the topic of one recent suppertime discussion, and the word was "stationery," which Mike said he had missed.

"How do you spell it," we asked. "Do you remember now?"

"Sure. s-t-a-t-i-o-n-e-r-y."

"What does it mean?"

"Means stuff like writing paper."

"Oh, no," we said. "It means it isn't moving—stuck in one place."

"No," said Mike his voice rising. "You spell that kind of stationary with an a-r-y."

"You have the two mixed up," we declared. "It's the other way around." And then, with sudden indecision, we added: "Or am I wrong?"

Mike chose an occasion some hours later, when there were guests in the house, to consult the dictionary and proclaim to one and all that his dad was dead wrong when it came to spelling stationery and stationary.

Of course it's embarrassing when a man who supports his family by putting down words is caught in the act of misspelling one by his fourth-grade son. But on the other hand, we're mighty pleased about his progress, and even more so by the fact that he is not shy about consulting a dictionary.

(April 22, 1950)

Pete, who was born in 1948, began to develop a personality about this time and appeared from time to time in Frying Pan:

Pete, our youngest, has just turned two and promises to be a blithe and adventurous youngster. Left to nap alone the other day, he awoke to find the house deserted. Somehow he crawled down off the bed, wandered through the house and finally got out through the open rear door. We found him tearless, barefoot, and scantily dressed, exploring the great outdoors and wondering where the hell his folks were.

At his tender age, Pete is indicating a more than normal interest in insects of all sorts. He picks up ants and smashes spiders with great abandon. He reaches futilely for moths and when the grasshoppers mature, he will have a grand time pursuing them.

The other day his mother found Pete chasing a bumble-bee in great delight, chortling and chuckling to himself as he followed the insect's erratic flight from flower to flower in the back yard. Kindly fate kept the bee out of reach and saved Pete from that searing, burning sting that would have struck him with terror.

Who knows but what Pete may grow into a bugologist, perhaps destined to come up with a better way to rid the earth of insect pests? But more probably, he'll just become a boy with a healthy but useless curiosity about living creatures.

(June 17, 1950)

Family life was simple, generally uncomplicated and happy, reflecting the experience of other Nisei families:

This is Alice's night out. Thanks to the generosity of friends, she's seeing a performance of "Finian's Rainbow." It's been a long, long time since she's seen a major show, and it isn't often that she gets to go out for an evening of entertainment.

Pretty soon she'll be home, bubbling with enthusiasm about the songs and the dance numbers. There will be a warm glow in her eyes reflecting the lightness that her heart feels. The magic of song and the rare pleasure of a carefree evening, far in spirit and distance from the scene of her daily chores, will have done wonders for her morale.

Meanwhile, for this evening at least, we've assumed those tasks and become a little better acquainted with home and children.

First, there was little Pete to put to bed. He played happily in his bath and was patient with unpracticed hands that tried to wash his apple cheeks. He didn't want to go to sleep. There was still so much to see, so much to do. The day is never long enough for a curious little boy. But gradually he relaxed and closed his eyes reluctantly, ever so reluctantly. And then he was asleep with the deep, even breathing of a healthy child.

Mike is old enough to put himself to bed, but he needs constant prodding. Usually it's comic books that just have to be finished before he can take off his clothes. But tonight it was arithmetic. He had a sheet of addition problems that he wanted to solve. Mike is slow in mathematics, just like his father, and he knows that he must practice. So there he was, trying to determine the sums of 17, 24 and 32, or the total when 12, 29 and 37 are added together.

Eventually even arithmetic palled, Mike peeled off his clothes in forty-five seconds (he asked me to time him) and leaped into the tub. There was a great splashing and thrashing around, followed by a long silence and an explanation: "I feel lazy tonight. I'm just laying here trying to soak the dirt off." Then he jumped out, scrambled into his pajamas after only partly drying himself, and trotted off to bed. He must have been sound asleep within fifteen seconds.

With Susan, it was another story again. She talked almost incessantly about school, about play, about her friends. She asked questions and dawdled along so she could ask still more questions.

After that came the dinner dishes, their chips the chevrons of long years of service; a host of pots and drinking glasses and greasy skillets. Dish-washing, we mused, is indeed an abominable necessity for us common folk who cannot afford a machine to take over the job.

Now all is quiet, the sink scrubbed out, the youngsters pinned in so they won't kick off the covers. There is time

103

to sit back and reflect and be thankful. Thankful for children and home and life's many blessings. Thankful for the opportunity to serve occasionally as substitute mother and housewife. And thankful that we don't have to do it every night.

8

Of Travel and Vittles

My work at the Post *involved considerable travel, especially in the early years. I went to places like Dalhart, Texas, and Alliance, Nebraska, in search of stories, to Paris to cover a Summit meeting, to Korea and Vietnam to look in on a couple of wars, and a lot of places in between.*

Many of these trips also provided material for Frying Pan, and a surprising number of these columns dealt with food. When a fellow is out on the road, a place to eat and a place to sleep are primary concerns. One bed is just about like another if they are clean. But travel often gives one an opportunity to try new and different foods, particularly if one is on expense account and cost is not an important factor. Incidentally, keep in mind that the prices mentioned here are in pre-inflation dollars. Here are some of those travel and food columns:

Edmonton, Alberta, Canada

One of the showiest eating places in this Canadian prairie metropolis is a Chinese restaurant called the Purple Lantern. It oozes more class, white linen and fancy chinaware than any chop suey house I've seen between Denver and the West Coast.

The waiter produced a long and attractive menu, and I chose a dish called Moo Goo Gai Pan, which, on reading the English version in parenthesis, was alleged to contain "fillet breast of young chicken sauteed and fried with mushrooms and Chinese vegetables." The tariff was $2, Canadian money.

But apparently something was wrong with my pronunciation because the waiter showed up with Farn Cur Shew Gai which turned out to be "fillet breast of chicken fried in batter with fresh tomatoes." That went for $1.65 so I gained 35 cents on the error. Besides, Farn Cur Shew Gai wasn't bad at all after it had been dressed up with a slug of soy sauce.

Two bowls of rice added thirty cents and a pot of tea was a dime, so the total bill ran $2.05. Plus a two-bit tip. Which wasn't excessive by any means.

The cashier turned out to be one of the bosses of the place. He was a shy little fellow who could have been thirty-five or fifty, it was that hard to guess his age. But he said his restaurant had been doing business for about fifty years.

I asked if he specialized in Cantonese food only, and he said no, he served American innovations like chop suey.

"No," I insisted. "How about Peking food. Do you serve any of that fine northern stuff?"

He said all he served was Cantonese food. Then he lifted an eyebrow and asked, "Are you from Peking?"

I couldn't miss the opportunity. "Yes," I lied, "and I sure miss that Peking food."

And then, feeling very wicked, I went back to the hotel and went to bed.

(August 5, 1950)

Liberal, Kansas

Jim Cinnamon, publisher of the local *Southwest Daily Times,* took me around town for an hour, then left while I went to the motel to wash up.

When I saw Cinnamon later he said, "You know, at least a dozen people wanted to know who you are. Some of them said, 'Hey, Jim, who's your Chinese friend?'

"I told them you're the Denver *Post* reporter. Say, what are you, anyhow?"

Hongkong

Fellow name of Jim Wilde, an Associated Press correspondent in Hongkong, escorted me one night to the Wah Mai restaurant which features spicy Szechuan style cooking. The food was fine but the English menu was priceless. In an effort to encourage English-speaking trade, someone had translated each of the several score items on the bill of fare. Here are a few of the more interesting samples:

Braised fish lips, $4

Braised fish head in pipkin, $3.80 (obviously pumpkin)

Been cured in pipkin, $3.40 (bean curd?)

Braised chicken blood, $1.20 (?)

Chicken and mushroam soup, $5.20

Turn over in soup, $1.20 (turnover?)

Before going further, let me explain the prices are in Hongkong dollars. You get about $5.80 in Hongkong money for every U.S. dollar.

While we were enjoying our repast, Wilde regaled me with stories about food he'd eaten in Indonesia. Once, he said, they served pig's blood soup at a banquet. He thought it was all black until someone waved his hand over the bowl, and up flew a swarm of flies. Wilde had to eat the soup to avoid offending his hosts. A strong stomach is a great asset in the Far East. Excuse me.

(October 17, 1958)

Of course not all the columns were about food. Some were about other matters of widespread interest that I had investigated:

Tokyo

If the ladies will pardon me, I'd like to comment this week on women of the Far East. That would mean, of course, the Chinese, for they are everywhere. The prettiest girls in the cabarets of Singapore are of Chinese descent. That's true of Bangkok where Hawaiian-born Shige Kameda of Japan Air Lines showed me the way around, and Taipei and Hongkong. And the men of Tokyo seem to think so highly of Chinese girls that the entire eighth floor (or was it the seventh?) of a building just off the Ginza is given to a cabaret that features 200 pretty young ladies all dressed in Chinese gowns. (It doesn't seem to really matter that all of them are Japanese. It must be the gowns, split high up the side, that fascinates the men.)

There is no denying that Chinese girls have eye-filling figures. Most of those in the nightclubs have long, shapely legs and many are busty even by Western standards. Add to these assets good skin, straight teeth, finely chiseled features and all-around good looks, which the girls have, and you've got some mighty attractive specimens.

What stops many a Western admirer of these young ladies are the sounds that emanate from shapely little mouths when they speak. Many of the Chinese dialects are far from euphonic to Western ears, and it's a little startling to hear the guttural noises these beautiful girls can produce.

108

Inch for inch and curve for curve, Japan's young women as a group don't seem to measure up to the Chinese. They are shorter-legged, for one thing. For another, they lack the erect carriage and graceful walk of Chinese girls. (Japanese girls waddle, says one observer who does not mean to be unkind.)

Nonetheless, the postwar generation of Japanese of both sexes is taller, better-proportioned than ever before. Some of the cabarets, especially those which cater largely to Westerners, have some shapely hostesses who stand from 5-foot-6 to 5-foot-9 inches in their high heels. And some of the strippers currently in vogue in Tokyo night clubs are wondrously endowed with curves where they are most effective.

The stripteasers are an amazing postwar Japanese phenomenon. In prewar Japan sex was accepted as a natural function and nudity wasn't considered particularly exciting. Babies were nursed in public and some baths and many public lavatories were co-educational. All of a sudden, perhaps due to American influences, a girl dancing with nothing but beads and sequins to protect her modesty becomes a big attraction. This is progress?

Many expert girl-watchers—and I know a lot of them—agree that the most attractive thing about young Japanese womanhood is its quiet, gentle, shy warmth that adds up to charm. This charm more than makes up for the greater physical assets of their sisters from the Asian mainland.

Unfortunately this charm is disappearing in the rush for emancipation. It will be a sad day indeed when the Japanese ideal of womanhood becomes a coarse, hard-boiled, tough-talking female. That day, however, would seem to be coming. The entertainers who get top billing and top money aren't the demure, blues-singing charmers. They're the brazen, fanny-waggling strippers and the gals who growl and shout and belt out the hot numbers like Ella Fitzgerald.

They do a fairly good imitation of Ella, too, and more's the pity. Japanese girls just weren't made to do those things. At least that's the way it seems to this middle-aging observer, and I hope you'll pardon me while I duck for the storm cellar.

(October 31, 1958)

The next item is out of time sequence, but the subject makes this the logical place for it:

This is most ungallant and probably uncalled for, but it seems that either *Time* erred (which it frequently does), or else Shirley Yoshiko (Rikoran) Yamaguchi has been very quick to adopt the old Hollywood custom of forgetting a few birthdays.

The pert and lovely Miss Yamaguchi, according to *Time,* is all of twenty-four years old.

Yet the film that made her a star, "Shina no Yoru" (China Night), was shot in 1939 or thereabouts and was the rage of Japan a decade ago.

Welly Shibata, who was among the pioneer editors of West Coast Nisei journalism, took me to see "Shina no Yoru" in an Osaka moviehouse during the early summer of '40. He recommended it as one of the best products of Japan's still shaky film industry, and later popular acclaim has borne out his good judgment. Miss Yamaguchi, as we recall, was no Ethel Barrymore when it came to emoting, but that wasn't required of her. All she had to do was look soulful and attractive, and in that department she was sensational.

A few months later Miss Yamaguchi had the misfortune to be caught in the same elevator with this reporter in a Shanghai hotel, with only the elevator operator as chaperone. During most of the twenty seconds of that ride she kept her eyes glued to the floor. This, no doubt, was a maneuver to avoid a certain person's rude but admiring stare.

If *Time*'s report is correct, Miss Yamaguchi was a mere fourteen years old at that time. And all I can say is that I've never seen another fourteen-year-old so lusciously curved.

(July 1, 1950)

Tokyo

One evening Hatch Kita took me to a second rate sushi shop where the prices aren't as fancy as at a first rate place, but the food is just about as good. A couple of fellows in short-sleeved shirts and aprons stand behind a bar and whip up any kind of sushi you order. Now, in case you've missed it, sushi in Japan is composed of a dab of rice about half the size of a Baby Ruth bar, delicately flavored with a little vinegar, on which is placed a slab of raw fish, squid, abalone, clam or other seafood. You hot it up with a little green horseradish, dunk it briefly in soy sauce, and consume. It's wonderful.

At this particular place, one of the fellows behind the bar came up with some huge shrimp which were still live enough to kick with considerable vigor. Hatch indicated he'd like one and I was game, too. The fellow grabbed one of the live shrimp, pulled off its head, shelled it, split it down the middle, slapped it on a lump of rice and placed it before me.

All this happened in a twinkling. One moment the shrimp had been kicking. The next, it was neatly served and still so fresh the shrimpmeat was quivering. Hatch was eating his with gusto. I stalled a moment waiting for the shrimp to become still, but it was a stubborn cuss and refused to quiet down. So, taking a firm grip on my insides, I ate my animated sushi, quivering shrimp and all.

111

One of Japan's gustatorial standbys is tempura in which shrimp and vegetables are dipped in batter and deep-fried in hot oil. The way the fancy places do it, a tempura-making outfit is wheeled into the room and the cook-san fries things up before your eyes. You get the goodies fresh out of the pot and eat them piping hot.

The shrimp tempura was particularly good at the place Naraichi Fujiyama of the Foreign Office took me. I noticed the cook fried them whole, without splitting them as is often done. And listen, girls, he had them in the hot oil no more than seventy seconds. Perhaps that was why they were so tender.

Incidentally, the Japanese like rich, oily foods in the summer. Baked eel on rice, for instance. In America we stick to salads and such when the temperature rises. The Japanese say their summer heat is so debilitating that they need rich foods to keep up their strength.

(November 7, 1958)

Paris

French hotelkeepers seem to figure soap is a luxury but breakfast is a necessity. At least the hotels I stayed in provided no soap; you had to go out and buy your own or ask the desk clerk for a bar at the time you registered.

On the other hand, one merely calls the desk in the morning and presently the maid traipses in with coffee, a roll, a small loaf of bread, butter and marmalade. It's all included in the price of the room. So is a shoeshine. Leave your shoes outside the door and some good elf comes along during the night and shines them up beautifully.

I wonder how many Frenchmen visiting the States have left their shoes out, only to discover that somebody swiped them.

One night in Paris I dropped into a Chinese restaurant to learn how French cuisine had influenced Cantonese-style chow. The food tastes just fine but the French language has done some horrible things to familiar old dishes.

Our dinner started with potage, or soup, which was called Bouillon Poulet aux Vermicelles Chinois. This turned out to be the French alias for chicken soup with clear noodles. Price: 200 Old Francs, or 2 New Francs, or 40 American cents.

We followed this up with Langoustines Sautees, which, as any Frenchman knows, is simply fried shrimp and vegetables. 4 New Francs.

Next, in the Viande Porc et Boeuf department, we ordered Porc Saute Pousses Bambou. That was fairly easy except for the Pousses. It was fried pork and sliced bamboo. That was 380 Old Francs, or 3.8 New Francs or 80 cents.

That was all we could put away. We had to skip such interesting sounding dishes as Shap Sui, Poisson Sauce Pekinoise, Salade Chinoise, Riz Saute, Omelette au Crabe (could this have been crab foo-yung?) Porc Sauce Piquante, and Porc Sauce 5 Parfums. Since the proprietor spoke no English and I understood no French or Chinese, the 5-perfumed pork sauce had to remain a mystery.

(May 27, 1960)

I was in Paris for the Summit meeting which went right straight down the drain when Nikita Khrushchev took after President Eisenhower for letting Gary Francis Powers fly his U-2 spy plane over the Soviet Union. Inadvertently, I was involved in a very minor incident which Eddy Gilmore thought interesting enough to write up, and the Associated Press put it out on its news wire. That shows how hard reporters covering the Summit were scratching for copy. However, inasmuch as this was one of the few times the AP has recognized my existence, and as a tribute to my friend Gilmore who died some years ago, his story will be reprinted here:

By Eddy Gilmore

PARIS, May 14 (AP)—Nikita Khrushchev's son-in-law warmly shook the hand of a U.S. citizen today and said "I'm glad you're an American—I thought you were somebody else."

Despite the American plane incident in Russia, Khrushchev's relative showed nothing but friendliness when he talked to several American newspapermen outside the U.S.S.R. embassy.

The son-in-law is Alexei Adzhubei, editor of *Izvestia*, official newspaper of the Soviet government.

The American Adzhubei greeted is Bill Hosokawa, assistant managing editor of the Denver *Post*.

American-born Hosokawa and Soviet-born Adzhubei are both here for the Summit conference.

Their meeting happened this way:

Late this afternoon newsmen from all over the world were standing outside the Soviet embassy, awaiting Khrushchev's arrival.

Inside the embassy Russian officials said:

"Mr. Khrushchev went sightseeing. We don't know where he is."

At this moment a Russian car drove up in the Rue Grenelle. Out hopped Adzhubei and Mikhail Satyukov, editor of *Pravda*.

"How's your mood?" asked Khrushchev's relative, smiling broadly.

"A little dull," replied this reporter.

"What's the trouble?" inquired Adzhubei.

"We can't find your father-in-law. Where is he?"

Adzhubei shook his head and looked at the editor of *Pravda*.

The editor of *Pravda* shook his head and looked at the editor of *Izvestia*.

At that moment, Khrushchev's son-in-law sighted Hosokawa.

The Russian stared at Hosokawa's Summit press card, which officials ask you to wear on your coat lapel.

"What nationality are you?" asked Adzhubei.

Hosokawa—who doesn't speak Russian—did not reply.

Khrushchev's relative looked belligerent.

"He's an American of Japanese ancestry," said this reporter.

A big smile broke over Adzhubei's face.

"Shake hands," he said. "I thought you were a colleague of Chiang Kai-shek. American, ah, that's horosho (good)."

Taipei

My host at dinner in Taipei beamed when the waiter brought a plate of piping hot food. "This is wonderful stuff," he said in Japanese. "Fresh hebi."

"Hebi," as any Japanese knows, means snake. I gulped and decided to be game.

But it wasn't snake at all. It was "ebi," which is nothing but shrimp, and probably for the same reason that Britain's cockneys add and drop their Hs, he had added one. It turned out to be a fine dinner.

This column should not be concluded without reproducing items from a menu we saw in a well-known Taipei restaurant. The prices are in New Taiwan dollars; since one U.S. dollar can be exchanged for forty Taiwan dollars, each Taiwan dollar is worth 2½ ¢:

Stewed duck feet with mushrooms $38
Stewed sea slugs with duck feet $60
Fried fish slices with distillery grains $30
Stewed fish tails and snout with brown sauce $40
Fried pig intestines (plain or with sauce) $32

Fried shrimp with gizzards $40
Sea slugs with shrimp roe $50
Cold dishes:
    spice gizzards, pig tripe, duck feet $45
Pig tender with crab meat $68
Sweet sow (sour?) pork $30
Chicken kidney and bean curd skin $42
Chicken feet and mushroom soup $32
Chicken hands (heads?) and mushroom soup ... $40

Although we were quite curious about what pig tender might be, and since we were afraid chicken hands was a printer's error for chicken heads, we settled for Chekiang pickle soup and shrimp with bean curd. Not bad, either.

(January 5, 1968)

In their formative years Japanese Americans worked vigorously to become "assimilated" and paid scant heed to the adjective "Japanese" in front of the noun "American." Then, in the Seventies, largely as a spinoff of the Black is Beautiful movement, it became fashionable among ethnic minorities to stress their ethnicity. It wasn't embarrassing, or shameful, or degrading anymore to be proud of one's background and spend a lot of time thinking and talking about it. That wasn't the case back in 1964 when, as a result of some experiences in Japan, the following column took shape:

If you read *Pacific Citizen* regularly, you may gain the impression the Nisei as a group are so deeply and perpetually concerned about themselves and their problems that they think the whole world revolves around them. At least that's the impression I get when I try to view this publication and its contents objectively.

Still, to be fair about it, it must be pointed out that the

116

PC is a special interest publication put out for a special interest group. It has a purpose. It is a house organ in the same sense that the Amalgamated Brewers' Journal or the Hogstickers' Fortnightly Review are house organs. Brewers and Nisei and hogstickers, as specific groups, have matters of special interest to themselves even though they may be more concerned about the outcome of the American League pennant chase. . . .

Generally, I've found, Nisei as a group think less and less frequently of themselves as Nisei or members of an American minority. And an increasingly large part of the time, when they have occasion to think about such matters at all, they identify themselves only as a segment of that astonishing conglomeration known as Americans. At least that is what I thought was in my mind.

So it was something of a shock, having said this, to learn this past summer that the Japanese in Japan have been thinking of us in the same way for some time.

I had a cab driver in Sendai call me *Gaijin-san,* or "Mr. Foreigner." In a Tokyo restaurant I was referred to as a *"Mukoo no hito,"* or "person from over there," or perhaps more correctly, "a person from the other side." Of course that was right, but somewhat unexpected.

To many contacts, I had to explain that I was a Nisei, then explain what a Nisei is in some detail. It was necessary to point out that my father left Hiroshima as a youngster and migrated to the United States, that I was born in America but my blood gave me an Oriental appearance.

Oddly enough, visual image seemed to make little impression on many of my Japanese contacts. I have straight black hair or, to be more precise, gray hair. My skin is not white. Still, because I spoke English with most of my associates, and my clothes were obviously not of Japanese cut, they saw me as a foreigner. The obvious visual fact of my ancestry didn't seem to make an impression.

I've often wondered why. Perhaps it's because the Japanese are accustomed to seeing many Asians who, while Oriental in appearance, are not Japanese. Take the Chinese, for instance, or the Koreans, the Manchurians, the Taiwanese, and even some Vietnamese and Thais. Many would pass for Japanese on appearance alone. So it may be that cab drivers and other Japanese have learned not to judge people solely on the basis of skin color or facial features.

For a Nisei to be called *Gaijin-san* in Tokyo is a far piece from what appears on page one of the *Pacific Citizen*. But there is a connection, and maybe you'll get it. At least I hope you will.

(September 25, 1964)

My duties took me to Washington and New York more often than to the Orient, but for Frying Pan columns I tried to find a "Nisei angle" no matter where I was. One Washington trip produced this item:

Washington, D.C.

Our visit to the nation's capital a week or so ago coincided with *Tenchosetsu,* the day the Japanese celebrate as the Emperor's birthday. The Japanese embassy was having its big annual cocktail party and reception, and Mike Masaoka suggested I might like to attend. Of course I would, never having experienced a full-fledged diplomatic reception such as Ambassador Shimoda was hosting.

Mike quickly arranged for an invitation, which was not a particularly easy thing to do, but neither could it be considered a great social coup. Invitations had gone out to some 800 Washingtonians—members of the diplomatic corps, top government officials, business leaders and the like, and sure they could squeeze in one more.

Squeeze they did. There was a monumental traffic jam outside the handsome embassy on Massachusetts Avenue as chauffeurs in long, black limousines came up to drop off Very Important People or returned to pick up these same VIPs after they had paid their respects and sipped the ambassador's booze. We had limousine service, too. Mike let me and his wife Etsu out a couple of hundred yards from the entrance while he went off to look for a parking place five or six blocks away.

Etsu, no stranger to diplomatic bashes and very attractive in a dress I don't know how to describe, was the perfect guide. The large gentleman who was making the introductions at the ambassador's side made an absolute mess of our names, but Ambassador Shimoda and his beautiful (that word is used advisedly) wife knew Etsu by sight and she straightened things out quickly.

Now, I've heard and read about the mad, glamorous, gay, diplomatic receptions in Washington, but I wasn't ready for what I saw next. The great hall was packed as solidly as the exit to a football stadium thirty seconds after the final gun in a closely contested game, and it was about as quiet. Elegant men and their elegant ladies were standing five deep in front of the bars and ten deep around the tables groaning with goodies, and everybody seemed to be talking at a pace close to Mach I with no one paying the slightest attention to what anybody else was saying. Why should they? You couldn't make out the words over all that noise.

Far as I could tell, the main function of this rite was to see and be seen by the correct people, and make vague promises to call you up sometime for lunch, okay? After a while, having found a place to park his car, Mike arrived and threaded his way expertly through the mob, revealing the benefit of his many seasons of experience in cocktail party scrimmages, and he took over the introductions, of which there were many more than could be handled even by that memory expert who wrote "How to Win Friends and Influence People," whatever his name was.

Eventually, having seen an astonishing number of cabinet ministers, ambassadors, State Department officials (Mike said he waved to Chief Justice Earl Warren but he got away before I could corner him), and others, we repaired to a much more sensible place, a quiet little restaurant called the Japan Inn. The specialty of the house is beef diced from an impressively formidable chunk of meat before your eyes and cooked on the steel top of your table by your own private chef, who has more moves than a maître d' tossing a salad. The showmanship was great and the food was even better, particularly after Mike explained that the Japan Inn tested all manner of sources for steaks whose quality would approximate that of the justly famous Kobe beef. Know what they finally selected? Colorado beef. Which showed that these folks know what the cooking business was all about. The dinner was no less than absolutely superb, and I soon quit feeling bad about not having made it up to the ambassador's table, pretty as it was.

(May 9, 1969)

A few weeks later we were off to the Far East again, this time with daughter Christie, by then a college student. The deepest impression was registered in Hiroshima:

Hiroshima, Japan

We had a choice in Hiroshima of visiting Miyajima, the justly famous shrine island, or Peace Park and the atomic bomb museum. There wasn't time to do both. Christie, who had seen plenty of temples and shrines, opted for the museum.

Hiroshima was still pretty much of a jerry-built shack town when I saw it in 1950, less than five years after it was devastated by the first atomic bomb ever used in warfare. Today, like most other cities, it is a place bustling with energetic activity, and the nuclear visitation seems like a nightmare of long ago.

But the memory is kept alive at Heiwa Koen (Peace Park), dedicated to peace among men, and the museum that displays the grim mementoes of that awesome day. The museum itself is housed in a handsome masonry and glass building and the admission fee is but twenty yen, a mere token. Generally, the displays are not grisly, although there are a few horror pictures that depict the suffering, the bewilderment, the agony of the time. There are exhibits of tile fused by the heat of the fire that followed the explosion, and of clothing charred by the nuclear flash, "brighter than the sun." Visible are stories of heroism and anguish, and the total effect is a new understanding of what makes so many Japanese such dedicated pacifists.

For a long time now we've been hearing the slogan, "No more Hiroshimas," a not particularly apt one. But it becomes meaningful as the horror of the unforgettable day sinks into the consciousness of the museum visitor.

And yet it is obvious that the number of persons who experienced the terror of that day, August 6, 1945, and lived to tell of it, is relatively few, that most here know of the agony only by hearsay, that recollections are short and nature has a merciful way of dulling with time the sharp edge of unpleasant memory. And so commerce races along at its heedless and headlong pace in Hiroshima, a city that rose as the phoenix, and a park and museum in the midst of his hubbub commemorates that ghastly dawning of the age of nuclear warfare.

Later during our visit to Hiroshima we got together with my cousin, Michizumi Fukeda, whose mother was my father's sister. Fukeda is a rice inspector, a minor bureaucratic post, I would guess, in a county about forty minutes by bus outside of Hiroshima. He brought along his wife, his twenty-two-year-old son Tetsuji, and his nephew, Tsutomu Matsumune who is an official in a Hiroshima bank. It was a time of happiness, for although I had met Fukeda and his family on several earlier visits, they had never met Alice and Christie. Donald Cieber and his wife Joann of Denver were with us and, although I forgot to ask to make sure, it was likely that never before had Fukeda and his family sat down to dinner with Caucasians.

Whatever shyness that existed soon broke down under the soothing of beer and sake and we were chatting like old friends. Fukeda, who served with the Japanese Army in China, was recalled for service after Japan attacked Pearl Harbor and he remembered that he was a non-com with a communications outfit in Kyushu when the war ended. Matsumune also was in Kyushu, an officer candidate undergoing training. But Matsumune's mother and sister were in Hiroshima that fateful day.

Their home was about a mile from the epicenter of the nuclear blast, and only the fact that they were indoors saved them. As he heard it later, there was a thunderous explosion and the ceiling of their home fell in. When Matsumune's mother made her way outdoors, flames were springing up in all directions. His sister was pinned down by a beam. His mother pulled a neighbor into the house, mainly by force, and with his help freed the girl. Cut and bleeding, they stumbled out of the city.

Fukeda's wife was working in the fields when she saw a flash of light, then heard the distant thunder of the explosion. Soon, clouds of smoke darkened the sky over Hiroshima, and soot-laden black rain began to fall. She hurried home, found the glass shattered and the roof askew, even though her farmhouse was a long way from Hiroshima.

Before long a stream of refugees, many of them horribly burned, began to appear on the road in front of her house, a pitiful stream of humanity seeking shelter, water, food, a place to rest. She helped them as best she could. Next day she and her father-in-law breasted the human tide and started for Hiroshima with their two-wheeled cart to look for Matsumune's family. By lucky chance they found them on Hiroshima's outskirts and took them back home.

Life has been relatively good for Fukeda. He has a comfortable home for his part of the country. His wife still farms a few acres. He has a married daughter and two grandchildren, a son who is learning to become a baker. The other son, Tetsuji, is working in a county job after completing two years of college. Fukeda is not a profound man, but he has the simple honesty and candor of the peasant stock from which he has sprung. Late in the evening he looked at Don and Joann Cieber and said to me in Japanese:

"I like them. They seem to be nice people. You know, you can never be sure what a foreigner is thinking, especially if he is a white man, but now that I know them, I like your friends very much."

Later I told Cieber what my cousin had said. He was delighted to discover that it isn't only Orientals that are inscrutable.

(July 25, 1969)

This section can best be concluded with some observations that came to mind as another trip to the Orient neared an end:

San Francisco

Old friend Hatch Kita and his wife Kyoko drove us to Haneda International Airport on a Monday night over the toll road that is the only antidote to Tokyo's horrendous traffic jams. The Japan Air Lines DC-8, heavy with fuel and freight, took off about 11 P.M. and nine and a half swift hours later we were over the golden hills south of San Francisco. This flight, boosted along by the racing winds of the jetstream, dramatizes as no other the magic of air travel. One leaves Tokyo as a day is drawing to a close, and because of the International Dateline he lands on the other side of the Pacific in mid-afternoon of the same day.

Our plane dipped low over the San Francisco peninsula, and it was hard to realize this was the homeland. It was easy to let one's imagination run as we floated down toward the airport. That scar across the landscape, marking the route of an advancing throughway, could easily be the raw earth ripped up for a new airfield in Vietnam. That line of trees—I saw a similar row that sheltered a Viet Cong patrol from prying eyes aboard an American helicopter gunship. The mudflats of South San Francisco Bay—from 2,000 feet in the air it well might have been the Mekong Delta in flood season.

But the land below us was a land of peace and security, troubled but not despairing. Its people were clean, well-fed, adequately clothed and sheltered for the most part. They feared no attack in the night, no midnight raids from police or guerrillas, no terrorist bombs. Food was to be had as close as the nearest supermarket, and one could drink from any tap without fear of dreadful diseases. What a blessed nation is ours.

Each trip abroad is an adventure, but it's always great to come home. And each journey makes this reporter more appreciative, more grateful for America, despite all its obvious shortcomings. We are a nation built on improvement, rising from dissent, but the dissenters and detractors in our midst might think more constructively if they could appreciate what we have.

(January 5, 1968)

124

9

Nostalgia

Seattle by the sea is my home town. There I first saw the light of day, and there I spent the first twenty-three years of my life. In 1947 I went back to Seattle for a very sad and special mission. I wrote about it in columns published September 20 and 27, which are condensed and combined here:

Seattle

There's a ramshackle old house which for so many years was home. It has acquired a concrete and brick porch since we left, and a bright, simulated brick sheathing for the clapboard that became decrepit with age and those Puget Sound rains.

But the structure itself is unchanged, and it looks strangely small. Nearby is the empty lot over which we raced in boyish games of cops and robbers, cowboys and Indians. It was an expansive natural playground then,

125

dotted with bushes that bore hazelnuts, and little thickets that were cool and convenient for hiding.

The lot is still there, unchanged except for a bit of one corner where someone started to excavate with a power shovel, but never finished. But where once it was roomy enough to stalk imaginary buffalo and Redskins, it looks confined and strangely inadequate for such goings-on.

Surely the proportions of that piece of real estate have not altered. The change is in our perspective—a viewpoint that has been modified by time and experience and growth —and I am not altogether sure that I like it that way.

At times during our years of exile—both forced and voluntary—I thought often of the old home town and how pleasant it would be to get back. I recalled the familiar streets and faces, the smell of salt air, the cold rains and the green of spring.

This week I returned and walked the old haunts. I strolled along the waterfront where once I fished for shiners and perch. I watched broad-flanked freighters loading, just as they did years ago when I dreamed of sailing to solve the mystery of what lay beyond the horizon.

I walked down sidewalks over which I had run years ago and saw little knots of Nisei and Sansei youngsters, no doubt talking about much the same things we talked about twenty years ago.

The purpose of the homecoming was to pay a last earthly tribute to a person who was very dear, and whom I held in great respect.

The Seattle sun shone brightly for four days, but on the fifth a Puget Sound rain closed in. It drizzled intermittently, not cold, but wet enough to be irritating. It was still raining at 7:30 P.M., the hour of the funeral.

Ten minutes before the appointed time all the seats were occupied, and the temple was filled to the doors when the priests began the first deep notes of their funeral chants.

In life she had been a person of simple tastes, a conservative and retiring woman who shunned ostentation. In death her friends and admirers pressed tributes upon her, tributes that she never would have dreamed of even if she were given to such idle flights of fancy.

The mourners came in limousines and afoot through the rain. They came in impeccable black, in muddy shoes, in trousers made baggy by wear, in rundown heels and crooked seams. They sent wreaths and flowers in great banks, gardenias, roses, carnations, mums, dahlias—and they came empty-handed with only the sorrow in their hearts to offer in tribute.

They paid their final respects to a woman who had touched the hearts of the humble—for she, too, was humble through unobtrusive, kindly ways. Their tribute was from the heart. It was a good funeral.

Spring has a way of hitting Colorado with a rush. One day it's winter, and almost before you know it, summer has come. Springtime in the Rockies is largely the figment of a songwriter's imagination. But if you are crafty, you can plant seeds in the waning days of winter and harvest a crop of garden vegetables, like radishes and spinach, before it becomes so hot they go to seed:

The garden out back yielded its first harvest this week. The radishes were thinned and, in the process we realized perhaps two dozen marble-size radishes of a beautiful crimson hue. We promptly served them on the Sunday dinner table along with some young green onions that Mike relishes.

The thinned-out radishes, too small to have developed eating-size roots, went with the other tops to make *tsuke-*

mono. Pickled radish tops are a kind of spring rite around our place. They are like a harbinger of spring, in the same fashion as bratwurst, bock beer and dandelion greens.

Radish top *tsukemono* is easy to make. Put a layer of radish tops in the bottom of a bowl, sprinkle liberally with salt, lay down another layer, salt again, and continue until you run out of tops. Put a dish over the greens and weight on top of the dish. Some families have a handy boulder around just for making these pickles. In our family we just take a half-gallon milk bottle and fill it with water. Works fine. Let it set overnight and you're in business. There's nothing finer with rice.

Back when I was a youngster in Seattle we used to go out on the empty lots and pick young ferns. The folks called them *warabi.* We knew that spring had come when fresh *warabi* shoots poked up through the tall, dry grass of the previous summer. *Warabi* were eaten boiled. Like olives and oysters, they took a little getting used to, but we kids thought they were pretty fine, especially if we'd spent a half day gathering them. I think the folks salted down *warabi,* too, and we even tried dehydrating them in the sun. They dried into something rather repulsive looking, but all they needed come winter was a good soaking before they were cooked.

We also used to go look for *fuki* (coltsfoot) and wild *gobo* (burdock root) but these were harder to find than ferns. Thanks to heavy spring rains, ferns seem to grow almost everywhere up Seattle way. But I'm afraid things are different now. The lots where we picked ferns have been occupied long since by houses. I wonder whether Sansei youngsters ever pick and eat *warabi* any more.

(May 21, 1954)

Springtime also stirred memories of my father and his passion for trout fishing. I wrote several columns on the

128

subject, and the following is a combination of two of them, the first published June 4, 1954, and the second on June 7 twenty years later:

This is the second spring since my father died. I remember him especially in the spring because of his love for fishing. He counted the weeks and hours until the season opened. I see him still, lovingly tieing leaders and shellacking his rod, oiling his reels, checking his line for weak spots that might have developed during a winter of disuse.

He (we called him Grandpa after the grandchildren came) was not a particularly patient man. But when he fished his patience was as that of Job. He forgot all else— business, personal anxieties, even his family—in the pleasure and concentration of fishing.

If my father had been a writer, he would have written amusing, touching, delightfully human stories about fishing. But he was not a writer; he was a raconteur. He could tell the most wonderful stories about his fishing experiences. He delighted his friends on many a rainy winter night back home in Seattle with tales about fish he had caught and fish that had escaped. Sadly, I don't remember any of them. I remember only that he had a way of making a fishing experience come alive, even though he spoke in Japanese and I understood the language only imperfectly.

One reason he could tell fishing stories so well was that he loved to fish so much. He not only loved it, he was good at it. He had little truck with the mystique of trout fishing which many writers worry to death. He just seemed to know where the fish lay hidden, and what would provoke their appetites on any given day. He would think like a trout, a facility that he must have gained by matching wits with them over a long period of time. In his later years he rarely came home skunked.

I think he would have liked very much to make a fisherman of me. I regret that he didn't and it was mostly my fault. At first I was much too impatient. I approached an outing with excitement, but before long I became bored to distraction with dunking worms or salmon eggs into a stream which obviously didn't contain a single dinky little trout. I suspect that my father was impatient, too, about trying to teach the fine points of casting or reading a stream to an obviously disinterested boy; if I wasn't going to try he had much more exciting things waiting for him at the base of the riffle, or in the backwaters behind a big boulder.

As I grew older and my patience improved, other interests got in the way of fishing. Baseball in the spring. Football in the fall and girls in the summer and the rest of the year. And before long it was time to leave home and make a living, and too late to try to learn a little something about the art of fishing.

My own two sons, Mike and Pete, are better at fishing than I am. I didn't have the know-how to teach them much about it. Perhaps it is true what they say about talents and interests skipping a generation before they re-appear in the genes. In any event, both Mike and Pete learned to fish, pretty much on their own, and enjoy it. By then, unfortunately, Grandpa was gone.

It was fitting then that the boys and I should spend Memorial Day on a fishing trip. Our companions, guides and mentors were Frank and Lil Fujita whose own love of the sport would have won Grandpa's approval.

It didn't make too much difference that we were skunked. We tried everything—wet flies, single salmon eggs, clusters, spinners, even lowly worms—but it wasn't our day. We darned near froze to death before we gave up, so it wasn't lack of persistence. Grandpa would have chuckled about that. He'd smile wryly when the fishing was bad, but he'd take the poor luck with the good and give it a whirl again the next week.

The night before we set out, Alice stayed up late to make us a fine lunch. She packed more than we could eat, not realizing perhaps that when fellows are trying to catch fish and they aren't biting, we don't get so hungry. We brought home the left-over sandwiches and the girls promptly opened the wax paper wrappers and ate them with as much gusto as if they'd been out in the mountain air all day.

We kids used to do that with Grandpa's left-over lunches, too. He'd have a pork sandwich, or perhaps a piece of apple pie all smashed flat, but they tasted mighty fine for having been out on the river.

Grandpa wasn't here with us on Memorial Day, but I'm sure he enjoyed it with us if he happened to be looking our way.

Picnics, in which the whole community took part, were a big event during boyhood summers. A picnic in a somewhat later time, 1954, inspired this column:

The Fourth of July dawned clear and hot, and we were up early to prepare the picnic lunch. There was chicken to be fried and sandwiches to be made, eggs to boil and the water jug to be iced and filled. What's a Fourth of July without a picnic?

We started out for Eldorado Springs where Frank Torizawa throws an annual picnic for his Granada Fish Market family and their friends. Anticipating the crowds, Frank had dispatched a task force two days before the Fourth to stake out a claim to the most desirable riverside location. George Nagai and his aides had pitched a tent to set up housekeeping and established squatters' rights. A second task force followed with stores of pop, ice, watermelon, wieners and buns, corn on the cob and other picnic fare. The entire operation had the air of an experienced, well-run military movement.

Which gets us to my point that the Issei certainly know how to hold and enjoy a picnic, and some of that knowledge must have rubbed off on the Nisei. I remember back on the Coast, when on a summer Sunday it seemed half the town descended on a tree-shaded meadow for the annual picnic of the Japanese association, or a Kenjin-kai (prefectural association). The committees must have worked like beavers, for by the time we kids arrived on the scene the banners were flying, the running course had been roped off, the free ice cream and lemonade stands had been set up, and there was an enormous pile of prizes in a tent ready to be given away to the fortunate and fleet of foot.

And when the day reached its close, we tired youngsters headed for home and bed. But a cleanup crew remained to pick up every last scrap of paper. So thoroughly did they scour the grounds that next day, except for the slightly trampled grass, one would never know that some hundreds of picnickers had enjoyed themselves there.

It was the same way at Eldorado Springs. Before sunset all hands pitched in to police the grounds. The rubbish formed the basis of a fine campfire, around which we sat munching on roasting ears and hotdogs heated up over the glowing charcoal of an adjoining cooking fire until they were fat, brown and juicy.

Kids have more fun than anybody at a picnic and ours were no exception. Mike's persistence paid off and he caught himself a trout in water that I would have sworn contained no fish. Susan made new friends, climbed rocks and went horseback riding. Pete went riding, too, even though, as he says, "I'm allergic of horses." He paid dearly for the pleasure, for before the hour's ride was over, his eyes were puffed and watery and his skin had begun to break out. Doesn't seem to be anything he can do, except stay away from horses. We washed him up, and after a while he began to

132

look more like himself again. As for Christie, she fought off weariness, refused to take a nap for fear of missing something, and enjoyed every bit of the outing.

Group picnics are a fine tradition and I can't think of a finer time to have them than the Fourth of July.

(July 9, 1954)

While picnics are both an American and Japanese tradition, the way my parents observed New Year's was strictly Japanese:

My folks were great ones for closing the books on the old year and, to mix a metaphor, starting the new one with a clean slate. At year's end, all possible unfinished business had to be taken care of before the dawning of January 1. This meant getting bills paid, chores finished, obligations retired, the house cleaned of last year's grime on December 31. And when all this was done, we kids would take a bath, wriggle into fresh pajamas, and be fit at least to face the new year.

Shortly before midnight Pa would come home from the office, where he had been sweeping and scrubbing and otherwise preparing for the coming year. Usually he brought home a huge, steaming pot of noodles in chicken soup which all of us helped dispose of. This, too, we were told, was an old Japanese custom, the idea being that a bowl of hot noodles was mighty fine for thawing out the inner man chilled during the debt-paying rounds on New Year's Eve.

The practice was a delightful one, but like so many other old world customs, it falls somewhat short of modern needs. Take the matter of debts. Sure would be nice to pay off the mortgage on the house, but it still has another thirteen years to run, and from the looks of things it will take every one of those years to get it paid off. And the

Christmas bills (shudder) won't even get here until after the first of January so how can we get them disposed of before the new year?

However, there's nothing wrong with hot noodles in chicken broth. They're a grand custom on New Year's Eve, or any eve for that matter.

(January 4, 1957)

In 1959 it was time to move again—to a house on the other side of town. Sifting through the stuff that had to be moved, I ran across an item that was rich in memories. It was a quarter-horsepower electric motor with a long main shaft and a crude aluminum fan fastened to it. The motor was screwed onto a piece of board:

I remembered buying that motor in Salt Lake City. The year was 1942. Home at that time was a black tarpaper-sheathed barracks at Heart Mountain, Wyoming. The Wyoming sun was intense and the tarpaper soaked up the heat. Those uninsulated barracks rooms stayed uncomfortably hot even after the cool of evening spread mercifully over the flats. An electric fan would push out the hot air and suck in the cool.

On a trip to Salt Lake, I prowled through the stores looking for a fan, but those were war years and none was to be found. One day, in a small electric shop, I found the motor. The man asked what seemed like an exorbitant price—it was something like $17.50—to a customer whose WRA "salary" was $19 a month. I bought it anyway, scrounged some wire, mounted it on a board, and we had a fan. What a blessing it was.

For some reason I kept the motor and fan over the years. Maybe it was sentiment. Perhaps I had planned to use the motor in some now forgotten project. The other day, cleaning out the garage, the motor came to light in the

134

bottom of an old packing crate. It was dust-coated, but it ran. I pondered over it a long time, then reluctantly placed it on the pile of discards. I gave it to one of the scavengers who eke out a living salvaging stuff that people throw away. Maybe it will help cool his family on a hot summer night.

(October 30, 1959)

As the Nisei grew older they were able to appreciate the wisdom of their Issei parents, and something Pat Suzuki said stirred recollections of my own:

Pat Suzuki, the little girl with the big voice who is cutting a wide swathe in the entertainment field these days, will be quoted in an upcoming issue of *This Week,* America's biggest syndicated Sunday newspaper supplement. Pat appears in a collection of prize quotations compiled by Bennett Cerf.

Says Pat, according to Cerf: "My father's philosophy will do till a better one comes along: Think big, work hard— have a dream."

The hope, courage and wisdom of the Issei shines through that simple philosophy. They had to think big, work hard, and have a dream to make their way and raise their families in a strange land.

Pat Suzuki, incidentally, is in fast company in Bennett Cerf's article. She shares space with such notables as Dr. Konrad Adenauer, Zsa Zsa Gabor, Maurice Chevalier, Winston Churchill, Anne Morrow Lindbergh, Mark Twain, and Benjamin Franklin.

Pat's recollection brings to mind something my own Dad used to say when my brother and I were in that perpetually hungry stage. He loved to see us put away the groceries even though at times it was a struggle to keep the bills paid.

"Eat first," he would say. "Eat first and work second."

He was remembering the hungry days of his own youth

135

when he urged us to eat our fill. He had come to America at age fifteen, equipped with little more than the great appetite that is characteristic of boys of those years. But food was hard to come by.

In mellow moments he recalled working first on a railroad section gang, and then as a houseboy. He was always hungry. The lady of the house would say: "Eat potatoes, Roy, they are good for you and filling." But he didn't like potatoes. He used to say his growth was stunted because he couldn't get enough to eat. That's why he wanted us to eat first and worry about the rest later.

(May 22, 1959)

Things that my father said or did or talked about were the basis of a couple of other columns:

Among my regrets, which are not many, is the fact that my father died before he could become a citizen of the United States. He lived in America for fifty-three of his sixty-nine years, from 1899 to 1952, yet he could never legally call it his own. The law denied him the right.

Once long ago he took out his first papers of intent to become a naturalized citizen. This was on the basis of a hitch with the U.S. Coast Guard. I'm sure that, being a Japanese, he was not entitled to these papers, but some clerk must have figured that if he served in the Coast Guard, he deserved to become an American. Of course he was never allowed to complete the procedure.

After World War II, when it appeared the Japanese American Citizens League's efforts to get the naturalization laws revised would be successful, he together with a good many Issei all over the country applied for first papers again. But he died before he could follow through.

All this comes to mind on the tenth anniversary of the

Walter-McCarran Act which, among other things, removes race as a bar to American citizenship.

Many parts of the Walter-McCarran Act have come under fire. Students of the immigration problem charge that the Act is discriminatory in favor of Anglo-Saxon countries. But few have challenged the justice of permitting qualified aliens, regardless of race or national origin, to become Americans. And that's what the Act does.

(June 29, 1962)

Among the bits of knowledge that my Dad failed to pass on to me was the way he picked ripe watermelons. He had an uncanny skill. He would pick out a likely looking melon, heft it, thunk it with his forefinger, and listen as intently as a robin stalking a worm. Every melon I ever tried would thunk with just about the same sound, one little different from another, but his ear was attuned to the resonance, the timbre, or something of each individual one. He could hear and interpret the fine nuances of sound. I never could. So we left the watermelon-selecting to him and he seldom failed us.

His skill was that of a virtuoso, his well-trained ear able to distinguish between a green thunk and a ripe thunk. Mine was crude, almost like killing a fly with a club, and it was developed under the circumstances related below.

One summer I worked in a wholesale produce house. The farmers brought their produce in at the crack of dawn if not before. My job was to unload their trucks. Shortly afterward buyers for grocery stores (there weren't any supermarkets in those days) would troop in to haggle and bargain for the produce. And if a deal was agreed upon, our crew would load their trucks. It was work that required a strong back but not much in the way of brains.

About this time of year the farmers across the Cascades

in the Yakima Valley would bring in great truckloads of watermelons. Coming over the mountains at night, the melons would be thoroughly chilled by the time they reached the market. And they were splendid melons—big, firm, sweet, juicy. And heavy. We workers unloaded them by forming a human chain, tossing the melons from one man to the next. Sometimes someone would drop a melon. Accidentally. When this happened everyone would stop work long enough to crowd around the shattered melon, grab a chunk out of the heart, and eat. Never were watermelons more tasty, more succulent.

When we had too many accidents the boss would become quite perturbed, so we tried not to be overly greedy. But it was then that I learned the only sure way to test the eating quality of a melon was to open it and sample it.

(July 28, 1967)

A visit to Portland, Oregon, resulted in this next column:

A good many Issei found Portland to their liking and they made it their home. Numbers of them sleep the eternal sleep in a segregated section of the Rose City cemetery. When I first saw it soon after the end of World War II, the Japanese portion was dusty and weed-grown, a dismal place showing the results of years of neglect.

Today the grass is green and thick. And there are many more tombstones laid out in orderly rows. The newer stones are larger and more pretentious, reflecting the new affluence. Some bear the names of both husband and wife, but only the birth date of one of them. The date of death will be carved into the stone when it occurs. A resting place beside the partner of a lifetime has been prepared and awaits the arrival of some elderly Issei.

The first time I saw the cemetery I resented the segregation of the Japanese into a special section, a resentment

138

sharpened by the starkness of the area compared to the cared-for appearance of the rest. But this time there seemed to be a kind of comfort and homeyness in old friends being buried close to those with whom they had lived and worked and struggled and with whom they had shared small triumphs. A misty rain floated down to emphasize the greenness and freshness of spring, and I felt no resentment.

(April 17, 1970)

I experienced another kind of homecoming when, on a visit to Powell, Wyoming, to speak at a college commencement, I drove a few miles to the site of the Heart Mountain WRA camp where I had lived fourteen months. The column was titled "Return to Elba":

Approached along the highway from the north and east, Heart Mountain looms above the haze like a tall Spanish galleon. The mountain is about all that remains recognizable of the War Relocation Camp that was erected on the parched benchlands between the towns of Powell and Cody.

The only exceptions are the tall brick chimney for the power plant that was part of the camp's hospital complex, and a weathered and forlorn signboard that once was the community honor roll listing the names of men and women who had gone off to war. The names were inscribed in black paint on gray asbestos board. Now most of the asbestos board has broken away, and not a trace of paint clings to the surface of those fragments that remain. The signboard is on a low pedestal built lovingly by placing flat fieldstones in concrete, a typically and unmistakable evacuee touch.

Where once some 10,000 evacuees had lived, griped, laughed, wept, and tried to make do, there is nothing but neatly tilled fields with the malting barley and alfalfa green with the vigor of spring. The high barbed wire fence is gone.

139

The watchtowers are gone. The scene, peopled by the ghosts of more than a quarter-century ago, is infinitely peaceful. Like a small-time Napoleon returning to his Elba, I walked through the buffalo grass around the war honor roll, trying in mind's eye to remember things as they had been.

For the casual passerby who knows nothing of the evacuation story, there is only one thing to identify the site, a bronze marker mounted in a stone monument which stands at the side of Wyoming Highway 14 that passed by the lower edge of the site. This is the legend on the bronze tablet:

"Heart Mountain Relocation Center, 1942–1945. During the World War II years, Heart Mountain Relocation Center was located on a 740-acre tract of land across the Burlington Railroad right-of-way westward from where you stand facing this monument and Heart Mountain itself on the Heart Mountain Division of the Shoshone Irrigation Project. Eleven thousand people of Japanese ancestry from the three West Coast states were loosely confined by the United States government in the center for about three years. They lived in barracks as singles or as families according to their marital status. The camp was equipped with modern waterworks and sewer system and a modern hospital and dental clinic staffed with people from the ranks of the evacuees. First-rate schooling was provided for the children of the evacuees through the high school grades. This monument was erected, 1963, by the American Legion Posts of Heart Mountain and Powell, Wyoming, and their auxiliaries in the interests of international peace and understanding, and as a memorial to the men and women who have died in the service of their country."

Apology is evident in almost every sentence of the inscription. In their awkward way, the sponsors of the memorial are trying to say the camp really wasn't too bad.

Any Nisei who went through the evacuation experience would have written a more honest appraisal. Only the good intentions of the sponsoring Legion posts saves the memorial from being insulting.

The way it was explained to us, the Legion post in Powell, which was friendly toward the evacuees during the camp period, and the post made up of World War II veterans who homesteaded the Heart Mountain area, wanted to raise a monument recognizing the sacrifices of the Japanese Americans. The post in nearby Cody refused to join the project, contending that nothing should be done to memorialize a shameful chapter of history that no Americans could be proud of. So Cody stayed out, and the other two Legion posts went ahead with the project with the best of intentions.

It's just a shame that some Nisei veterans weren't consulted about a more appropriate wording to be cast permanently in bronze. Maybe it's still not too late to change, or amend, the plaque as a matter of putting a sorry historical event into proper perspective.

(July 16, 1970)

Change also came to familiar haunts in Denver. This sentimental memorial to the passing of a landmark was titled "Requiem to a Service Station":

They came the other day, unhooked the pumps from the gasoline storage tanks hidden underground, and took them away to wherever it is they take old gas pumps. It was the final emasculating act that changed George Kuramoto's Texaco service station to just another little brick shell awaiting the demolition crews under contract to the Urban Renewal people.

The service station stood at the corner of 20th and Lawrence streets. It was a decaying area even before World

War II. That's probably the reason the handful of Issei in prewar Denver were able to concentrate their businesses there, and why the evacuees also settled there when they sought refuge from the West Coast's hysteria and the boredom of camp life.

After the evacuees arrived the service station quickly became one of the landmarks of Denver's crumbling Nippon Town. Even with ration cards, one had to buy gas, right? And if you couldn't buy a new car, you needed expert help from a mechanic to keep the old one running. So you went to the gas station. At first George was just one of the fellows running the place. Then the others went back to California, or some other place, and George remained as the proprietor. He remembered the humid heat of Walnut Grove, near Sacramento, where he used to live, and the dead-end economic opportunity there and decided Denver was a better place to bring up his family.

So he stayed, and as the community dwindled, the gas station became a sort of greasy, cluttered community center. You left the car there to be gassed while you walked a half block to shop at the Granada Fish Market or at Pacific Mercantile, or walked across the street for a bite to eat. You stopped by for the latest gossip, and you left packages for a friend to pick up. You knew they would be dropping in, sooner or later.

For the Methodist ministers like Paul Hagiya and Jonathan Fujita, whose base of operations was on the other side of town, George's gas station served as a second office. If you couldn't find the preachers at the church, you telephoned the gas station and left word because if they weren't there at the moment they were likely to drop by later in the day to pick up any messages.

Over the years George's spot won a place in the community that was far more important than just a service station to get gas, a lube job, or a set of tires. The loafers

142

hung out there, sitting in the shade in summer and huddling around the heater in winter. The young bucks would come by in their hopped-up cars and use the hose to wash the dust off spotless finishes, or borrow the jack to change the tires. The fishermen came by to get a tank of gas and find out where the trout were biting. The mushroom hunters got the latest word about moisture conditions in the mountains.

In season Nisei farmers with big trucks of melons from Rocky Ford and lettuce from the San Luis Valley and truck crops from up north would stop in, too, on their way to or from market. This was where you could get the latest news about weddings and funerals, and word about job openings and new businesses and people moving into town or back to California, and youngsters who got drafted, and who had been in the hospital and a lot of other incidental intelligence. In other words, the gas station was a kind of general store for all the folks of the community where one picked up the news along with the gasoline.

Well, the Urban Renewal people have big ideas for renovating the area. But to build fine new structures it is necessary to demolish the old ones. One by one the crummy, rickety, outmoded old buildings have been knocked to the ground and their unsightly remains trucked away. George Kuramoto's gas station, the physical shell, will be leveled shortly to make way for a handsome complex planned by the Buddhist Church. And the corner will never be the same again.

(January 22, 1971)

And finally, to wind up this chapter, there is a sort of requiem for the Issei:

I suppose the tradition of gala New Year's parties will continue to thrive as long as there are Issei among us. The dwindling number of Issei here in Denver made it necessary

143

to combine the resources of three organizations to hold a New Year's party on the last day of January. (Some of the oldtimers were going around saying "Happy New Year" even though the next day would be the first of February, and somehow the greeting seemed not inappropriate since they hadn't seen each other since the new year dawned.)

These parties are happy affairs with plenty of Chinese chow to be stowed away, and a lot of home talent entertainment. It doesn't take much persuasion to get the old folks up before the microphone to perform, and one gathers that they've been practicing for the event for some considerable time in advance.

The Issei, even after all these years, are by and large a humble looking lot. The men wear their best suits, which look like they were first bought twenty years ago. The suits probably didn't fit too well in the first place and time hasn't helped much. The ladies, bless them, favor house dresses and the thought of being stylish would probably frighten them half to death. They are, to put it kindly, not a physically impressive people, and one knows that their occupations are far from prestigious.

Yet they have culture, dignity and pride. An old gentleman who puts on khaki britches and a sweat-stained jacket and mows other people's lawns for a living can stand before a crowd and sing a classical number. Another old-timer who operates a third-rate hotel composes poetry to fit special occasions and recites heroic ballads. An elderly lady who has struggled to make ends meet most of her life sings a beautiful folk song. In the eyes of the world, particularly the Caucasian world, these humble little people are, perhaps, looked upon as strange foreigners who never really learned to speak English. But if they could look below the surface they would find pride, yes, and culture and dignity.

144

10

Of Language and Things

Japanese immigrants had a perfectly miserable time with the English language. There was nothing common to the grammar of the two languages, and the sounds required in speaking English posed almost impossible challenges for Japanese tongues. Thus it was that not many Japanese immigrants learned to speak English well. Their children, on the other hand, going to American public schools and associating with English-speaking playmates, seldom progressed beyond baby-talk in Japanese. It is something of a marvel that the two generations could communicate, which they did after a fashion with the Issei speaking to their children in Japanese and the Nisei replying in English.

This section will be devoted mostly to Frying Pan columns commenting on the confusing and amusing situations created by language difficulties.

Larry Tajiri in a recent *Pacific Citizen* column held forth at length on the word *skibby*. The word, he noted, is listed by H. L. Mencken in his *The American Language: Supplement I,* as being used on the West Coast as a racially derogatory term referring to persons of Japanese ancestry. Mencken says *skibby* was originally applied to a loose woman "though now it means, at least in California, any Japanese, male or female." *Skibby,* he adds, seems to have been borrowed from a Japanese word, "though what that word was is uncertain."

Tajiri observed correctly that *skibby* is a word alien to the experience of most Nisei. But it was used more commonly in an earlier era before Nisei ears became attuned to racial insults. I remember being called a *skibby* in grade school a good three decades ago. The name fell on deaf ears because I was too dumb to be insulted.

"What's *skibby* mean?" I asked in all innocence. The name-caller too, was caught flat-footed. He replied: "Don't you know what *skibby* means? It means, well, it means you're a *skibby.*" That's all he could say.

The word remained in the back of my head and after another encounter with it some years later I looked it up in a Japanese-English dictionary. I found it at the bottom of page 1839, *sukebei,* a noun meaning "lechery, bawdiness, lewdness, prurience, a satyr, a bawdy person, a hot-stuff." As an adjective, *sukebei-na,* it becomes "bawdy, lecherous, lewd, lustful, lascivious, incontinent, concupiscent." The dictionary goes on to explain unsmilingly that the sentence, *Kare was sukebei da,* means "He is susceptible to female charms."

If I had a spare Japanese-English dictionary, I'd send it along to Mr. Mencken for his edification. He could also use a round-trip ticket to the West Coast to learn for himself that *skibby* is not a commonly used word among the "Jap-haters." Indeed, he may find considerable difficulty trying to locate them.

(May 28, 1954)

From studying the dictionary definitions of the word sukebei, *one gets the idea that the editors were groping for a precise meaning. Well, the Japanese language is often like that, lacking in profanity and depending on inflection to get the idea across as illustrated in the following:*

According to the newspapers, Shigeru Yoshida is in danger of losing his job as Japan's premier because he said a bad word. In the heat of legislative debate, he called a heckler *bakayaro.*

That, as most Nisei know, is very naughty although in translation it comes out an innocuous "stupid fellow," or as the press dispatches have it, "stupid fool."

Now that seems to be a pretty mild epithet for determining the life or death of a cabinet, but the severity of *bakayaro* stems from a fact little known among Americans —that it is impossible to swear in Japanese because there are no cuss words.

Even Mr. Takenobu's Kenkyusha Japanese-English dictionary, which has been gathering dust for a long time on my bookshelves, has trouble translating bad-word Japanese into English. *Baka,* for instance, is defined as meaning the following: "a fool, a simpleton, a dupe; an ass; a donkey, a moon-calf, a goose, a dunce, a blockhead; a dullard; a dolt; a ninny; an oaf; a booby; a chump; an idiot." In adjective form, *baka* becomes "foolish, silly, dull, stupid; weak-minded; dull-witted; thick-headed; idiotic, imbecilic."

If anyone calls you *baka,* you take your pick of the above, and get as angry as you like—depending of course on how big the name-caller happens to be.

In the case of Mr. Yoshida, it might be helpful to know that he is a tiny, slight and somewhat elderly individual.

The real effect of *bakayaro* rests in the inflection. Shouted by a military officer it sounds half way between a pistol shot and a whipcrack. There's no mistaking the meaning when an expert in the *bakayaro* business uses the word.

Early in my encounters with the English language I discovered the word "crazy." Someone described a playmate by saying, "Aw, he's crazy." It sounded like a pretty good word and subsequently all of us used it frequently and indiscriminately.

Because we were a cosmopolitan gang, one of the fellows asked me how to say "crazy" in Japanese. *Baka,* I told him. It was the only bad word I knew in Japanese.

My parents, however, were scandalized. A person could be *baka,* they explained, and sometimes it wasn't too bad. But to be crazy, why that was *kichigai,* and *kichigai* people were put away in the booby hatch. I've never forgotten that lesson in trans-Pacific semantics.

Since our Sansei youngsters don't speak any Japanese at all, the things they pick up sometimes are little short of weird. One day they came back from a visit with some black-haired friends and one of them—I forget which one —remarked:

"Dad, I know how to say 'shut up' in Japanese."

"How?"

"*Yakamashii.* That's what the old man said when we were hollering and running around."

(The literal meaning of *yakamashii* is "noisy," but it is often used to mean "be quiet.")

(April 3, 1953)

American efforts to cope with the Japanese language can be just as amusing as Japanese problems with English:

Last week I ran into a situation that knocked me off stride for a moment. I was introduced to a girl who was paying more attention to the handsome guy next to me.

148

When he drifted away, she turned to me and said: "I can say your name. I ran into it in Honolulu last spring, Mr. Sukiyaki."

She was sober, too.

That reminds me of a story I saw in an old number of the *American Legion* magazine. It's by William C. Todd and I hope he won't mind if I repeat the essence of it here.

It seems a young G.I. came home to the U.S. after serving a hitch in Japan and let it be known that he was pretty hot stuff with the Japanese language. Word of his ability as a linguist got around, and one Sunday in church the pastor asked if he wouldn't honor the congregation with a rendering of the Lord's Prayer in Japanese. Todd continues:

"As the congregation bowed their heads, our hero intoned: *Ohayoo gozaimasu, konnichi wa, konban wa, oyasumninasai.* (Good morning, good day, good evening, good night.) *Domo arigato gozaimasu, doo itashimashite.* (Thank you very much, you're welcome.) *Anone, benjo wa doko desuka, sukoshi, takusan, ikaga desuka.* (Say, where is the toilet? Little, much, how are you?)

"Rolling his tones sonorously, he concluded with: *Musumesan, watakushi wa anata no tomodachi—okusan.* (Young lady, I am your friend—wife.)

"As he sat down, the congregation stirred respectfully and awaited the parson's amen.

"But before this could be uttered, another voice spoke up from among the rear pews. Very softly, very reverently, it said, '*Ah so desuka*' (that so?)."

(July 17, 1953)

It wasn't always words that caused problems. Sometimes the sight of an unfamiliar face led to confusion, and sometimes it didn't, as related in the two following items:

Having moved recently, I went down to the schoolhouse this week to register anew as a voter. The registrar got along fine until she came to the blank that called for the voter's complexion.

She cast a sidelong glance my way, then wrote "dark." No one had ever referred to me before as dark, but no matter. Let it pass.

Then I registered for my spouse, which is permitted under the laws. Once again the registrar asked such pertinent questions as place of birth, present age, height, etcetera. When she came to the blank marked complexion, she stopped.

"Is your wife dark?" she ventured.

"Well, now," I replied, "I guess that would depend on the season. In the winter she's quite fair, but she picks up a pretty good tan during the summer."

This seemed to fluster the good lady and she turned to her companion for help. "I wouldn't say this man's dark," the second woman said. "He's more medium dark."

Suddenly she seemed embarrassed and hurried to add: "I get awfully dark in the summer, too." And the first registrar, a Nordic type, said with a nervous titter: "And I get freckled."

And with that, they decided I was just "medium dark." They listed my wife that way, too, and I hope it's all right with her.

(May 13, 1960)

Spearfish, S.D.

A gentle-looking elderly lady (what other kind does one meet at a writers' conference?), apparently with adequate eyesight, approached me and asked: "Mr. Hosokawa, how do you spell your name?" I showed her the identification badge on my lapel and spelled it out for her.

150

"Oh, yes," she responded. "A very unusual name. Is it Polish?"

The only thing I could think of to say was: "No, ma'm, it isn't Polish. Do you think I look Polish?"

I think I was more flustered than she. I've been asked if I were Chinese, Korean, Manchurian and Indian, but never have I been mistaken for a Slav. Later, thinking it over, I wondered whether the little old lady was simply befuddled. Or, living in the splendid isolation of the Black Hills country of South Dakota, had she been so completely insulated from the shifting cross currents of American life that she could not distinguish a Japanese face from the face of any other "foreigner," in this case a Pole. Or was she such a completely democratic cosmopolite that her eyes did not register, nor her brain distinguish, whether a person's skin was black, brown, white or yellow, whether his features were flat or aquiline, his hair straight or curly?

What had brought me to Spearfish was an invitation to speak at an area-wide workshop of aspiring writers at Black Hills State College. If there was any irony in the fact of a Japanese American, offspring of immigrants, lecturing to a group of whites on the fine points of writing in the English language, and writing so the product would be salable, it seemed to have escaped all concerned.

The elderly lady mentioned above made it clear, however, that she was aware of the existence of Japanese Americans. After I had informed her that Hosokawa had Japanese rather than Polish origins, she was kind enough to remark: "Oh, you're one of those smart Japs."

After that I could not bring myself to tell her that we aren't Japs, that we don't like the term, that many people consider it offensive and a vulgarism. Perhaps I should have.

(July 5, 1968)

151

"Jap" is a fighting word for many Japanese Americans. They do not consider it an acceptable shortened form of Japanese. They feel it is an ethnic slur, harking back to the bitter days of what someone has called California's war against the Japanese, when the word was pronounced with a sneer. However, in decrying its use, some Japanese Americans over-reacted, shouting insult and claiming affront even when the term was used innocently and out of ignorance. One Japanese American writer, in expressing his outrage against the use of the word, inadvertently slurred another group and I felt the need for pointing this out in a column published July 23, 1971. Although the writer was named in the original column, I am omitting it here since it is not necessary in making my point:

"First, I need a dirty word. Since there aren't any good dirty words that we can use in print, we'll settle for the word 'bannock,' a term I'm sure you never heard of. A bannock is a flat oatmeal cake. Now the next time you slam your thumb with a hammer, or hit your shin on a low-standing coffee table, scream to yourself, 'I'm a dirty, rotten bannock.' You'll probably laugh, since you know you've just called yourself a dirty, rotten, flat oatmeal cake."
—A writer in the July 9 *Pacific Citizen* discussing the use of hate words, like "Jap."

"Bannock Indians once roamed throughout southeastern Idaho and western Wyoming. They traveled in small bands hunting buffalo and other animals. The U.S. government placed the Bannock on a reservation in the 1870s. Poor living conditions led to an armed outbreak in 1878. Troops under Maj. Gen. Oliver O. Howard defeated the Indians in September 1878. The surviving Bannocks intermarried with the Shoshoni, and their descendants live in Idaho."—The World Book Encyclopedia.

The writer quoted above was looking for an unfamiliar, inoffensive word in order to make a very valid point when he chose "bannock." He meant to offend no one. It turns out, however, that the Bannocks were once a prominent Indian tribe. Their memory is honored by a Bannock street in Denver. In Pocatello, Idaho, there was and undoubtedly still is a Bannock Hotel, and there probably are some Bannock tribesmen left who quite likely would not look kindly on the suggestion in a Japanese American journal that their name be substituted for a more offensive oath.

There seems to be a lesson in this little incident. Sometimes those who offend by the use of racial epithets do so intentionally. But more often the offense is unintended and the result of ignorance. A case in point is the term "Jap."

Once it was used as a hate word. It had the same derogatory connotation as "sheenie," "kike," "dago," "wop," "spik," "nigger," and other terms that have no place in our language.

Despite our efforts, many well-meaning Americans still do not understand this about "Jap." So they use it, intending no more offense than when they call a person from Sweden a Swede, a person from Turkey a Turk, a person of the Jewish faith a Jew, all of which are accepted terms.

What do you do when you encounter ignorance? Why, you try to educate. This is the approach taken by JACL in its pamphlet, *Please Don't*. The fact that the word keeps popping up every so often is not necessarily an indictment against the approach. It merely points up the fact that a lot of educating needs to be done and constant vigilance is necessary.

In view of our experience as a people it is natural that the blood pressure rises when we hear "Jap" used, no matter how innocently. But the crux of the matter is the intent, and we must concede the possibility of an unintended slur when even a Japanese American writer, commenting on the subject in moderate fashion, inadvertently slurs still another minority. As for the bigots, I think it was Ernie Banks, the superb Chicago Cubs' black baseball player, who said something very like: "You can't convince a fool against his will by shouting at him."

Meanwhile, the important thing is that we be as quick to protest slurs against others as we are to speak out in anger at the use of the word "Jap." Negroes are not "niggers," Jews are not "kikes," officers of the law are not "pigs," any more than Japanese Americans are "Japs."

(July 13, 1971)

A point that I tried to make in other columns on this subject is that some of us are excessively thin-skinned; we go looking for insults where none was intended. Some of us are constantly searching for opportunities to clobber some poor, inoffensive slob who refers to someone as a "Jap" without ever realizing that it's a no-no. A well-known comedian helped make the point for me:

One of the speakers at our meetings in San Diego was Arte Johnson, the little comedian of the highly successful "Laugh-In" TV show who, making like a German soldier, says "Verrry eenteresting." Johnson told us he speaks nothing but English, but he has made a lucrative living with dialect roles. This isn't too easy these days because people are so quick to become offended.

Not long ago, Johnson recalled, he pretended on a program to be telling an off-color story in Polish. He leered and gestured and laughed lewdly while mouthing a lot of gibberish that he thought sounded the way Polish ought to sound. A few days later he was astonished to receive a letter from some sort of ethnic organization protesting what was described as an unspeakably obscene performance that offended all Polish-speaking Americans.

154

Johnson wrote back asking for a translation of the story he had told and predictably he never did get a reply. Johnson told the story simply as an anecdote about his experiences, but the moral was only too obvious. Too many folks these days are protesting too much about too many affronts, real and imagined. And when one becomes overly sensitive, a lot of the fun drains out of life which is a pretty grim business without our purposely making it even more that way.

(October 11, 1968)

But getting back to the Issei, it was inevitable that they should adopt convenient English terms into their daily language. The pronunciation they gave some of these words was unique. Note that their language is referred to below as "Issei-ese." On a later occasion I called it "Japlish," a combination of "Japanese" and "English," and was taken to task by some thin-skinned readers who prefer to see it not as a contraction, but an ethnic slur.

Before it is too late, someone ought to compile what might be titled a lexicon of Issei-ese, or a list of words and expressions that were peculiar to the conversation of Japanese immigrants as they tried to cope with the English language. They did strange and wonderful things with English that are quite different from the "*katakana* English" that characterizes the pronunciation of many Japanese. As an example, let's take the simple sentence, "That is no good." In *katakana* English, based on the Japanese *katakana* system of writing, it would emerge something like this: "Zatto izu no goodo." But in Issei-ese it might sound this way: "Datto no guru."

The degree to which an Issei mutilated the language depended on his education, the extent to which English was necessary to his livelihood, whether he lived and worked in a Japanese community or elsewhere, and many other factors. Just for beginners, here are ten expressions I recall from my boyhood. Perhaps they were peculiar to my own father's vocabulary, but I remember them vividly and I hope others can add to the list:

Donguri pantsu—Obviously a corruption of "dungaree pants," which are known today as blue jeans or Levi's. Being for the most part blue collar workers, at least in their earlier days, Issei had plenty of opportunities to make the acquaintance of dungarees.

Dorosu—Drawers, or underwear.

Holu-dappu—Hold-up, or stickup. Since the Issei lived and worked in what is now called the ghettoes, they were often victimized by thieves and bandits.

Humboku stekki—Hamburger steak, a staple in the Issei diet because it was cheaper than meat that hadn't been ground up.

Oh lie—All right. Just the opposite of no guru.

Oh-tohn-beeru—That's an easy one. The Japanese word for automobiles is jidosha (self-moving vehicle) and the Issei also referred to them as "caw," the way some Bostonians do.

Osumala you—Mouthed in an accusing manner, the Issei was asking: "What's the matter with you?"

Panku taiya—If you found it difficult to say your tire was "punctured," you said panku.

Waya—Things were "waya" when they were haywire.

Yongu—Used as in "Oi, Yongu," meaning "Hey, young fellow." The implication was deprecatory in that young fellows, even though they spoke English well, were considered wet behind the ears, unversed in practical matters, and altogether rather dumb.

(March 8, 1974)

My request for reader contributions to the Lexicon of Issei-ese brought in several:

156

George Mits Kaneko of Denver contributes *Go tsu heh-ru,* which of course translates to "go to hell," no doubt uttered often in frustration. And in happier times they cried out *Ha-ro,* which is easily recognizable as "hello."

Charles Kamayatsu of Los Angeles suggests other expressions that reflect Issei life and times. *Go-home kutta* literally "swallowed (or told to) go home" meant the person was fired from his job. And *basto-uppu* or "bust up" meant to go bankrupt.

June K. Tanaka of Montreal, who like most Canadian Nisei grew up in British Columbia, suggested these additions:

Compa—Together, in partnership, probably shortened from "in company."

Contsuraiki—Contract, as in contsuraiki with a cannery.

Dan-buro—Basement, corruption of "down below."

Hohsu-behta—No, it doesn't have anything to do with betting on a horse. That's the way some Issei pronounced hospital.

Meriken—A punch in the face. This must be a Canadian expression, possibly derived from getting beaten up by a pugnacious American.

Washi-dekki—Cleaning the floor, from washing the deck. Perhaps a naval term, but I remember hearing it at cleanup time in the salmon canneries.

Just as the Issei found difficulties with English, Nisei and Sansei tripped often and amusingly in their efforts to speak Japanese.

Jean Pearce, columnist for the *Japan Times* in Tokyo, wrote recently about Ni/Sansei who go to Japan in search of their roots and find language an insurmountable barrier. "We're Japanese until we open our mouths," one girl told her. This leads to disillusion and frustration, but also to

157

some hilarious situations, somewhat like the experiences of Issei when they first came to the United States. So, taking a cue from Jean Pearce, it seems only fair to relate some stories about linguistic misadventures of Ni/Sansei in Japan.

One Sansei Miss Pearce writes about went to a Tokyo confectionery and asked for three pastries. But she made the mistake of using the counter for animals, presumably saying "Give me san-biki (three animal) pastries." The shopkeeper, Miss Pearce says, was incredulous, and no wonder.

A Sansei I know, DeDe Torizawa of Denver, was in Tokyo last summer with her brother, Mike, to take a language study course. One day Mike ran a fever and DeDe, being the motherly sort, thought it wise to pick up a thermometer and take his temperature.

DeDe found a pharmacy, all right, but suddenly realized she didn't know the word for fever thermometer. Somehow she got over the idea that someone was ill. She went into elaborate play-acting to depict her brother's problem, dramatically clasping her forehead to project the idea that his head was burning with fever. The clerk came up with aspirins, antihistamines and various pills.

Then DeDe remembered that the Japanese customarily place the thermometer under the armpit instead of the mouth, so she demonstrated that point with further pantomiming. This time the clerk produced a deodorant.

Eventually DeDe recalled the Japanese word for temperature, or fever, which is *netsu,* and that one word solved her problem.

The Japanese language has so many different constructions that words which mean the same cannot be used interchangeably in different situations. Jim Yoshida remembers a Nisei GI who asked a waitress for *samui mizu. Samui* means cold and *mizu* is water but you just don't say *samui mizu.* A person can be *samui,* but water that is chilled is *hiyai* and the proper term for cold water is *o-hiya*, literally "honorable cold." I'll be darned if I know how to explain these differences in usage. You just have to know; there don't seem to be any rules to cover these situations.

Charles Kamayatsu likes to tell about the time he visited the city of Nara in Japan. Everywhere he went he made it a point to sample the various foods for which the area was famous, and he assumed with considerable logic that Nara would be well-known for *nara-zuke*, which is a kind of sweet pickle, *zuke* meaning pickled.

Kamayatsu made his big mistake when he decided to speak very politely. Instead of asking the clerk in the store for just plain *nara-zuke*, he put the honorific *o* in front of the word. What he said was that he would like some *o-nara-zuke* which, to his utter mystification, caused the clerk to explode in unladylike laughter.

Only later did Kamayatsu discover that *o-nara* is what happens inevitably when one eats too many beans.

(November 19, 1976)

This final item isn't directly concerned with language, but in a way it does, or more correctly, it deals with the deeper meaning of differences of culture and nationality:

My friend Hatch Kita from Tokyo, who has been visiting us together with his wife Kyoko, had only two matters he wanted to take care of during his week's stay in Denver. The first was to get in a day of skiing. The second, and more important, was to see that Kyoko was naturalized as an American citizen.

The first was relatively easily taken care of. We drove up to Vail, one of Colorado's more glamorous ski resorts.

The second matter was somewhat more involved, but the outcome more satisfying. To explain, Hatch is a Nisei who went to Japan soon after VJ-Day as a GI interpreter and translator. He took his discharge in Japan and is now a civilian employed by the U.S. Army, doing much the same kind of work he did while in uniform. Kyoko is a Tokyo girl who married him about fifteen years ago. Although she had expected to become an American citizen, somehow she had never gotten around to it. This trip to the United States, her second, provided an opportunity to make application for "expedited" procedure. And this she did through the Denver office of the Immigration and Naturalization Service. It was a big step, and one not to be taken lightly.

But once the decision was made, the fates seemed to be arrayed against its consummation. First, a very important form was lacking, and it was necessary to get it from the personnel officer in Hatch's outfit in Japan. Then, after the Kitas had come to Denver, it was discovered that for some reason the entire file had been sent to Honolulu.

By the time the file was returned to Denver, Kyoko was in pretty much of a state about the impending examination even though one would never have known it. Her composure appeared unshatterable. After she learned the file was back safely, she had only three hours to present herself for the citizenship examination. Having studied the manual, she knew that the three branches of government in the United States are the executive, legislative and judicial. She knew the first ten amendments to the Constitution are known as the Bill of Rights, that the Declaration of Independence was signed in 1776, but the Constitution was not drawn up until 1787, that the Senate is the upper house and each state has two senators regardless of population.

Well, as it turned out, the examiner didn't ask her anything about these matters, which frustrated her just a bit. First, he asked why in filling out a questionnaire she had said she would refuse to bear arms in defense of the United States. She had an answer to that one: "I wrote that because I am a woman," she replied, "and women do not fight."

That must have set the proper tone because the examiner then asked who Christopher Columbus and Abraham Lincoln were. That was easy. Then he asked who is the Vice President of the United States, and she had to reply: "I know, but I forgot his name." The examiner laughed about that and told her, so she would not forget again, and passed her so that the last barrier to citizenship was removed.

Later, we talked about the awesome responsibilities of citizenship, and what a momentous matter it is for a person to renounce his or her allegiance to the country of birth and voluntarily seek membership in the family of another nation. And in the case of the Japanese, naturalization as an American is an even more sacred event because not so many years ago that privilege was not extended to them. And Kyoko Kita, realizing all this, and having sought American citizenship of her own volition, will make a good American.

(April 26, 1968)

Do you *remember who was Vice President in 1968? How could you forget Hubert Horatio Humphrey?*

11

The Growing Family

The children, growing rapidly, continued to be a favorite and prolific source of column material. There were amusing episodes, and tender ones like this:

Susan sidled up coyly the other day and, looking at me with wide open eyes, asked if I could beat up Buster Crabbe. I knew by the expression on her face that she expected me to say yes. I disappointed her. I asked her who Buster Crabbe happened to be.

Patiently, she explained. It seems that Buster currently is a TV-type cowboy. Buster is very strong. He vanquishes bad guys with skill and dispatch. He can ride like the wind and he has a wallop in his right that should make Rocky Marciano quiver with fear.

The cobwebs fell away and I remembered Buster. He used to be an Olympic swimmer. After that, I recalled, he played a movie Tarzan for a while, leaping through trees, strangling lions and outswimming crocodiles. He was quite a man.

Perhaps I should have been flattered that my daughter thinks I am in the same physical class, more or less, with Buster. And yet there is a little sadness in the thought because all too soon she will grow up and lose her child's faith.

Soon she will realize that her daddy is a chair-borne softy who gets winded running for the bus. And even in his prime, she'll come to learn, he couldn't have qualified to carry Buster's towel for him.

Today, though, through the adoring magic of her nine-year-old eyes, her daddy has stature. She is sure he can do anything. She thinks that perhaps he too can perform all the brave and wonderful feats that Buster Crabbe demonstrates so well on television.

As adolescence opens her eyes, she will discover the horrible truth. Her daddy is not superman. He will crumble in her estimation, an adobe god with feet of clay. He never again will quite approach her ideal of what a man should be like—never, that is, until she is grown and wise.

But in adolescence she will see only that his suit always wrinkles across the back, that his hair sticks up no matter how he combs it. That his shoes usually need a shine and that he lacks the courtly manner that all young women expect in elderly men. Elderly men? Why, that's me. . . .

Just for a while, though, I shall stand a little straighter and talk a little lower down in my throat. I shall flex my muscles under the layer of fat, and try to walk with just a little spring in my flattened arches. All because Susan, in her childish way, thinks that perhaps her daddy is big enough and strong enough and brave enough to beat up Buster Crabbe.

(March 20, 1953)

163

*Not all the children were so kind and adoring. Witness
this next experience with Christie, who was three years old
at the time:*

The other afternoon Christie went with me to buy a load
of gas at George Kuramoto's service station.

George has made it a custom to slip a penny into a
machine and take out a handful of peanuts for the kids
each time we drop by. This time, when it appeared that
George had overlooked the peanuts, Christie pulled at my
pantlegs and in a loud whisper made it known that she
wasn't willing to abandon custom. George caught the hint,
all right, and produced.

On the way home Christie sat beside me and munched
nuts happily. But she made no effort to share them with me.

"Christie," I said after a while, "aren't you going to offer
me some peanuts?"

She gave me a reproachful look and replied: "I didn't
know you were hungry." Then she pulled one tiny peanut
from her pocket and presented it to me.

"Here," she said. "And next time be sure to eat all your
lunch so you won't get hungry."

(July 31, 1953)

*Although they shared the same genetic heritage, each of
our four children developed highly individualized personalities and reacted differently to life's experiences and
crises, like losing a tooth:*

Mike, our first-grader, has a front tooth coming loose.
It is his first and he is intrigued and thrilled by the prospect
of losing it. Yet he is a little apprehensive for he hates pain
and he is afraid it might hurt. He practically has sworn off
eating apples for fear of further loosening that tooth. . . .

(February 8, 1947)

164

Our Susan lost the last of her frontline baby teeth recently on a day when I didn't come home for dinner. Next morning, as I was reading the newspaper, she told me about it. The conversation went about like this:

"Daddy, remember the loose tooth I had? Well, it came out yesterday."

"That's fine."

"Didn't Mommy tell you about it when you came home last night?"

"Nope."

"Oh. Well, I put the tooth under my pillow last night. The tooth was still there this morning and there wasn't any money."

"Oh, that's too bad."

A light begins to dawn.

"Daddy, I think I'll put it under my pillow again tonight."

"That sounds like a very good idea."

Funny thing happened. Susan found a quarter under her pillow the following morning although the regular rate for discarded teeth around our house is a dime.

(November 20, 1953)

Our Pete noticed some weeks ago that his front teeth were getting loose and he worked on them diligently. Eventually one of them got pretty wobbly, but it just wouldn't drop out. One night last week he asked me to pull it out for him. "Don't want to bother with it any more," he said with great unconcern.

Pete and I went to Mom's sewing basket and requisitioned a length of white thread. He opened his mouth and as carefully as clumsy fingers would let me, I wound the thread around the soon to be dispossessed tooth.

"Ready?" I asked. Pete nodded. I jerked. The thread slipped off and the tooth was still in Pete's head. I tried a

165

second time and failed again. I could see that Pete was growing a little nervous.

The third time I took an extra hitch around the tooth, and yanked vigorously. The tooth flew through the air and rattled to the floor. Now that the deed was done, Pete was dumfounded. I steered him over to a mirror and let him see the gap in his smile.

"It's bleeding," he observed in an awe-stricken voice. He rinsed out his mouth. The bleeding stopped, and he had passed another milestone.

(January 13, 1956)

Got home late the other night and found a note left for me by Christie, the seven-year-old. It said: "Dear Dad. I got my loose tooth out all by myself. Please leave 25 cents here."

(February 23, 1958)

Christie seemed to be quite precocious about leaving notes. Like the one that was the basis for this item:

Just before we went out the other evening, Christie, the seven-year-old, ran out to play. The last word she heard was to be sure and come in within a half-hour since it was fast becoming dark.

When we got home late that night there was a penciled note in our room. It read: "Dear Momy, I'm sorry I was late coming in. Please do not scold me in the morning and do not talk to me about it any time."

At least she's discovering early in life that the printed word is a most useful form of communication.

(March 28, 1958)

School lessons posed a series of problems for the young-sters and helping them provided an education for us, too:

166

Our Mike is having fraction trouble. You know, stuff that goes like: "What is the sum of nine-sixteenths and five-eighths?" "What is two-thirds of four and one-half wormy apples and why?" "If Farmer Jones had two-tenths of an acre under cultivation in spinach and Farmer Brown three-fourths of an acre under water, what is the legal limit on rainbow trout in Colorado?"

That sort of sixth grade mathematics baffles Mike, which is probably a weakness that he inherited from his father. Even dime store clerks can beat Mike's dad in figuring the amount of change due on a dollar bill tendered for a 39-cent purchase. With the kind of clerks they're getting these days that's saying quite a bit.

So Mike persuaded his mother to help him bone up on fractions and they had a long session together one night last week. After the lesson, Mike's mother was in a reminiscent mood and she told about her own troubles with arithmetic. The story as she related it was an experience that was shared by most Nisei.

"When I was a little girl," she said, "my biggest problem was story problems."

That's the kind where Johnny Jones has a four-bit piece burning his pocket and he goes on a shopping expedition. After he buys this, that and other things, how much change has he left?

"My mother was very good about helping me, but that's where a lot of the trouble came. First I'd have to read the problem until I understood it, then I'd translate it into Japanese for my mother.

"Then, speaking in Japanese, she'd explain step by step how to solve the problem. When I got that digested, I'd have to translate that back into English in my head, and finally put the answer down. It was a lesson in language as well as arithmetic."

As I recall now, a somewhat related problem presented

itself to me when I reached long division. My mother got the correct answer, all right, but she arrived at it in a fashion that wasn't taught in Washington Grade School, U.S.A. We never did get that situation ironed out, but her answers were convenient for double checking mine.

The problem was much more acute when it came to asking parental guidance in grammar. Tense, gender, person, dangling participles, prepositional phrases, proper nouns and conjugated verbs were just so much Greek (or English) to Pa and Ma, so we kids had to figure those things out for ourselves after class hours.

(May 3, 1952)

Baseball provided the boys fun as well as learning experiences which are reported in a couple of columns:

Mike's current passion is sports, which he courts with a fanatic's zeal. At school he rapidly is catching on to the rudiments of baseball, and getting his share of the knocks and hip-strawberries on the playground. Once in a while I get around to giving him some firsthand fatherly coaching. One of the pearls of wisdom I have imparted is the trick of choking the bat.

"Hold that bat up high," I told him. "It's too heavy for you. So choke it and you'll have better control over it. You'll hit the ball more often."

Then, the other day at school, Mike's gym teacher saw him choking up and advised him to grip the bat at the end and swing like mad.

Now, any sandlot Durocher will tell you that a batter can get distance by swinging from the end, but the chances are he'll strike out more often, too. Maybe Mike's just lucky. He came home a firm believer in the long swing, and full of scorn for his father's conservatism.

168

"I did just like the teacher told me," he exclaimed. "And I got a triple. No more of that choking baloney for me."

(May 13, 1950)

When and how does one teach a child honesty? I had occasion to wonder the other day when Mike and I went into a sporting goods store to buy a bat. Mike had been saving his dimes and nickles—no one seems to bother much with pennies any more—to buy a bat and it was a big event for him. He had been blaming his inability to hit on his not having a good bat of his own. He figured that if he had a real good bat, he'd be slamming out homers like Mickey Mantle.

So we went to the store and Mike hefted a few bats and found one he liked. The price was $2.65, which seems like a pretty fat price to pay for a little old softball bat.

The clerk said: "Do you play for a league team?"

I learned a long time ago that league teams always get discounts on equipment. I would have said: "Sure, and what's the discount?" whether I played on a league team or not. You get shrewd that way when you have to count your pennies, as most of us Nisei did when we were kids.

But Mike, he had to be honest. He mumbled, "No," and I saw visions of the discount flying out the window.

Maybe the clerk was hard of hearing. Maybe he wasn't listening. Anyway, he just said: "Okay, league players get a 55¢ discount. For you, the bat is $2.10." So Mike paid $2.10 plus 6¢ tax, and got his discount even though he wasn't trying to.

What should I have said and done? Darned if I know. What's the moral of this story? I don't know that either. Sometimes it's tough being a parent.

(May 21, 1953)

The next two items have to do with Pete, at the time of kindergarten age:

Our Peter (age five) and Christie (three) were arguing about something trivial the other day when Pete gave way to exasperation and called his sister stupid.

"I am not stupid," she retorted. "I'm smart."

"All right," said Pete, "if you're so smart, what's two and two?"

Without a second's hesitation Christie replied: "Two and two is three."

I waited to hear what Pete would say to this mathematical falsehood. But of course he didn't know the answer and it seemed he was overwhelmed by the authoritative ring in Christie's voice. He lapsed into the gloomy silence of a small boy who has been outwitted by an even smaller sister.

(August 21, 1953)

On the last day of school, Pete, the kindergartener, brought home a "report card." Since it was the first time we'd come across a kindergarten-size report, we examined it with special interest. It read:

Child's name: Peter
Knows name: √
Knows address: √
Knows phone No.: √
Knows birthday: √
Can recognize colors and
  name them: √
Can tie a bow: √
Recognizes printed
  name: √
Can print name: √
Can count to: 40
Recognizes numbers
  to: 10
Can skip: √

At first glance it appeared that Pete had passed kindergarten with flying colors. But, when I showed proper parental interest and began to check him out, we discovered Pete's teacher was either mighty lenient with her young charges or else Pete has a distressingly short memory.

He knew his name, all right. He knew his address, too, but the telephone number stumped him. We could forgive him, though, because he's never had occasion to call home. He knew his birthday, since that's the time he gets presents. Colors were easy and skipping was a lead pipe cinch.

But when I asked him to tie a bow, he threw up his hands, cried, "Oh, no," and demanded that the investigation be called off immediately. I could see two reasons for this. He (1) really didn't know how to tie a bow, or (2) he didn't want to give up a small piece of graft, namely that of getting his mother or Mike or Susan to tie his shoestrings for him every morning.

So we skipped the bow-tieing test and he demonstrated that he could both print and recognize his printed name. Then the fun started. He must have tried to count to forty at least a half dozen times and each time he had either too many numbers or not enough when he got through. We gave that up for a bad job and decided Pete would have to get someone to fill out his income tax return for him when he is old enough for a job. After this last fiasco we just passed up the number recognition test and Pete went off to play, mumbling to himself about child labor laws, or something.

(June 18, 1954)

Odd thing about all this is that Pete grew up into the smartest kid in the family when it comes to figures. He majored in finance at the University of Denver and was graduated cum laude. *He became the youngest assistant vice president of the Union Bank of California and manager of their corporate services department for northern California. His department was responsible for the computerized* *accounting systems and cash management services offered by the bank, and in two years helped bring in more than $70 million in new demand deposits. Then he went on to new challenges at the 1st National of Oregon in Portland. If your youngsters demonstrate a deplorable weakness in math, don't worry. Things probably will work out okay.*

Pete also distinguished himself in another fashion:

In our family there are two schools of thought about the least unpleasant manner of rising. The majority holds to the idea that ten or twenty winks snatched after the alarm sounds is a pleasure and a privilege. But Pete, our sixth grader, has another theory.

He insists that he be routed out at 7 A.M. sharp. He struggles manfully to come awake, washes hurriedly, and quickly downs what passes for breakfast. After that he climbs back into bed. There he wallows in sheer luxury for a quarter of an hour or so, just enjoying the sensation of being in bed.

Then, reluctantly, he climbs out, dresses and starts out to slay dragons, fractions, prepositional phrases and other problems of a young man of eleven years.

(February 19, 1960)

Let's back up a few years and take you with us on a Sunday outing. This was in the nervous period after the Korean War when defense was much on everyone's mind and the Air National Guard had invited us to watch them in action:

The jet fighter-bomber poised for a moment high in the blue, blue sky. Then it nosed earthward and swooped down, down, down in a sharp, swift, breath-taking dive. A thousand feet, maybe 800 feet off the ground, two arrow-like projectiles freed themselves from the aircraft's wings and shot off in a burst of yellowish flame. Trailing fiery tails, they swept downward far faster than even the speeding plane, smashed into the target with a brilliant flash. Moments later we felt the shock wave and heard the bellowing kaaaroom of rockets smacking home. The plane, agile as an eagle, had pulled easily out of its dive and was thundering back toward the heavens.

I looked at the boys and their eyes glistened in excitement. In their imagination they were eagles, too, soaring with infinite ease, racing through the skies at the speed of sound, strewing thunder and lightning and death and destruction at will. We had witnessed the Colorado Air National Guard's demonstration of aerial firepower, and a brilliant exhibition it was.

Later, on the way home, I asked a question that never had entered the boys' minds. "What do you suppose it would be like," I said, "if you were a civilian, or an infantry soldier, dug in on the hillside those jets were strafing and bombing?"

The question wasn't quite cricket. It broke an illusion and shattered a daydream. We weren't eagles any more, just some earthlings staring apprehensively into the sky.

Later that evening, the jet fighters forgotten, Pete wanted to know what kind of noises dinosaurs made. He's a pretty fair hand, thanks to television, at imitating elephant sounds, horse sounds, cow sounds and sundry other sound effects such as jet aircraft, a heavy weapons company leveling an enemy strongpoint, or the Pacific fleet softening Okinawa prior to invasion.

"Nobody," I told him, "knows what dinosaurs sounded like because the dinosaurs were all dead before men came along to hear them." That satisfied him only partially. So we got out the encyclopedia and I read aloud, paraphrasing into basic English as I went along.

The way it came out, some dinosaurs were longer than a semi-trailer, and so tall they could poke their noses into a TV antenna on top of a two-story house. They had teeth six inches long set in a mouth half as big as a house doorway. They first came around about 180 million years ago ("That's a long, long, long, long time ago") and finally all of them died about 60 million years ago. The fiercest of all the dinosaurs was a fellow called Tyrannosaurus who probably could eat up a lion and a tiger and a bear in one gulp apiece, and snap up a gorilla for dessert. And the stupidest dinosaur was one called Stegosaurus who was twice as long as a Cadillac but had a brain only as big as a walnut. He couldn't remember nothin' and probably didn't even know it if another dinosaur came along and started chewing on his tail.

Now, you didn't know all that, did you?

After the session with natural history, Mike and I went to the mat with algebra. The subject was how to multiply a polynomial by a signed number and the instructions said: "When a quantity in parentheses is preceded by a plus sign, the parentheses may be removed if the sign of every term within the parentheses is changed."

Oh, we worked it out, all right, but it made me wonder how I ever got out of high school.

(November 19, 1954)

In addition to his studies, Mike kept extremely busy with sports, hobbies like building model airplanes and collecting all manner of things. One of these hobbies led to an interesting experience:

Mike's rock collection, assembled at considerable cost and effort last winter, has been set aside temporarily for stamps. Seems every kid in school is collecting stamps, and Mike is not one to be left behind by a fad.

Lately, instead of raising hob around the house after

supper, Mike spends his time poring over his stamp book and casting covetous eyes at the stamp advertisements in the magazines. Since his budget is limited, he cannot go out and buy every eye-catching stamp on the market, much as he would like to. So he looks for bargains.

Now, it seems the stamp sellers are well acquainted with kids like Mike who have big ideas and little money. So they offer a set of "rare Hitler stamps" for a nickel, or a Presidential series for a dime, provided they can send you more costly stamps which you look at, and pay for if you want to keep.

Of course putting stamps under a young collector's nose is like catnip to a cat. They can't let go. So they scout around for money, and buy.

Mike, a cautious sort of fellow, is well aware of the power of temptation. He also would like to cash in on all the loss leader bargains. So he reads the ads like a lawyer going through the small print of a contract, and figures all manner of angles whereby he'll get stamps for next to nothing without exposing himself to the sellers' lures.

I'm afraid it's a losing proposition. After all Mike is only an amateur at this business, while the stamp dealers are old pros. Currently the largest part of Mike's earnings and allowance is going into stamps. And he even tries to borrow uncancelled stamps from his parents as a business expense.

(March 15, 1952)

In the mail last week was a fat and mysterious letter addressed to Mike in care of his father. It was postmarked Chicago, and the envelope bore a University of Chicago imprint.

I took it home and gave it to Mike, who was properly puzzled because he figured he didn't know anyone in Chicago outside of his Uncle Kenny. But he opened the envelope and found it stuffed full of exotic postage stamps torn off envelopes—a haul to delight any small boy philatelist.

Mike was tickled several shades of pink, but completely puzzled as to why anyone should send him such a treasure. So I explained that I had mentioned his hobby in Frying Pan some weeks ago, and that someone probably read the column, thought kindly of Mike's efforts, and took the time, trouble and interest to save a batch for him.

Too pleased to say the obvious, he refrained from remarking: "Well, your column has at least one reader."

"Why don't you write me a report about your mysterious friend and his gift?" I said to Mike. "I'll put it into the column, and maybe you'll find the answer to the mystery."

So Mike borrowed the typewriter and pecked out the following:

"I received Saterday, April 5, a envelope containing about 200 or more stamps. There were stamps from Japan, Germany, Finland, Peru, and about every place in South America, and any other place you can think of.

"I don't know who sent them to me, all I know is that the letter come from Chicago. I thank the person very much and if he would send his address I would like to send him or her a letter."

So there it is in the column, and maybe Mike will learn the identity of his mysterious friend.

At last report the new batch of stamps had been painstakingly soaked off the envelope fragments, separated by nations, and most of them pasted in an album. A few duplicates have been saved for trading. Other parents may be interested to know that Mike is showing more diligence, persistence and neatness with his stamps than with any other hobby he's ever dabbled with.

(April 12, 1952)

176

We never did learn the donor's identity, unfortunately.
Susan, too, was growing up as the next two items indicate:

For about eight months now, our eight-year-old Susan has been studying piano. She went through the various stages. First, there was anticipation, followed by the thrill of actually playing a simple tune. Then came disinterest. She wept before she would practice. She hated piano. Later came apprehension. How could she ever, ever learn to play those difficult pieces in the back of the book?

Somehow the difficulties ironed themselves out. She made good progress, got over her psychological hurdles, even played for the fun of it, practiced without being told. Last week Susan had her first recital, along with a score or more boys and girls of various sizes, shapes and musical skills.

The recital was held on a Sunday afternoon in a small auditorium well filled with proud parents and restless little brothers and sisters. The performers sat in the front row, most of them in their week-old Easter finery, and all of them with hair neatly combed and faces diligently scrubbed.

Susan's piece was a tuneful little number called "Monkeys in the Trees." It was neither too simple nor too complicated; it was just right for her current abilities. I don't think there is too much fatherly prejudice in evidence when I say she played it well. Aside from her musical skill, she displayed fine poise. She took the entire performance in stride.

As I watched her leave the platform and walk back to her seat, I wondered at the speed with which children grow and develop. It was only a few years ago, it seemed, that she was born. She was a difficult baby—hard to put to sleep and forever plagued with colds. She was shy—wouldn't have anything to do with her grandmother the first time they met.

She didn't get the attention that the first-born did. The second child never does. Maybe the parents are just reacting from having fussed and worried over the first child. At any rate, the second child just sort of grows up by itself after infancy, and that's the way it was with Susan.

And now, calmly and with assurance, she had mounted a platform before strangers and played a musical instrument. And with equal poise she had accepted their applause and returned to her seat.

I asked myself where the years had gone, and what I had been doing as Susan changed from a fat and wobbly baby into a young lady.

Oh, she isn't grown up, of course. She still throws an occasional tantrum, refuses to give in to her younger brother, helps around the house only as a concession to parental authority, and neglects to pick up her clothes. She likes to hang from a horizontal bar, would follow her big brother everywhere if he let her, talks to herself as she plays with dolls, sasses her mother once in a while and has weepy spells. Withal, she can be sweet as honey and live up to the very letter of the Brownie credo.

All this and more came home to me as I watched this child, and marveled at the goodness that the years bring. Chances are Susan will not be a great pianist. But if she can acquire a skill that she can enjoy, the lessons will not have been in vain. As for me, they have proven their worth manyfold already.

(April 26, 1952)

Susan was teaching Pete a new game the other day. It consists of holding your hand behind your back and counting, one, two, three. On three, you fling your hand out in front of you, with the fingers held in one of three positions. The hand may be clenched in a fist, which is the symbol for rock. The first two fingers may be extended in a symbol

178

for scissors. Or the hand may be held out open, the symbol for paper.

Rock can be wrapped up by paper, but cannot be cut by scissors. Scissors can cut paper, but cannot cut rock. Paper can wrap up rock, but can be cut to shreds by scissors. The idea is that you try to outguess your opponent as you select the symbol you'll show on the count of three.

All at once I recognized the game as "Jon, ken, poh," a Japanese child's and parlor pastime that we played as kids. I tried to explain it to the youngsters, and to teach them to say: "Jon, ken, poh. Ai go no hoi."

They looked at me dubiously and stuck to something they understood: "One, two, three."

(November 6, 1953)

This chapter will be wrapped up with a couple of columns about what was concerning the youngest and the oldest of the brood:

There was a mess of material demanding attention last Sunday, but I decided to ignore everything and just take things easy. I turned on the television to the Cleveland Browns-Pittsburgh Steelers football game and witnessed a rugged and well-played contest.

In reality, though, there was more excitement and action going on in front of the picture tube than in it. One of the prices I had to pay for loafing was to watch over Christie, our youngest, and she put on a tremendous show, talking sixty miles a minute all the while.

First, she played barber. She got out a comb, ran it through my hair, messed it up good and proper, and then ventured on into more interesting things. She took off my slippers, polished them on her overalls, suddenly saw herself as a shoe salesman. She tried the slippers on my feet and in a loud voice demanded to know—just as Otto Graham threw a touchdown pass—whether I would buy them or wanted to see something else.

When she tired of this game, she climbed on my lap and made like the Lone Ranger riding Silver. Since she doesn't weigh very much, this wasn't too bad except for her ponytail tickling my nose and blurring the vision just about the time Graham cut a long one loose to Dante Lavelli.

Next, she assumed the character of a masseuse. She worked over the back of my neck, massaging my shoulder muscles and finally got around to tickling me. That inspired a new game—buttoning and unbuttoning my shirt, all the while obscuring the view of the picture screen.

About this time she decided to be nature girl. She took off her shoes and sox, then put them back on. That meant she needed help in tieing her laces, except that I had to search under the chair for the shoestrings which somehow had become divorced from the shoes.

Fortunately, the football game ended shortly afterward and I was able to stop relaxing. Next day I read in the newspapers that the Browns had defeated the Steelers 20 to 16.

(November 27, 1953)

The other Friday night Mike went to his first church teen canteen social. He slicked down his hair, donned his good slacks and went off to join the others of his generation. It didn't happen without a good deal of coaxing for, until now, he'd rather putter around at home than go chasing off to a social. Besides, he took a rather dim view of girls, or at least he professed to.

At first we had been under the impression Mike was going to a movie Friday night with the vague possibility he and his friend were going to meet a couple of girls at the theater. Then I supposed they'd share popcorn, giggle, and feel they were having a fine time. But somehow this arrangement must have gone awry because he came home Friday afternoon and announced:

"I'm going to the social at the teen canteen tonight. We're going with some girls who're having potluck over at Linda's house. They want to play us football for a while after they eat, and then we're going down and maybe we'll dance."

A game of football with girls? And a dance after that?

It caught this old fogey somewhat off balance. I couldn't remember disporting myself in such a manner when I was entering my teens. But Mike was off before I could collect my wits sufficiently to question him.

As I got the story later they didn't play football. But they did dance for a while in the church basement. One of the mothers picked them up after the festivities were over and delivered the kids to their homes. Mike was back home and in bed shortly after 10 P.M.

After Mike came home I sat around and tried to remember what I did for social diversion when I was an eighth grader. Some individuals can remember thousands of small details of their childhood. Not I. I couldn't recall going on parties, neither could I remember girls having much of a part in my activities.

There was one party. The girls and the boys showed up separately. When it was time to go home, all the boys got together into one big band and escorted the girls home, one by one. The bolder boys walked right with the girls, but the shy ones walked on the other side of the street. That was about as close as we dared come to girls, those strange creatures.

I can see even now Mike's generation has a much better understanding of this boy-girl business than its parents had.

(November 6, 1953)

12

Unscrambling the World

As both the column and its conductor matured, Frying Pan roamed far and wide for subjects of interest to the Nisei. Frequently, topics of widespread general concern were found to have unique Japanese American angles. For example, the Valachi hearings about organized crime in 1963:

In recent weeks a convicted felon and confessed gangster named Joseph Valachi has been getting an enormous amount of newspaper space and television time. Valachi has been singing like the well-known canary before a Senate committee looking into organized crime. He related in great detail—such great detail, in fact, that some officials suspect he was making up history as he went along—the bloody rivalry between Neapolitan and Sicilian factions of the Cosa Nostra crime ring, and citing dozens of Italian-sounding names.

Some Americans were fascinated by Valachi's recital, some were bored, and presumably some were embarrassed simply because this hoarse-voiced, ungrammatical hoodlum was airing dirty linen in the public gaze. I suppose there were some Nisei in each of these three categories.

Now, just for fun, let's make a wild assumption. Let's say that rather than an Italian American named Valachi on the stand, it is a Japanese American named Yamadama or Nakagada or Morogoto spilling his guts about gang and gambling activity in the Li'l Tokyos of the American West Coast thirty and forty years ago. Let's say he named the gambling overlords, the enemies that were rubbed out, the illicit fortunes that were assembled, the blood-brotherhoods that enforced the law of the underworld.

How would you feel about the airing of this sort of dirty linen? Would you be more fascinated by Yamadama's confessions than Valachi's? Would you be more bored? Would you be more embarrassed because the canary's name was Nakagada or Morogoto rather than Valachi? And if so, why?

Just out of curiosity, I asked a second generation American of Italian descent what he thought about the Valachi hearings. His reaction may or may not be typical, but at least it was revealing.

Sure, he was interested in what Valachi had to say, he admitted, but he guessed his interest was no more and no less intense than that of any other American. Was he embarrassed because Valachi's confessions had to do with Italo-American criminals? Not particularly. My friend pointed out that there are criminal elements in every society, and it was just too bad if some of them had Italian names. And even though his name had Italian origins, and he still enjoyed spaghetti two or three times a week, he saw no reason to associate himself in any way with a bunch of New York thugs.

"I'm a law-abiding family man," he said. "I've never been in jail. Once in a while I get a traffic ticket. I like a game of poker and I buy chances in the office pool, but that's about the extent of my law-breaking and gambling. There is no reason to feel I'm associated with gangsters just because of our mutual origins. And I don't think my friends and associates look at me in an odd way just because another spaghetti-eater happens to be named as the boss of the Mafia."

Would the majority of Japanese Americans be in a similarly objective position if they were in a similar situation? I don't know. Would their non-Nisei associates? It's a good bet that they would be somewhat more objective than the Nisei themselves because the Nisei as a group tend to be deeply introspective.

There are, of course, no answers to these questions, but the questions themselves make for interesting pondering.

(October 18, 1963)

Nearly five years later this column surfaced again in a peculiar manner. Chicago police cracked down on what the newspapers described as a million-dollar bolita gambling racket controlled by crime syndicate gangsters. Bolita is a form of lottery said to flourish in Chicago's Puerto Rican community. The Tribune *and* Sun-Times *reported that among those arrested was one Thomas (Mitch) Yoshii. The* Tribune *also said someone named Ken Eto was being sought, and indeed he was apprehended several days after the item appeared. Some reader in Chicago sent me clippings about these arrests, plus a clipping of my Valachi column. How he happened to keep that column over such a period of time, I'll never know. He sent the clippings along with a question: "How do you feel about the airing of this sort of dirty linen?"*

I replied in the column of February 2, 1968:

This, I guess, is the way I feel about the two unfortunates with Japanese names who were involved in a Chicago gambling crackdown.

The press, of course, has an obligation to report the news whether the subject's name is Valachi or O'Brien or anything else, although perhaps it could be done in a less lurid manner than the *Tribune* employed in this case. However, in the edition I saw, the story was back on page 14, which cannot be considered sensational display.

The Nisei are now part and parcel of American life. Some of them get elected to public office and others get tossed into jail. Some of them win distinguished service awards, design magnificent buildings, make successes of their businesses, discover ways of eliminating dangerous germs, and otherwise win the plaudits of their fellows.

Others get drunk and wreck cars on occasion, abscond with someone else's money, defraud widows, or get caught in a gambling crackdown. Human nature being what it is, these variations in behavior must be considered inevitable, and so long as Nisei make news, their activities whether praiseworthy or otherwise will be reported.

The Nisei press has much the same responsibility as the general press with one notable exception. The Nisei press is inclined to play up the constructive, to play down the sensational and deplorable. In this respect the Nisei press tries to be a constructive force. But it has the responsibility of reporting the news, and sometimes that means airing dirty linen in public—not luridly, not sensationally—but fairly and in the proper perspective. What would be the result of failing to report the facts? An immediate loss of confidence in the integrity of the press, a suspicion that other information of importance is being overlooked or suppressed, and a diminution of public respect and regard for the press.

(February 2, 1968)

185

The matter of Nisei press comment, as differentiated from reporting the news, had come up in Los Angeles in 1963. Li'l Tokyo had been invaded by an old Japanese custom, namely nomiya *(literally "drinking places"). Its primary difference from an American bar is that* nomiya *come equipped with females, usually young, whose primary function is to attract customers into the place, and once they're there, to persuade them to stay longer and drink more. Upstanding elements in Li'l Tokyo were upset by the proliferating number of* nomiya *and things came to a head as a result of a triple murder and suicide in which war bride waitresses were the victims.*

William T. Hiroto, editor of Crossroads, *an all-English Japanese-American weekly, published a series of signed editorials decrying the situation. Frying Pan was moved to applaud this rare demonstration of Nisei journalistic enterprise:*

I am impressed when a Nisei editor names names and speaks out in a forthright manner about an issue close to home which he feels affects the welfare of the people of his community. This is journalism in the best American tradition and something that is too seldom seen in the Nisei press. The question as to whether Hiroto is right or wrong is not the issue; the point is that he has expressed his opinion and thereby refused to yield by default his rights and responsibilities as an editor.

The Nisei press has been afflicted over the years by an understandable Afghanistanism, which is a term coined for editors who write boldly about problems in such remote areas but are mute about controversies on Main Street. Thus the Nisei press has waxed eloquent about discrimination, which is safe, but has seldom commented on issues closer to home.

As a matter of fact, I would guess the average reader of

the Nisei press would be made vaguely uncomfortable by a strong editorial position on a local issue, and would be inclined to wish the newspaper would quit stirring things up. Perhaps sensing this, and sharing in the feeling themselves, the editors, generally speaking, have run bland publications which have been scarcely more than bulletin boards. It is a rare and refreshing journal that has been otherwise.

I have no idea how Hiroto will fare . . . but I salute him and his newspaper for editorial courage that has given a community leadership.

(May 17, 1963)

The question of how Hiroto would fare was answered in 1971. His newspaper went broke:

It was with characteristic flair that editor William Hiroto announced the impending death of his twenty-three-year-old Los Angeles Nisei weekly newspaper, *Crossroads.* The entire front page of the July 30 issue was devoted to a black-bordered box containing the large black letters, R.I.P., under which in more modest type were instructions to see page 2. There he announced that *Crossroads,* age twenty-three years and three months, will die Wednesday, August 25, 1971, with funeral services to be held the following Friday, publication date of the final issue. There was no further explanation although Hiroto puckishly requested that flowers be omitted.

Still, it would not be fitting to permit a publication like *Crossroads* to vanish from the scene without an eulogy of sorts, even though its death may be noticed by few and mourned by even fewer.

It was typical of *Crossroads'* casual and charming approach to matters at hand that even while Hiroto was announcing suspension of publication on page 2, he should

187

also print a subscription form on page 5 inviting one and all to send $5 to get the newspaper for a year.

The news contained in *Crossroads* was minimal, and in this sense it was hardly a newspaper at all.

Page 6 of the eight-page tabloid largely was given to hints for the home handyman and questions and answers for women worried about bad skin, brittle fingernails, acne scars, falling hair, and other misfortunes. Page 8 was generally a bulletin board for various Nisei golf clubs, and perhaps one reason for the publication's demise is that golfers either don't read or there simply weren't enough of them to maintain circulation.

Much of the rest of the paper was turned over lately to some dreadfully earnest columnists who loved to pontificate about almost anything, some chronically indignant letter-writers who would have been dismissed as crackpots by an editor less hard up for material with which to plug the columns, and a Bay Area essayist, one of whose avocations seemed to be issuing press releases about his own activities.

All this notwithstanding, *Crossroads* was a delightfully entertaining paper reflecting many aspects of Nisei community life usually ignored by other publications. Perhaps the best part was Hiroto's own column, made up largely of chatty, irreverent observations about the foibles of the mortals about him. Hiroto's columnists could work up a sweat scolding eloquently for hundreds of words. Hiroto could puncture egos in a paragraph, wink knowingly and slyly in a sentence, set tongues to wagging with a dropped hint. He was fun to read, and I hope some Los Angeles editor has the perspicacity to sign him up to continue his observations.

Perhaps there was little "value" in Hiroto's form of journalism or else it would have survived the economic demons that do in newspapers. Yet *Crossroads* did serve a function and the tiny, strictured world of Nisei journalism will be the poorer for its passing. There were, I'm afraid, too many readers like me who enjoyed the paper from afar and failed to support it. For years Hiroto had me on his mailing list. He never bothered to send me a bill, or if he did I managed to ignore it, and still the paper arrived regularly each week. And if this is a sample of the way the business was run, it was inevitable that malnutrition should take over.

The least I can do, then, is to make note of *Crossroads'* untimely but foreordained death. Rest in Peace.

(August 13, 1971)

While the column could comment on such matters as the responsibility of the press, memories of the Evacuation were not far below the surface, as indicated by the next two columns:

One of the more memorable characters of postwar American fiction is Captain Queeg of Herman Wouk's masterfully told story of the mutiny aboard the U.S. destroyer *Caine.* You may recall Queeg, played by Humphrey Bogart in the movie version of the *Caine Mutiny.* Queeg is essentially a weakling, overburdened by the responsibilities of running his ship. He seeks refuge and support in the Navy's regulations, enforcing them to the letter, performing like a tyrant, and perpetually fearful that an error of judgment will be detected and entered on his record. It's altogether possible that you have encountered Queegs of various types in your everyday lives.

Well, I got to thinking of poor old Captain Queeg the other Sunday afternoon while watching the Columbia Broadcasting System's *Twentieth Century* program about the Great Evacuation of 1942. That was the occasion, as some of you may recall, when a preoccupied nation accepted the idea that some of its citizens should be tossed into concentration camps without being charged or tried of any crime, simply because they happened to have the wrong kind of ancestors. I thought about Captain Queeg and came up with an idea for a somewhat similar novel, but different enough so that it wouldn't be strictly identifiable with the *Caine Mutiny* story.

This novel would be set on the Pacific Coast of the United States in December, 1941. Our principal character would be the military commander charged with the defense of the western United States. Suddenly he is faced with the fact of Pearl Harbor, and he realizes that it might have been the coast of California or Oregon or Washington that could have been attacked on December 7. This scares the dickens out of him because he realizes his command was no more prepared to meet attack than were the luckless forces in Hawaii. So, to make up for lost time he hastens to do everything possible to insure that his command will not be caught with its collective pants down.

About this time one of his aides points out that the "Japanese" on the West Coast are potential saboteurs and espionage agents, a mighty dangerous Fifth Column. This aide, according to my idea for the novel, has his reasons for hating the "Japanese." Maybe one of them got better grades than he did in high school and became the valedictorian, or maybe he lost out in the all-conference wrestling meet to a sneaky little judo expert named Watanabe. It would be easy to build up this part of it.

At any rate, this aide keeps warning the commander that he will be guilty of dereliction of duty unless he takes every precaution to safeguard the West Coast, and that he faces an unfathomable hazard in the inscrutable "Japanese" who are demonstrating their treachery by buying war bonds, trying to enlist in the Army, cooperating with local authorities, denouncing the attack on Pearl Harbor, and refraining from committing sabotage.

This commander, as I see him, is a pretty decent sort of fellow at heart, but like Queeg, he's frightened. He's afraid of what might happen if he doesn't listen to his aide, and he's afraid of what will happen if he does. And so, like Queeg, he's torn by his fears until he almost goes out of his mind, partly because he read something somewhere about the Bill of Rights.

In the end he decides that the aide is right—he just cannot take a chance—and so he orders the Great Evacuation. And just as he expected, his order is approved right up the line because all his superiors are so desperately involved with the Big Decisions of fighting the war that a basic breach of civil rights somehow escapes their attention and a great tragedy is approved.

Well, that's the idea, and since I haven't copyrighted it, it's free for anyone to pick up and develop into a best seller. You're welcome.

(February 12, 1965)

I can't remember just when it was that I learned there were such people as the Eta, the untouchables in Japan. It probably was after I had reached the age of reason, whenever that might be, and my mother mentioned them with some reluctance and embarrassment. Come to think of it, she probably was warning me so I wouldn't get interested in a girl from an Eta family, but the warning was lost because no one could distinguish an Eta from any other Japanese. They're the same kind of people.

I got the vague idea that Eta were Japan's pariahs, and that they had become that way because at some distant time in the past, they were assigned the work of butchering animals and tanning leather and doing other things that were beneath the dignity of more fortunate folk. Well, since I didn't know any Eta, and would not have been aware of the stigma if I did, I didn't press the matter further.

And since my folks were kindly people, tolerant about most things and probably uneasy about prejudices acquired in their youth, they didn't bring up the subject again, either.

It took an American to dig into this unfortunate social phenomenon in Japan and give us the unhappy details. He is Dr. George DeVos, professor of anthropology and social welfare at the University of California in Berkeley, and he has written a book, *Japan's Invisible Race.*

Dr. DeVos reports that there are still some two million Eta, or Burakumin, which is another name for them, in Japan although they were emancipated by law in 1871. He says they live in approximately 6,000 ghettoes sprinkled around more than half of the country. Some of the ghettoes are middle class, but others are unspeakable slums even though there has been considerable job integration. Few non-Eta Japanese visit these ghettoes and certainly no American tourists.

Since Eta are physically indistinguishable from other Japanese, unlike the Negro who is different from the American majority, why do they remain in segregated communities? Dr. DeVos says some of them do "pass" into the mainstream, but the majority don't try. He makes the point that many Eta regard themselves as inferior, and their position in Japanese society is predetermined, and that no one can do anything about it.

One of his researchers interviewed an Eta, asking if he were the same as common people. The reply was: "No, we kill animals. We are dirty, and some people think we are not human." When asked if he thought he was not human, the Eta replied, "I don't know." The interview went on like this:

"Do you think you or your children will ever leave the district or change occupations?"

"No."

"Do you think outsiders will ever come to this village and treat you as friends?"

"No, people on the outside don't like us. They haven't changed for a hundred years."

"Do you believe this right or fair?"

After a long pause: "I don't know, we are bad people and we are dirty."

The point the book makes is that this man, presumably typical, has been beaten down psychologically until he feels himself incapable of being anything more than dirty and bad. There is an application in the American Negro, Dr. DeVos points out, where "the social and psychological stigmas of a hundred years of oppression after slavery are still visible and will remain so for some time to come."

After reading this, I couldn't help but wonder if prolonged confinement in relocation camps wouldn't have affected us Nisei in similar fashion. The first symptoms were becoming visible when the camps were being closed. "People on the outside don't like us. They think we're bad."

(June 7, 1968)

The matter of civil rights came up sporadically over the years in Frying Pan columns. Here is a sampling:

If you've been reading newspaper reports of the Judith Coplon spy trial, you no doubt detected a faint, unpleasantly familiar odor when confidential FBI reports were introduced as evidence. But to start at the beginning, Miss Coplon is accused of stealing secret government information for delivery to Russian agents. A large part of the government's case hangs on notes alleged to have been found in Miss Coplon's purse.

The government charges these were excerpts from confidential FBI reports. The prosecution introduced the original reports and urged that they be kept confidential. But the court ruled that if the FBI reports were entered as evidence, they must be made public. Miss Coplon's attorney read them to the jury.

These confidential reports included serious charges against a number of persons. These charges were made by unidentified informants who may, or may not, have known what they were talking about. In other words, the confidential FBI reports included serious accusations against individuals who apparently did not know they were so suspected, and never had a chance to answer their accusers.

In these perilous times it unquestionably is necessary for an internal security agency to keep tab on potential domestic enemies. However, it is a duty that inevitably becomes fouled up by many false leads and unreliable reports—none of which can be entirely discounted if the service is conscientious.

Your name and mine may well be in FBI files. In fact, because of the Evacuation, chances are a large percentage of Nisei have been investigated. Someone may have taken a dislike to the way I part my hair, gone to the FBI and told them I was seen drinking coffee in Joe's Chop Suey Shoppe with a long-haired character who was wearing a red necktie and had a copy of the *Daily Worker* sticking out of his coat pocket. Mighty suspicious. Without knowing a thing about the workings of the FBI, a citizen could logically assume that any security agency worth its beans would enter that report in its files for future reference.

The fact that you and I may have a dossier is not a disgrace in itself. But we'd have a mighty difficult time salvaging our reputations if baseless charges—perhaps most of them discounted entirely by the FBI—were suddenly made public as straight from FBI files.

The similarity may not be readily apparent, but the unsubstantiated accusations and the whole aura of diligent and secret police activity is reminiscent of those hectic weeks after Pearl Harbor. Remember? The Issei were walking around expecting arrest at any moment, and the newspapers were scare-lining their stories with heads like: FBI DRAGNET NABS 115 JAP SUBVERSIVES.

(June 18, 1949)

I am no political seer, but it seems that anyone who has been reading the newspapers can discern the handwriting on the wall. We are going to be in for the darndest siege of red-baiting we're ever witnessed. The chief red-baiter will be, of course, Senator Joseph McCarthy of Wisconsin who has returned to congress by an impressively large vote.

Senator McCarthy has demonstrated that he has scant regard for facts. He is a master of innuendo, the unsubstantiated accusation and the irresponsible slur. He has a fine sense of timing. And whether they intend to or not, the nation's newspapers lend him support by publishing his utterances under sensational headlines.

If the Nisei have profited at all from their bitter wartime experiences, they should be the first to realize McCarthy's tactics for what they are—trial by headline with falsehoods and half-truths artfully woven into the net of dubious evidence for political purposes.

One short decade ago it was not McCarthy, but men like Martin Dies, John Costello, Parnell Thomas, and Bob Reynolds who cast themselves in the role of keepers of the public conscience. And the victims then were the Nisei— not liberal educators, left-wing thinkers, and public officials who were friendly to the Soviet Union at the time it was national policy to support "our brave Soviet comrades in arms."

Trial by headline began with the first faint rumblings that demanded the evacuation of all "Japs." It continued even after we were safely corralled behind barbed wire. Do you remember the fantastic charges mouthed by supposedly responsible congressmen?

Here are a few that come to mind: We were buying up all the knives in towns near the camps to prepare for an uprising. We were caching food in the Arizona desert to supply an invading force of Japanese paratroops. We were being pampered by the WRA, provided with a daily one-quart whiskey ration. We were stuffing ourselves on meat and other rationed commodities while American troops went without.

Preposterous? Yes. But millions heard and read these charges and they were willing to believe. And the truth was a long time in catching up with falsehood.

Senator McCarthy has adopted and improved on these tactics whose basis is the big lie. We who were slandered and injured by demagogues should be the first to expose them. Oust those who would overthrow the government by violence, but let us take care to separate the sheep from the goats.

(February 13, 1953)

Simply as an exercise in conjecture, serving no useful purpose, let us project what is happening today in places like Selma, Alabama, backward almost a quarter-century. Let us suppose that in 1942 the more militant Nisei, led by a Christian minister, staged demonstrations protesting that their civil rights had been abridged by the evacuation order.

Let us suppose that those Nisei, affirming their complete loyalty to the United States and all its institutions, pledging to defend the nation against all enemies foreign and domestic, demanded as American citizens that they be permitted to live in their homes in the three western states without harassment. Let us suppose that they marched on General John L. DeWitt's military headquarters demanding that

196

they be properly charged individually as required by law, or be given their freedom.

Would there have been Caucasian Americans, moved by the legal justice of the Nisei cause, joining them in their protest march? Would there have been prayers in the streets and men on horseback clubbing the marchers and expressions of horror from the White House? Or would there have been a nationwide wave of anger and hysteria, fanned by war fever, directed against the Nisei?

As it was, the Nisei demonstrated their loyalty by co-operating in their own incarceration. And partly as a consequence of this cooperation they won acceptance in their own country perhaps a generation earlier than if history had run its course peacefully. The difference is that the Negroes have been waiting a hundred years for their deliverance and measured in the lifespan of men, that is a long time in which to be patient.

(April 9, 1965)

The Nisei attitude toward Iva Toguri d'Aquino, convicted of treason as the mythical Tokyo Rose, makes an interesting study. At the time she was convicted in 1949, the Nisei themselves were still so insecure that most chose to ignore her plight. Not until the Seventies was the community's social conscience awakened to the point where an effort was made to win a pardon for her. Under the leadership of Dr. Clifford Uyeda, a San Francisco pediatrician, a volunteer committee launched a campaign to disseminate the truth about how she was railroaded into prison. President Gerald Ford signed an unconditional pardon for her on his last full day in the White House. Frying Pan commented on her problems on at least two earlier occasions:

A favorite device among authors of 19th Century melodrama was the wayward girl who had brought shame upon her family. In these stories it was forbidden to mention her name. It was reasoned that if no one acknowledged that she existed, perhaps even the memory of her would go away. But inevitably the disgraced sister would come back. And in an encouraging number of instances there were extenuating circumstances to clear her of disgrace and restore her fair name.

The disgraced sister of the Nisei family is a woman named Iva Toguri d'Aquino, a native-born American convicted as "Tokyo Rose" of treason. Mrs. d'Aquino was tried before a federal jury in 1949 on eight charges of treason and convicted on one count. Sentenced to ten years in prison, she was released in January of 1957, just a year ago. Soon after her release the department of immigration opened deportation proceedings against her. So far as we know, these proceedings are still under way.

For a variety of reasons which we need not go into here, the Nisei in general have chosen not to speak Mrs. d'Aquino's name. Perhaps like the relatives of the soiled doves of melodrama, they hoped even her memory would be erased. Recently, however, there has been a piercing and eloquent voice raised on her behalf. The voice is that of William A. Reuben, a thrice-wounded lieutenant of infantry in World War II. He speaks through the pages of the February issue of *Frontier,* a small, liberal monthly think-type magazine published in Los Angeles, in an article titled "The Strange Case of Tokyo Rose."

Reuben probes into the background of the Tokyo Rose trial and comes up with some disturbing information. There never was, he says, a Tokyo Rose. That was a name invented by Americans for English-speaking women announcers employed by Radio Tokyo during the war. And there were eighteen of these from among whom Iva Toguri d'Aquino was singled out for prosecution.

Testimony during her trial, Reuben reports, brought out that Mrs. d'Aquino was a Nisei caught in Japan by the war, forced to stay against her will, suspected as an American spy by the Japanese secret police. She refused to give up her American citizenship, and finally took a job as typist in the accounting department of Radio Tokyo.

Further, Mrs. d'Aquino did not become an announcer until she was requested to do so by a captured Australian, Major Charles Cousens, who had been ordered by the Japanese to produce a radio program. Cousens testified at the trial that when Iva Toguri protested against broadcasting, he told her: "This is a straight-out entertainment program. I have written it and I know what I am doing. All you have got to do is look on yourself as a soldier under my orders. Do exactly what you are told to do. Don't try anything for yourself and you will do nothing that you do not want to do. You will do nothing against your own people."

Reuben says the government's case hinged on the "oral and uncorroborated testimony of two native-born Americans, Kenneth Oki and George Mitsushio, both of whom admittedly became Japanese propagandists. They were the only witnesses to the one act of which she was convicted."

Reuben makes a strong case on behalf of Mrs. d'Aquino. What's more, in addition to pointing out the injustices of her conviction, he argues that if the government wins its deportation case, "an ominous precedent will have been established, based on a treason conviction resting entirely on a disputed and undocumented allegation concerning twenty-five words."

Perhaps it is time for the Nisei to stop being so coy about their disgraced sister, a woman who has paid her penalty for an action which may or may not have been a crime. Perhaps it is time to acknowledge that she does indeed

199

exist, and say firmly that we are interested in seeing that she gains justice.

(February 15, 1957)

The news services report that the United States government in all its dignity and majesty is trying to collect the balance of the $10,000 fine imposed on Mrs. Iva Toguri d'Aquino after her conviction nearly twenty-two years ago on treason charges. . . .

The background of the case is that Mrs. d'Aquino, a Nisei, served her sentence in a federal prison and was released. She has been living quietly in Chicago. In 1968 the U.S. attorney's office attached two insurance policies held by Mrs. d'Aquino. The cash value, according to dispatches from Chicago, was $4,745. Now the government is trying to get the balance which, if my arithmetic is correct, amounts to $5,255. In other words, the United States government is seeking to extract the last full measure of retribution on a judgment reached back in 1949.

A lot of things have happened since that time. Many Japanese and German war criminals, convicted of far more heinous crimes than that which Mrs. d'Aquino was accused of, have served their terms and were freed to go their way. The wisdom and justice of the war crimes trials that resulted in the execution of Japanese Gen. Tomoyuki Yamashita by the United States have been cast into doubt as a result of the My Lai massacre in Vietnam. General Yamashita was found responsible for the atrocities committed by combat troops under his command. Students of the law contend that if we are to be consistent, the same principle of responsibility should be applied to the American generals whose troops committed the My Lai atrocities.

Since 1949 our standards of patriotism have changed. It is not my intention at this point to pass judgment, but only to report fact. For example, on several occasions U.S.

troops in Vietnam have refused direct orders to launch an attack and have gone unpunished. Under other circumstances they might have been executed. American deserters have fled into the rabbit warrens of Saigon and made their way with impunity to the sanctuary of Sweden. Draft-dodgers have fled to Canada. Revolutionaries in our midst have preached violent overthrow of the government, a treasonous act in other times. The Supreme Court has ruled aliens may not be kept out of the country because of Marxist beliefs.

And Professor Roger Daniels of the University of Wyoming history department, in a book to be published soon, suggests that the Nisei in the WRA camps who refused to respond to draft calls in 1944 were more heroic than those who stepped forward to serve their nation. At this rate it would not be at all surprising to be told some day that Benedict Arnold had good and sufficient reason for doing what he did and should take his place in the gallery of patriotic champions of democracy.

Mrs. d'Aquino's treason trial lasted fifty-seven days. There was considerable doubt that she should have been tried at all. And it was never adequately explained why she should be singled out for punishment from among the many who took turns at the job of playing sentimental American songs and trying to break down the morale of American troops in the Pacific Theatre. Now, at this late date, it is difficult to understand why the federal government is suddenly so zealous about collecting its due.

Delinquent taxpayers can reach a compromise settlement with their government. Indian militants can seize and hold Alcatraz Island without being punished. Police are cautioned not to "overreact" when radicals shatter the windows of campus buildings or race through the streets of Chicago smashing cars and plate glass. But Iva Toguri d'Aquino, a middle-aged woman who has paid her penalty with many years of her life and bitter memories that cannot be erased, must be hounded for the last dollars of a fine that a magnanimous government could well afford to forget. Something is wrong with our sense of justice and values.

(April 2, 1971)

During the early 1970s it became fashionable for young people to critize the values of their elders. I had thought I was fairly liberal, but by the standards of the day I apparently was a reactionary. Editor Honda rightfully printed all the letters he received criticizing my views. After publication of one scathing, and I thought unreasonable criticism, I responded as follows:

I crawled out of bed at the usual time one morning recently, staggered to the bathroom and sadly contemplated the bleary-eyed image in the mirror.

"Good morning, Hosokawa," said the image. "How are you, you tradition-bound, no-good, quiet, conservative running dog of the majority establishment?"

"Now that's a hellava way to greet me at this time of day," I replied. "What have I done to deserve such vilification?"

"You made some disparaging remarks about drunken Japanese tourists at the Los Angeles Farmers' Market in your Frying Pan column."

"Oh that," I said. "You mean I shouldn't have tut-tutted them?"

"Did you read the letters in last week's *Pacific Citizen?*" the image asked. "Some fellow takes you to task for your remarks."

"You mean he's in favor of public drunkenness?"

"No, he doesn't say that. What he seems to be saying is that sobriety is the lifestyle of the Establishment, and the majority is being inequitable when it demands that minority groups conform to their lifestyle as the price of acceptance."

"I'm not sure I understand that," I said, splashing some water on my face. "Besides, some establishment types I know are the worst damned boozers I've ever had the misfortune to encounter, and I as a member of a minority have no wish to seek their approval if it means guzzling the sauce as a way of living. Matter of fact, I don't give much of a damn what they think of me. I just happen to think public drunkenness isn't a very good idea for anybody regardless of skin color, and I'm a little surprised that anyone wants to argue that point."

"That shows what a hidebound, moss-backed, anachronistic relic you are, Hosokawa," the image jeered. "When you say you're surprised, that shows you have hardening of the arteries of the brain. If you're with it these days, you shouldn't be surprised at anything."

"Well, you've got a point," I agreed. "When some people these days demonstrate their independence and disdain for convention by fornicating in public, I suppose public drunkenness is a rather small transgression of what we've been taught to regard as desirable behavior."

"Hosokawa," the image said, "you're using some awfully big words for so early in the morning."

"Sorry about that," I replied. "Seems I've been associating with establishment types too long, living with the philosophy of winning the approval of the majority through exemplary behavior, or stoically bearing the indignities of discrimination, and trying to remain sober in public."

"Now let's not get sarcastic," the image scolded. "You're not being relevant. How do you expect to establish a meaningful dialogue when you react that way?"

"I'm not sure it's possible any more. Everybody's so darned sensitive, so uptight about everything that a fellow gets criticized no matter what he says or writes about. Maybe I'd better just stick to safe subjects—like the flag, motherhood, and apple pie."

"That shows how far you're out of step with the times, Hosokawa, you dumb-dumb," the image said with a snicker. "You know what's happened to the flag. And motherhood is a very controversial subject, what with the Woman's Lib movement and the concerns over population pressure on the environment. As for apple pie, aren't you aware that saturated fats in the crusts cause cholesterol to clog your blood vessels? If you want to play it safe, you have to get mad at things like people using the word 'Jap.' "

I stared back at the image in the mirror for a long time. Then I went back to bed. It just didn't seem worth the effort to stay up and try to unscramble the world.

(July 2, 1971)

13

More Observations

Jimmie Sakamoto gave me my first writing job on his little weekly, The Japanese American Courier. *With blindness closing in as a result of injuries in the professional boxing ring, Jimmie had returned to Seattle from New York and founded the newspaper on January 1, 1928. As editor and publisher, and as a JACL leader, he was an eloquent spokesman for Japanese Americans. I worked on his paper part-time from 1933 to 1936 while going to college. The paper, never robust, succumbed along with a lot of other businesses during the Evacuation in 1942. Jimmie never went back to newspapering. In 1955, on his way to work as director of the telephone soliciting section of St. Vincent de Paul, Jimmie was hit by a car and died shortly afterward. I wrote about Jimmie in the columns of December 9 and December 16:*

Late of a wintry Saturday afternoon the telephone rang. It was Johnny, at the office. "Telegram just came for you," he said. In my business telegrams are routine things. They come, and they go.

"Do you want me to read it to you?" Johnny asked. I almost told him not to bother, that I'd catch it Monday morning. But that would have been ungrateful after Johnny had taken the time and effort to telephone. "Sure, go ahead," I said.

There was a small pause as Johnny tore open the envelope. "Oh-oh," I heard him say. "I'm afraid this is bad news."

Bad news has a habit of coming unexpectedly. Suddenly concerned now, I waited for the details. Johnny read the terse message. It was from Chet Gibbon, Sunday editor of the Seattle *Times*. Jimmie Sakamoto had been struck by an automobile and killed.

Saturday night, while I was out of the house, George Ishihara telephoned from Nampa, Idaho. George had been a boyhood friend of Jimmie's. He knew Jimmie as few men did. He wanted to let me know. A few hours after that, the *Pacific Citizen's* Harry Honda notified me by wire. Now there were more details.

And so the news spread, and there would be many who would grieve. Welly Shibata and Tadao Kimura in Tokyo. They had helped Jimmie launch the *Courier* in Seattle back on New Year's Day, 1928. Tooru Kanazawa in New York, Jimmie's managing editor of long years. Takeo Nogaki in New Jersey. Toshio Hoshide in Washington, D.C., friends and pioneers together in the JACL movement. John Funai, who somehow got type set on the ancient linotype machine in *The Courier's* backshop. And in Kyoto, Father Leopold Tibesar, the man who converted Jimmie to Catholicism with all its implications for the spiritual life of James Yoshinori Sakamoto.

A few months ago Editor Honda, preparing for *PC's* holiday issue, asked me to put together a profile of Jimmie.

206

He had been my boss, wise and good, and friend a long time ago. He was still my friend, but I hadn't had a chance to see much of him for many years. So I wrote to Jimmie for updated information.

He replied promptly, saying that if it weren't for the 25th anniversary of JACL, he would prefer not to be written up in any prominent way. But a request was a request, so he sent me some notes. Throughout those notes ran a single theme—Jimmie Sakamoto's love and regard for JACL.

JACL was everything in Jimmie's life. He helped found it. He launched and kept alive an eminently unprofitable newspaper to promote and advance JACL. Jimmie's devotion to JACL was like that of a priest to his church; all other matters were secondary, and that's the way I tried to write the Sakamoto story.

The nicest thing that ever happened to Jimmie was his marriage to Misao Nishitani. She was, and is, a woman of exceptional kindness, wisdom, patience and courage. She was always at Jimmie's side. Their lean years were hard on her, but I don't ever remember hearing her complain. As Jimmie's widow, she can take comfort in the knowledge that she was a tower of strength in Jimmie's darkest hours, that her companionship made Jimmie's life more full, more meaningful. She helped him gain his destiny as none other could do. . . .

(December 9, 1955)

Sometimes one small anecdote tells more about a man's character than a column of type. Such an anecdote was relayed to me this week by Chet Gibbon of the Seattle *Times*. It had to do with Jimmie Sakamoto's death.

John Closs, a Seattle *Times* photographer, was on his way to work when he noticed what appeared to be a car-pedestrian accident. Closs stopped his vehicle, grabbed his camera, and jumped out. He was shooting a picture of the victim, lying in the street with a blanket over his shoulders and being comforted by a police officer, when he recognized the man as Jimmie Sakamoto. They were long-time friends.

"This is Johnny Closs, Jimmie," said the photographer. "You'd better lie real still until the ambulance gets here."

"Oh, hello Johnny," said Jimmie. "What happened?"

"You got hit by a car."

"Can I get up now?"

"No, you'd better stay where you are. They've phoned for an ambulance."

"Are you taking a picture, Johnny?"

"Yes."

"Good work! Attaboy, Johnny. Anything I can do for you?"

"No, just lie still, Jimmie. You'll be okay. I'll phone your wife and tell her you had an accident."

"That's a good idea, Johnny. Thanks a lot."

But the St. Vincent de Paul salvage bureau, where Jimmie was going to work, already had telephoned her. Four hours later Jimmie Sakamoto was dead, his skull fractured.

It was characteristic of Jimmie that he should wax enthusiastic—"Good work! Attaboy Johnny"—on hearing that a friend was engaged in carrying out his professional duties, even though Jimmie himself was the victim to be photographed. Jimmie Sakamoto was the most selfless man I ever knew. That, no doubt, was one of the main reasons his newspaper was never a financial success. He was too busy helping others, thinking of the welfare of others, to do much about his own troubles. That was the very reason he made such a success of the job with the salvage bureau. He never considered himself unfortunate; there were so many others who needed his help.

"Anything I can do for you?" Let that stand as an epitaph in memory of one of the most remarkable personalities it has been my privilege to know. Let me remember those words when I'm feeling sorry for myself.

(December 16, 1955)

It probably is safe to say no American ethnic minority spends more time than Japanese Americans in introspective study, discussing their "problems" and seeking to improve themselves. Two columns published more than a decade apart touched on the subject:

From way back, the Nisei have been great ones for self-analysis. Perhaps this trait is an indication of their insecurity and immaturity. On the other hand, it may be evidence of superior desire for improvement and advancement. At any rate, individual and collective soul-searching was an inevitable part of all prewar Nisei convention, of which there was a plentitude.

It's not surprising then that the Chicago JACL chapter should have sponsored a series of discussions under the general title, "Let's Look at Ourselves." Highlights and conclusions of these discussions have been mimeographed by the chapter. It would take much more than the space available here to analyze all points in the report, but a few are worthy of special notice. For example, the first session, which was called "The Trouble With Us Nisei," in which these traits were offered as typical of the Nisei:

1. He desires to remain in the background as evidenced by his preference for anonymity and marked reluctance to speak up at public meetings.

2. He has a tendency to conform to prevailing standards.

3. He is over-eager to please Caucasians and agree with their views.

4. He smiles to cover embarrassment.

5. He is sensitive to slights and slurs.

6. He arrives late to social affairs, in other words observes "Japanese time."

7. He avoids fellow Nisei in public. Passers-by look the other way.

8. He has strong inhibitions.

Those taking part in the discussion believed that "these characteristics stemmed from excessive reserve (*enryo*), a sense of obligation and duty, and racial pride as well as the factor of Nisei introversion due to dominant fathers."

If all the above personality quirks were true of any single Nisei, he would be a Sad Saki indeed. I would prefer to believe that some Nisei display some of the listed traits, but many Nisei don't have any of them.

Obviously the hazard in making broad generalizations, such as drawing up a list of "typical" traits, is that you're trying to analyze a fine watch with a hammer for a tool. The fact that the list was drawn up at all proves how unreliable and fallacious it is. Witness:

If Nisei desire anonymity and are reluctant to speak up, if they are sensitive to slights and slurs, how were they able to hold a meeting and make a list of their own shortcomings? It they smile to cover embarrassment, it must have been a jolly meeting indeed. If they avoid fellow Nisei, how come 131 of them showed up? If they have strong inhibitions, how were they able to take down their hair in public and figuratively mortify their own flesh?

I suppose there's no harm in sitting down with one's kind and making an inventory if one is careful not to take the whole business too seriously. In any self-appraisal it seems to me that the main thing for the Nisei to remember is that they, like all humans, are individuals beset by individual problems. If they have group problems and weaknesses, why they're just incidental to the far more complicated matter of overcoming individual shortcomings. And far less serious.

(July 26, 1957)

After last summer's quick trip to Japan there were more than the usual number of questions that began with, "What do the Japanese think about . . . ?"

That's a question that's virtually impossible to answer because there are 100 million Japanese and they represent virtually every shade of opinion on virtually every subject under the sun. There are Japanese radicals and there are Japanese conservatives. Some think the United States can do no wrong and others contend we can do no right. When you get a large number of educated people and give them the freedom to think as they want, it is inevitable that there should be differences of opinion, and there is no reason why all the Japanese should think alike, any more than all Americans should think alike.

For a long time, particularly in the prewar Oriental ghettoes on the West Coast, ethnic ties were more important in holding the Nisei together than education, occupation, personal interest or almost any other factor. The fact that two fellows were Nisei, sprang from the same heritage, faced the same prejudices and liked the same kind of food was more important to their ability to get along and enjoy each other's company than the fact that one had advanced degrees and the other was a high school drop-out, that one was an attorney and the other a dishwasher, that one played golf while the other played pool. Well, maybe we're exaggerating a bit, but you get the idea.

It was concerns and problems springing from ethnic origins that led to the founding and growth of the Japanese American Citizens League movement.

211

Today, those strictly ethnic concerns seem to be less important than other matters the Nisei are interested in. So the once fairly solid Nisei consensus has been broken down, and we find Nisei both applauding and jeering Dr. S. I. Hayakawa's efforts to bring peace to San Francisco State. We find Nisei supporting and opposing the California table grape boycott. We find Nisei who share a substantial part of the action in what is known as the Establishment and want to protect the system. And there are others who could destroy it in their zeal for reform.

What this amounts to is that more and more Nisei are beginning to think and act as individuals and not as racial or ethnic stereotypes, and this is the essence of integration. But corollary to this observation should be the understanding that zeal ought to be tempered with tolerance, and that the other fellow isn't necessarily a fink because he refuses to see things your way.

Most Nisei have spent a lifetime fighting for tolerance and understanding for themselves. Now it would be ironic indeed if the Nisei, having won a large measure of the tolerance they sought, should deny that same tolerance to those who hold views opposed to their own, whether on the right or the left.

For some reason, perhaps for the reason that civil wars usually are the bitterest kind of conflicts, the intra-mural dissents among Nisei generate a great amount of heat. To a conservative Nisei, any radical may be a fink but a Japanese American radical is a double fink, and the compliments are returned with interest from the other side. Thus confrontation between left and right, conservative and activist among the Nisei is likely to be more abrasive than in the greater community. All the more need for tolerance if the JACL as an organization is to survive as an effective and (to employ an overused term) relevant organization.

(September 12, 1969)

Contrary to the earnest soul-searching evident in the above two columns, the Nisei were moving forward in their occupations and distinguishing themselves in many ways. A number of columns were written on this theme, and here are several of them:

"Someday," the man said, "a Nisei will be elected to Congress. Just wait, you'll see."

This was nearly thirty years ago. The nation was deep in the economic chaos of the Great Depression. For the Nisei it was not a time of optimism. In their efforts to find a place in the sun they had to scale the high stone wall of discrimination in addition to the depressed economy.

The man who made the prediction was my father. I don't remember the circumstances of our discussion, but we must have been talking about opportunity and the future of the Nisei. Now, I can't recall whether he was trying to be prophetic or was just attempting to encourage me. But I do remember my reactions. As teen-agers often do, I dismissed the parental prediction as a lot of unlikely bunk.

I wish my Dad could have lived long enough to see Daniel K. Inouye, first member of the United States House of Representatives from the state of Hawaii, make his prediction come true. It would have made him glow with pride.

Congressman Inouye was sworn in early this week. A few days prior to the ceremony he was among the special guests at the White House as President Eisenhower signed the papers that made Hawaiian statehood official. Photographs of these events were distributed to hundreds of newspapers and television stations in this country and abroad. They showed the newest congressman to be a photogenic young man with an engaging smile.

Perhaps the swearing in of Congressman Inouye was not of extraordinary significance to the general public, but it was a memorable milestone in the history of Americans of Japanese origins.

The Japanese are among the youngest of this nation's immigrant groups. No large numbers of them arrived until shortly after the turn of the century. Of their offspring, the Nisei, relatively few have advanced beyond middle age. Most Nisei have yet to enter their most productive years. But now their achievements are impressive. Their achievements are certain to grow in coming years.

Even now, in the arts and sciences, medicine, business, research, agriculture, finance, trade—select the field; there's likely to be a Nisei making a name for himself.

A Nisei in Congress—he is a Congressman representing all the people, and only incidentally a Nisei—completes the picture. Someone once remarked that political activity is the finest essence of a democracy in action, and if this is so the growth to maturity of the Nisei would not have been complete without it.

It is altogether likely that Congressman Inouye's election will spur political interest among mainland Nisei. I hope it will. Certainly the time is ripe and there are men of competent talents. There is nothing standing in their way today except their own reluctance.

Pa would have been astonished and delighted to see how far we have come in so short a time.

(August 28, 1959)

When Dan Inouye moved up to the Senate, he was succeeded in the House by Spark Matsunaga, another war veteran from Hawaii. And when Hawaii was granted two House seats, Patsy Takemoto Mink was elected to fill the post. In 1976, when Senator Hiram Fong, of Chinese ancestry, decided not to run for re-election, Matsunaga and Mrs. Mink opposed each other for the Senate seat. Mat-

sunaga won, Mrs. Mink was named an assistant secretary of state.

Meanwhile, Norman Mineta, mayor of San Jose, California, ran for the House in 1974 and won. He was the first Oriental to be elected to Congress from a mainland state. Mineta was re-elected in 1976 when Dr. Samuel Ichiye Hayakawa, the redoubtable educator, was elected to represent California in the Senate. These two events will be treated in a later section.

Along with the good news there was the sad, and these chronicles would not be balanced without recognizing that fact. Like the week that Larry Tajiri died:

One of the great talents of the Nisei world ended his labors last week. Larry Tajiri, nationally respected drama editor of the Denver *Post*, died of a stroke after a five-day illness. He was fifty years old.

It is a trite thing to say, but an accurate one: Larry was a newspaperman's newspaperman, an old pro who knew every facet of the business and could do everything well. His province at the *Post* was the movies and the stage, but he knew music and books and politics. When there was an obscure fact about sports that needed clearing up, the fellows in the sports department would ask Larry. He would have been as outstanding a sports editor, or an editorial writer, as he was a drama critic.

In the field of drama comment he left a lasting and probably indelible mark on Denver, a city of long and honorable traditions in the theater. The *Post* said editorially in tribute:

"His effect on our community was profound—and profoundly beneficial. No man in Denver's recent history accomplished more in informing and elevating the public taste. All those who knew Larry Tajiri, either as a reporter

215

or as a friend, are immensely the richer because he lived."

The above is certainly an accurate appraisal of Larry's impact on Denver. Yet it is the Nisei who benefited most from his labors, his talents, his courage and ideals as a newspaperman.

Larry's professional life started more than thirty years ago in Los Angeles on the *Kashu Mainichi,* in the infancy of Nisei journalism. He brought standards of enterprise and competence to the English section of that paper unknown at that time. The Nisei were a struggling group then, uncertain of their destiny, torn by doubts and fears, in need of a strong press to inform and lead. More than anyone else, Larry provided that kind of press. He took his talents to the *Japanese American News* in San Francisco, and quickly that newspaper took on a widely recognized excellence.

But it was during the war years, as editor of the *Pacific Citizen,* that Larry served the Nisei most nobly. The strong fearless voice of the *PC* penetrated the barbed wire of the relocation camps, rose above the hysterical babble of hate mongers and their press. The *PC* under Larry's leadership was the focus of hope, courage, and above all, the information necessary to make individual judgments in a confused time. He, assisted by his wife Guyo, edited the *PC* in the finest traditions of the free and militant American press. More than any single factor, the *PC* was responsible for maintaining the morale of the Nisei community in the time of their greatest trial.

Larry had many opportunities to take more glamorous, more profitable jobs during this period, but he turned them down because of his sense of responsibility to the Nisei. He left the *PC* only after the good fight had been fought and victory assured.

This tribute to Larry has concentrated largely on his professional accomplishments. It is likely, however, that he will be remembered by those who knew him best as Larry the man, the kindly, fun-loving, gentle, generous, intensely curious human being. He was constitutionally incapable of arrogance, meanness or pettiness, and by his example he taught me many lessons in living life to its limit of fullness. That's the way he lived it, so that his fifty years were the equivalent of many more.

So long, Larry. It was great knowing you. And thanks for everything.

(February 19, 1965)

Public tribute of another sort, voiced while the recipient was able to enjoy it, was paid to Mike Masaoka, and Frying Pan joined in the praise:

They will be singing hosannas for Mike Masaoka at his testimonial banquet in Chicago this week. The nicest part of it is that every elaborate tribute delivered by some very accomplished orators will be thoroughly deserved. Most men are dead by the time anybody gets around to saying anything nice about them. Mike will have the pleasure of being present in the flesh, hale and hearty, when the eulogies are spoken. Who could wish for more?

Mike Masaoka is the classic example of the right man in the right place at the right time. The Japanese Americans needed him in the worst way in the quarter of a century between 1940 and 1965. Even so, it is possible that if he had been born ten years earlier, and had appeared on the Nisei scene in 1930 instead of a decade later, the Evacuation might never have taken place. That, of course, is purely conjecture and no one is ever going to prove the statement either right or wrong.

What is indisputable is that in 1941 when Saburo Kido was looking for an aggressive, articulate, inventive, forthright, ingenious, and far-sighted individual to take over as executive secretary of JACL, he found precisely the right man in Masaoka. He was young and inexperienced, as were all Nisei at that point in history. But he had all the other necessary attributes and he learned quickly. I shudder to think what course Nisei history might have taken had Masaoka not been on the scene to lead the way.

It is natural that the speakers at the testimonial will dwell on Masaoka's triumphs, which are many and impressive. It will be equally pertinent, I think, to remember his frustrations and trials, which he had the fortitude to overcome. Like the time he and George Inagaki were thrown into separate cells of a Louisiana jail by over-zealous deputies who suspected them of being Japanese spies. And fearing a lynching, how they signaled each other—by flushing the toilet—to keep up their spirits. And like the time he followed an elusive congressman into the men's room and engaged him in conversation while he couldn't get away, finally winning promise of a more formal audience.

I hope also that the speakers will not forget the people who made Mike possible. His mother, Haruye, for instance, who kept the family of eight children together when her husband Eijiro was killed in an automobile accident when Mike was only nine years old. And the oldest of the brood, Joe Grant (who just died of cancer this past week), who took over the burden of supporting the family and seeing to it that Mike and the others got their education. And of course Mike's patient, understanding and long-suffering wife Etsu, who has been his loyal helpmate and who uncomplainingly has shared him with his duties. Mike's night of triumph and acclaim also is theirs.

Which of Masaoka's many accomplishments on behalf of the Japanese Americans were the most notable? I would pick two. First, the campaign to extend naturalization rights to the Issei, which he masterminded to a successful conclusion. Wartime hatreds still smoldered at the time the campaign was launched. Some members of Congress confused the issue by attaching the citizenship measure to the controversial Walter-McCarran Immigration and Naturalization Act. The bill was vetoed by President Truman for reasons not connected with the Japanese Americans. Masaoka stirred up a floodtide of sentiment that overrode the veto, provided naturalization for the Issei, and at the same time accomplished his second most notable feat—repealing the disastrous Oriental Exclusion Act of 1924 and extending the dignity of immigration quotas to Asian nations. He had accomplished what had appeared to be the impossible.

In more recent years it would have been understandable if Masaoka, like so many other "successful" Nisei, had turned away from his colleagues to concentrate on his growing business and to follow his inclinations and personal interests. In truth, however, he has not forgotten his constituents, nor is he likely to. The testimonial this week is not necessarily the climax to the Masaoka career. It is, I hope, only another bright milestone along a route that leads inevitably to greater achievements.

(July 17, 1970)

I will wind up this chapter with a column about a movie that had no direct reference to Japanese Americans, but nonetheless held a poignant indirect message for them:

Someone told Alice that we ought to go see a movie titled "Kotch." Now what kind of a title is that? Is it something like M*A*S*H, whatever that was? Or did it have something to do with crotch, the way so many movies today seem to do; at least one gets that impression.

No, said Alice, nothing like that. It had to do with an old man, and because I'm getting closer and closer to that stage of life, her friend suggested it was a good movie for me to see. So we went. The last time we'd been to a movie was about a year ago when we saw "Tora! Tora! Tora!" so you can see we aren't being much help to the motion picture industry.

The first thing that astonished me was the price. Admission to this neighborhood cinema was $2.50! Per person. They were right about me getting older. Why, I can remember back on Jackson Street in Seattle when a fellow could treat a girl to a first-run movie and take her out afterward for a bowl of Chinese noodles, all for a buck and a half. The second surprise was the refreshment stand. It was closer to a cafeteria than a snackbar, with a popcorn popper lit up like a jukebox, all manner of beverages, and a battery of coin-operated vending machines large enough to meet the needs of the labor force at a General Motors assembly plant. Motion pictures these days must do something to whet the appetite.

But to get back to the movie. It starred an old gaffer named Walter Matthau, much older than I am likely to become for a good many years. Matthau is Mr. Kotch, or Kotcher—I was never quite sure—who is a good-hearted, garrulous retired salesman and widower. He has moved in with his son, daughter-in-law, and young grandson and even though he tries to be helpful and unobstructive, things have reached the point where everything he does grates on the daughter-in-law's nerves. When she finally persuades her husband to send the old man off to a retirement village, he gets the point and strikes out on his own.

All this may sound melodramatic, but it's done in good taste and with considerable dramatic skill. Mr. Kotch is portrayed as a harmless old duffer, still fully in control of his senses but inclined to be terribly long-winded as many older folks are. He also has a great capacity for love and compassion, which has been rebuffed by his own family, and so he befriends a teen-age babysitter who has been abandoned by society after becoming pregnant. In the course

220

of helping the girl find herself, old Mr. Kotch also learns that he, too, must make his independent way.

What makes this story particularly poignant from the Nisei point of view is that many of us are at that point in life in which we are, or soon will be, facing situations not very different from Mr. Kotch's. The Nisei are in a somewhat peculiar position. They knew that their parents, the Issei, expected their Nisei offspring to look after them in old age. In fact, in the Oriental tradition old age is a time to look forward to, when one can enjoy leisure while being supported by one's children and also enjoy the grandchildren. And the Nisei expected to assume this responsibility.

But now as the Nisei in turn reach retirement age, they realize that times have changed. While some may cling to the old traditions, others find themselves anxious to maintain their independence as long as possible. And even those who don't hold this point of view may change their minds after viewing this film. The infrequent times I go to a movie I expect to be entertained rather than to be exposed to a moral commentary, but Kotch was both.

(November 26, 1971)

14

Dispersal

The years slipped by more swiftly than we realized. Our Mike became a high-schooler with all those teen-age joys and afflictions. Christie was no longer a toddler. There were ten years of difference between the oldest and the youngest, and this fact exposed their parents to a wide spectrum of offspring activity. In the summer of 1957, when Mike was not quite seventeen years of age, he left home to take a summer job. That was a year when part-time jobs were easy to find. The occasion gave me reason to comment:

The summer job is a tradition as American as Horatio Alger. Youngsters freed from academic confinement seek profitable outlets for their energy, and our economy is such that they can find work without too much difficulty. Perhaps it was necessity, but the Nisei took to this custom. Some of them, back in the days before child labor laws, were going off in the summer to do men's work at the tender age of twelve; fourteen was a good average for leaving home to labor for two and a half months in the fields and canneries.

This year our Mike, now going on seventeen, figured it was time for him to seek out employment while working himself into shape for the coming football season. So, with three buddies, he headed for Wyoming to spend the next ten weeks on the power end of a shovel. The work will be good for him. So will the experience. And the money he'll bring home should pay for a half-year of college if not more.

Last weekend we watched him drive off, proud of our fledgling's departure and yet with a twinge of parental concern. I thought back, too, over the years to the first time I left home and I could understand a little of what my own folks must have felt.

It might be considerably more lonesome at home now if there weren't three other youngsters doing their noisy best to fill the void left by Mike's departure. On top of this, we've discovered that during the last few months Mike was out of the house so much of the time we hardly miss him any more. So far the most serious aspect of his departure is that he took the family's only decent can opener. Its loss has crippled the culinary efforts of those who are left.

(June 14, 1957)

A long time ago when I was a teen-ager, Pa and I used to test the strength that was in our right arms. We'd face each other across a table and clasp right hands. The idea was to keep elbow on table and wrestle your opponent's arm down. Pa, having been a railroad section hand among other things, was a mighty stout fellow and didn't have much trouble disposing of his stripling son. Then one day I discovered to my elation that I could pin him. Either I'd grown so strong, or he had grown so old and decrepit, that I could handle him. We laughed and made much of it.

I didn't know how he felt that day. But now I know because my own son, Mike, visiting at home from his pick and shovel job, tangled with me in a test of strength and forced my arm back. After he won once, we tried again just to make sure it was no fluke. He laughed and won even easier, not even breathing hard.

This is how a father feels: A small touch of regret and disappointment that the good right arm is no longer sure. And a great surge of pride and elation that the fledgling is now a man.

(August 2, 1957)

The next spring, Mike was graduated from high school. We all trooped down to the auditorium to witness the rite, and when that was over I came home and wrote a column:

Last Monday evening, East Denver High School's class of 1958 was graduated with all the pomp and ceremony that has come to be associated with high school commencement. The graduating class, numbering more than 750 bright-eyed young men and women, marched in cadence into the auditorium. The boys were in black gowns and mortarboard hats, the girls in pristine white, and a handsome lot they were.

For these youngsters it was the biggest day of their young lives, and the ceremonies were appropriately solemn and impressive. In fact, they were staged with such precision and competence that it made one wonder if their college commencement, four years hence, wouldn't be something of an anticlimax. Yet today's youngsters are so precocious even in their adolescent years that less sophisticated rites would be flat.

Our Mike was one of the throng that marched up to claim diplomas. (The appropriate thing to say at this point is, "How times does fly." Fly it has, indeed. It was just a few

224

years ago, it seems, that he trudged off purposefully, with his hand in his mother's, for his first day in kindergarten.) We watched him, tall and straight, walk up to a member of the school board who shook his hand and handed over a handsome leatherbound diploma. For a moment they exchanged pleasantries and from high in the balcony we could see them smiling at their own private joke.

Then it was time for us to go home, but we didn't see Mike until the next day. He went off to a party with some of his chums, and since this was a very special occasion— celebrating the attainment of maturity, of a sort—there was no telling when he'd be home. The rest of us went to bed, marveling a little at what a wonderful day this had been for our Mike.

Before sleep came, I tried to remember back over the years to my own high school graduation, trying to recall what that day had meant for me. Had it been a memorable, unforgettable, wonderful experience? Perhaps it had seemed so at the time. But this night, it was disappointing to discover that I could not recall a single detail of that event. Time had obliterated those memories, as cleanly as the tide washing the sands of the seashore, and perhaps it was just as well.

(June 13, 1958)

That fall, Mike went off to college. It was a small four-year institution called Adams State. A lot of Coloradans have never heard of it. It is in Alamosa (Dogpatch, U.S.A., according to Mike's little brother) in the south-central part of the state, a five-hour drive from Denver. That left three young ones at home.

We had a siege of cold weather not long ago, the temperature falling as low as 5° below zero. Our Christie, now

225

eight years old, was out playing in the snow until suddenly she became aware that her ears had become painfully chilled.

"Gosh," she remarked, "I wish I could put my ears in my pocket."

She is perhaps the most imaginative of our youngsters and often she amuses herself by making believe. One day she cut some small slips of paper and proceeded to print "fortunes" on them—the kind that one finds in the fortune cookies passed out for dessert at Chinese and Japanese restaurants. Here is a small sampling, her spelling intact:

"You will marry a man and then will divorice him. Poor girl."

"You will birth a brat. Poor lady."

"You will go on a long trip and will meet a handsome man."

"You will have a horse to ride. Lucky duck."

"Your child will die if its birthday is in July. Too bad."

"You will kill your wife after you are marryed 25 years. Bad boy."

"You will be poor when you marry."

The bane of Christie's existence is her brother, Pete, two years her senior, who takes a particularly fiendish delight in tormenting her. She makes her feelings quite apparent with this fortune:

"You will kiss Peter Hosokawa. Poor kid."

It might be interesting to get a psychologist to analyze her literary efforts. On the other hand, the findings may be more frightening than her parents can bear up under at this time.

(December 5, 1958)

When our nine-year-old Christie heard that we weren't planning to attend the P.T.A. meeting, she went into a pout and declared:

"I was born too late. You went to P.T.A. meetings for Mike and Susan and Pete. And now when it's my turn you're all pooped out. I guess it's just my hard luck."

So we went to the P.T.A. meeting. And we're still pooped out.

(April 15, 1960)

Our Number 2 son, Pete, is a fairly husky lad for his thirteen years, which really isn't anything startling in these days of super-potent vitamins and scientific diets. His pediatrician, who doesn't see many youngsters of Oriental descent, apparently was quite impressed by Pete's development. He seemed to be under the impression northern Japanese, like northern Europeans, are larger physically than southern types, and so he asked:

"Pete, do your people come from the north?"

"Yes," he responded solemnly, "my father was born in Seattle and my mother comes from Portland."

Just for the record, Pete's grandparents came from the southwestern part of Japan, Hiroshima and Okayama.

(June 20, 1961)

In his sophomore year Mike transferred from Adams State to Colorado State College. Almost before we knew what had happened, Mike was being graduated. That was an event worth noting:

Having completed the prescribed course of study and paid the required fees, our Mike was graduated last Sunday from Colorado State College. Looking just a bit self-conscious in cap and gown, he stepped forward to accept the diploma which attests to his academic accomplishments.

It is difficult to describe the emotions we felt. There was pride, of course, happiness, relief and anticipation, and perhaps even a bit of regret that we are losing our first-born. He is no longer ours in the sense that was true for twenty-

227

one years; he is an independent young man who hereafter must rely on his own intelligence, energies and other resources to make his own way.

This is a sort of landmark year for us. In addition to Mike, the other three are passing rather important academic milestones. Susan will be graduating from high school in a few days and is preparing to go on to college. Pete will be entering the ninth grade in the fall, which doesn't mean much any more in these days of junior highs, but in other times the ninth grade was the beginning of high school. And Christie will be leaving elementary school for junior high come September. A landmark year, indeed. And only one P.T.A. to go to in the fall.

I suppose it would not be entirely appropriate to recall that my commencement took place just twenty-five years ago this month; a sheepskin, which cost $5 even in those depressed times, attests to that fact. I haven't seen it in some years. It must be stored away somewhere in the piles of junk that one collects.

The memories of that day are somewhat dim. What remains are largely inconsequential things, like how hot it was in the arena in our rented gowns, how hard the seats became as the program dragged on, and more vividly, the light of pride in parental eyes as we met them after the program. They had sacrificed much to make education possible.

Looking back now, it is more obvious than ever that commencement, as the word says, was only the beginning. The real process of learning came after classroom courses were completed. If our youngsters learn only this lesson while they are wrestling with their academic challenges the time and money invested in their educations will have been well spent.

In trying to analyze the fascination of rearing a child to adulthood, the real satisfaction seems to be in watching a personality and an individual develop. In our family we've never tried to shape a child into our own images, or to experience the things we missed through them. And so the youngsters have grown up as distinct individuals with opinions of their own, reacting to situations on the basis of their own glands and brain cells and whatever else goes into the creation of personality.

All four of the youngsters have started with basically decent instincts, and we've tried to build on that foundation. But they're all different and will continue to become more different as they develop.

If all this sounds a bit bewildering, the subject matter a trifle alien from the usual column that appears in this space, I hope you'll be indulgent. This is a special sort of day, and I wanted to share a few thoughts with you about some kids we've reported on in the Frying Pan from time to time over the past twenty years. They don't do "cute" things any more, but they're still interesting, I think.

(June 1, 1962)

Last Saturday morning Christie, our youngest, went to work for the first time in an honest-to-goodness money-paying job, not counting her occasional baby-sitting. Gene Side, who runs the two Madam Butterfly shops hereabouts, agreed to take her on for Saturday and perhaps summer employment, and just about the first thing he wanted to know was Christie's Social Security account number.

Of course she didn't have one, but it would be a simple matter to apply. So I dropped down to the Federal Building where the local branch of the vast Social Security apparatus is housed and picked up an application. Christie filled out the card and signed it and I, being her parent and guardian, provided the 5¢ stamp to guarantee its delivery.

The last of the brood is now duly registered as a person, officially recognized as a potential wage-earner and taxpayer by the United States government and entitled, when the time comes, to share in the benefits as may be provided by the Social Security system. As the Japanese would say, *Christie mo ichinin-mai ni natta,* although she is only a high school sophomore and it will be some years before she is really *ichinin-mai,* which might be translated roughly into "full-fledged person."

Although only Mike, the eldest of the four, is out on his own, all of the offspring found gainful summer employment at a relatively early age. Somehow, as the baby of the family, it had seemed Christie would remain a child for a long time to come. Not so. Another family milestone has been passed.

(March 11, 1966)

A few hours ago we climbed into the sedan and drove up to Boulder to pick up our Susan. From where we live the most direct route to Boulder stretches northward along the foothills of the Rockies. Recent rains have greened the fields, and it is a pleasant forty-minute drive. We have driven the route many times, but it has not lost its charm. At sunset the peaks are a sawtooth silhouette against the sky. On the homeward leg, the lights of Denver stretch across the horizon, winking and twinkling in the distance.

This day is a special occasion, for Susan has completed her schooling at the University of Colorado and we are bringing her home. It seems incredible that we took her there on a hot September Sunday nearly five years ago and delivered her to a dormitory bustling with other excited freshman girls and their somewhat bewildered parents. But now those five years are irrevocably gone, and to show for it Susan has a diploma testifying to the fact that she has earned a bachelor of arts degree, a certificate entitling her to teach school, and a few hours toward a master's degree for which she will continue to study as she teaches.

And so the second of our brood has become, as the Japanese say, *ichinin-mai,* meaning literally "one person's portion," an oddly expressive phrase. It's been a long road.

(June 9, 1967)

Why should a person, on a hurried business trip to the Pacific Northwest, want to travel some scores of miles out of his way to visit Eugene, Oregon? To see his grandchildren, of course.

Ashlyn, who is three years old, and her younger brother Mikey, who is a little (but not tiny) toddler, were at the airport with their Pa and Ma in a driving rainstorm to welcome their Grandpa. Maybe it was the darkness of the night, or the sudden appearance of the stranger that caused the young ones to be somewhat shy and cautious. Little Mike, who does not find it necessary to speak yet, was suspicious of the visitor's intentions and insisted on giving him a wide berth.

But presently, particularly after gifts had been distributed, the atmosphere became more cordial and we proceeded to become acquainted. Grandchildren are a wonderful institution, especially since it is their Pa or Ma and not Grandpa who has to stagger out of bed and minister to their demands when they decide 5 A.M. is a good time for getting up.

Big Mike (187 pounds), the Pa in the paragraphs above, had been teaching at Lewis & Clark College in Portland. This year, however, he has taken a fellowship at the University of Oregon in Eugene to complete his academic work on his doctorate. (Who would have thought a dozen years ago when we were trying to get him to open a book that Mike some day would be a doctoral candidate?)

Among the courses he is taking is one in sociology. Mike chose to make a study of the Evacuation. Like a good many other Sansei he was too young to recall the experience, although he went through it. Now he is becoming curious about that sad episode. So we sent him some books, and he learned for the first time the incredible thing that had happened.

After the grandchildren had been put to bed, we talked for a while about the evacuation years—how we went to Heart Mountain, Wyoming, and from that desolate place to Des Moines, Iowa, where we found a warm welcome from the people in the American heartland. We talked about Pauline and Ronald Lynam next door, who at first looked askance at their new neighbors because they didn't know what to expect, and how they became two of our closest friends. And Mike remembered that Pauline's sister, who lives in Eugene, had called on his family and we wondered at the warm human ties that stretched across half a continent, and span two and a half decades in time. Mike had been a kindergartener when we left Des Moines; how Pauline would enjoy seeing him and his family now.

All too soon it was time to be on the way again. We bundled up the grandchildren, put the suitcase in the car trunk, and headed through the pleasant green countryside to the airport. Ashlyn was wide-eyed, fascinated by the aircraft, but sensing that Grandpa was about to fly away out of her life. No one had taught her what it meant to be lonely, but she knew nonetheless that she would feel that way when Grandpa left.

I started up the ramp to the plane as a rain squall swept the field, and Mike wisely hurried his family into the shelter of the terminal. Shortly we were airborne and what was there for a man to do but relive his memories of long ago and of the twenty-four hours that had just passed.

(November 10, 1967)

You'd think that with the fourth one, we'd be used to having youngsters going off to college. But parents never get accustomed to having the offspring leaving hearth and

232

home to try their wings in the great, wide, exciting world of independence.

We knew since last spring that Christie would be enrolling this fall at the University of Colorado. Still, the campus is a long way from home in respects other than geographical distance, and Christie was looking forward all summer long to the day she would move into her dormitory room at the university.

And finally the day came. All her things were packed. (She had looked with consternation on the vast tonnage of material that she would have to take to college and she observed only partly in jest: "It would be easier to move the University of Colorado down here than for me to get all this junk up there.") The trip to the campus was made, and she was safely established in the room that she will be sharing with a freckled young lady from Los Angeles.

Christie is a self-reliant sort, perhaps the result of being fourth in a family of four youngsters and therefore having been the subject of less parental attention (perhaps "concern" is a better word) than the others. She will get along and she will enjoy experiencing campus life. Yet, even knowing her anticipation, we left her at the dormitory entrance with not a little sadness and began the empty journey homeward.

The home that once sheltered six of us has a bit of a hollow feel to it now that only three remain. Pete is living at home while he attends Denver University, which is a sensible thing since tuition plus rent would add up to a frightening figure. But Pete is a quiet sort, busy with his own interests, and he has not moved into the vacuum left by Christie's departure. Nor will he. You would think that if the population of a home is reduced by one-fourth, the sound and activity level would drop by 25 per cent. But it doesn't work that way. When a teen-age girl leaves, the activity level falls off by something closer to 50 per cent.

The telephone doesn't ring nearly as often. The laughter and squeals are heard no more. The door to her room stands ajar and even though it appears just about the way it did when she was here, it has an abandoned look.

We'd been talking semi-seriously about selling the house and moving into an apartment, which is what many people seem to do when the brood has left the nest. But Christie protested, saying it wouldn't be like coming home if she were to visit us in an apartment. So we've put off thoughts of moving away, for a while at least.

(September 27, 1968)

It was her first dinner for her folks in her new home, and our newlywed Susan was particularly anxious that everything should go right, even though she and her husband, Warren, live in a tiny apartment on the ground floor of an elderly dwelling. She served something called beef fondue, wherein we speared little cubes of sirloin on a long fork and dipped them into a pot of oil bubbling over an alcohol flame. The beef was tender and the sauces tasty, and the meal was well on its way to success.

Then it was time for dessert, and what happened next was not her fault. She had ordered a strawberry cream cake, which has to be kept cool. The bakery gave her a strawberry ice cream cake, which has to be kept frozen. Not knowing this, she put the cake out on the back porch. Now she opened the box and removed the plastic collar around the cake preparatory to cutting it. That's when the cake sort of collapsed, for the ice cream had melted. And so we ate our mushy cake with a spoon, which was no hardship at all but a matter of considerable chagrin to our hostess.

Later, when we suggested that what remained of the cake ought to be hustled into the freezer, she confessed that the freezer compartment was so small there was no room for the cake. Furthermore, the freezer had an obnoxious

234

way of failing to keep ice cream firm while lettuce in the bottom of the refrigerator frequently froze so it couldn't be used.

Well, such are the trials of housekeeping in a rented apartment, particularly an old one. Before too long, we hope, they'll be able to move into a more comfortable place, where the bathtub doesn't sit on legs and the pole lamp doesn't have to be placed atop an empty paint can in order to reach the ceiling.

We live in a fairly comfortable home now, but it was not always like this. When Alice and I were first married, we had a room in the house where the folks lived. What more could a young couple afford when the total income was $75 a month?

When we were relocated to Des Moines, the only house we could find within our means was an ancient two-story clapboard dwelling heated with a coal furnace. Still, it was far better than a barracks unit. The house seemed to have seams that had ceased to become airtight. When it stormed, which was frequently, the curtains fluttered in the breeze that swept through the house, blowing in great drafts of cold and driving out whatever warmth we had been able to hoard. My recollection is that we bought twenty-two tons of coal that winter to satisfy the furnace's insatiable appetite, and hauled out twenty-three tons of ashes. An Iowa winter is not something to be taken lightly. The cold was one reason we left an otherwise friendly and hospitable state.

This was the home to which we brought Susan after she was born in a hospital. She spent the first half-dozen months of her life in that miserable place, and perhaps the experience helped her take later hardships in stride.

Having reminded ourselves of some of the dumps we've lived in, and were happy in because we were young and doing the things we wanted to do, we did not feel overly sorry for Susan. She is happy in her new home. She is embarking on a new life. The comforts and luxuries that we have come to take for granted are not particularly important to her now. They will come with time, just as they came to us with the passage of years. Years from now they will remember the melted cake and the overcrowded freezer, and they will laugh and be warmed by the memory.

(October 18, 1968)

Our usually well-ordered household was in a happy state of confusion over the holidays. The credit would go to two very small bundles of energy, Ashyln who is now five years old, and Mikey who is three and a half, and who happen to be our only grandchildren so far. They persuaded their folks to drive down from Eugene, Oregon, where they live, to visit Grandpa and Grandma for Christmas.

Christmas morning was the highlight. Ashlyn had asked for a longhaired doll, and there it was alongside the stocking she had left for Santa to fill. Her face mirrored an emotion that was a combination of delight and awe; for once she was speechless when she saw it. Mikey had his heart set on a cowboy hat, among other things. But when he discovered his wish had come true, he was all but overwhelmed. He could only gaze at that beautiful red hat in wordless delight; he could not bring himself to wear it until an hour or two had passed.

Later that morning, after the debris of the gift opening had been cleared away, the entire clan sat around to admire each other's presents and reminisce a bit. There was Mike, of course, with his wife Jackie, and children. Susan and her husband, Warren, had driven across town to be with us before hurrying down to Colorado Springs to spend the balance of the day with his folks. Pete pulled himself out of his bachelor pad to be with the family. And Christie, the youngest, was close by the side of her fiancé, Lloyd. Let's

236

see. Four children, two spouses, one fiancé, two grand-children, and Grandpa and Grandma. Eleven in all. And here I was, the patriarch of the clan, feeling far from patriarchal but proud of the brood and happy with what they've made of their lives so far.

And yet there was a touch of sentimental sadness, too. One by one the youngsters have left the nest. Eugene, in western Oregon, is a long way to drive and a trip back to Denver is hardly for every Christmas. Susan and Warren are likely to remain in Denver where both teach in the public schools, but Pete is casting his eyes California-ward in planning his career after he gets his degree in June. Christie's young man, Lloyd, is an Air Force cadet soon to win his commission, and duty will take them to far away places. When would we all be together again? Perhaps next year, and then again perhaps never.

The development of our brood is a measure of the way the years have sped by. Big Mike, soon to be thirty, was a toddler on Pearl Harbor Day when the shape of the world changed for all of us. Susan was born after we were re-located to Iowa. Pete and Christie came along after the war when we had moved to Denver. In fact, Christie was born just a few days after the outbreak of the Korean War.

Where have the years gone? There are moments of soul-searching when we ask this question, not really expecting to find an answer. But the answer was there in substantial flesh and blood at the gathering of the clan on Christmas morning.

And so, hi ho, into the Seventies we shall go.

(January 16, 1970)

It was just about a year ago that Pete, the Number 2 son, came to us and announced that he thought it was about time he struck out on his own. He was making pretty good

237

money at his parttime job at the bank, he said, and he and a couple of other fellows could get a good deal on an apartment. The clincher to his argument was that he probably could study a lot harder in the privacy of his own apartment, away from the distractions of home, and it'd be good for him to take on a little independence.

Well, shucks, he was nearly twenty-one years old and if he wanted to try his fledgling wings, why not let him? Of course it wouldn't have done a bit of good to try to talk him out of it. Parents don't talk their kids out of anything these days; you just act philosophical and roll with the punches.

So Pete moved into his apartment and even though it was only two or three miles from the old homestead, he didn't show up very often. He fixed his own meals and took care of his own laundry, and he usually was too busy to come when we invited him to dinner. After a while it occurred to us that the only reason he seemed to be avoiding us was that he had to assert his independence, and he couldn't very well be doing that if he were running home every day or so.

Sure enough, after a goodly number of months had passed and Pete had proved his independence to his satisfaction, he found he could accept our invitations to dinner without compromising himself. He even began to drop around for social visits, although he rarely tarried for long. It was a normal and comfortable relationship.

Some days before Christmas he brought a young lady to see us, and she skillfully wrapped some presents that Pete was going to distribute. She seemed to be a very nice sort although we didn't get much of an opportunity to know her.

The inevitable next step, of course, is marriage, and I guess we were half-way prepared when a few days after Christmas Pete announced he was now ready to commit matrimony.

What do you say to a son under those circumstances? Do

you urge him to put off marriage a few more months until he gets his college degree? No, when the son is as mature and as sure of himself as Pete is, you shake his hand and congratulate him and wish him happiness and ask if there is anything you can do to help.

The marriage ceremony took place last weekend. Pete, who had scorned church attendance, yielded to Vickie's wishes and agreed to a church wedding. He would have preferred, I think, a very simple civil ceremony. Instead, he had attendants decked out in white jackets and black bow ties, just the way she wanted it. The ceremony was brief but dignified and proper, and it turned out very well.

Pete is the first of our offspring to be born in Denver. That shows how long we have lived here, and how deeply our roots have been sunk in Colorado soil. As we waited on the unyielding wood of the church pews, it was difficult not to think back to the day so long ago—and yet so recent —when we made Pete's acquaintance through the glass of the hospital nursery window. We remembered how he hated to wear shoes, how he was entranced with toy trucks, and the way he became so fascinated with nature that he was determined to become a forest ranger when he grew up. We remembered those times when fate dealt with him cruelly—it seemed he was forever getting hurt—and how he went on to a certain prominence that set him a niche above most of his high-school mates. And there was the day when he gave up a menial but well-paying summer job and asked for help in lining up other work, any kind of work, where he could learn something useful. That, it is evident now, was the day he grew up.

And so now he is a married man shouldering the responsibilities of an adult. One more of our burdens is terminated and today I'm not certain that it is a good feeling.

(February 13, 1970)

The last of the brood has departed the nest. One recent Saturday Christie and I walked down the long church aisle together. I was uncomfortable in a rented dinner jacket, she radiant in a bridal gown. The man of her choice awaited together with the minister, and I delivered her into his hands. When the minister asked who gives the bride in marriage, I said firmly as I had been instructed: "Her mother and I do," and, my responsibility completed for the moment, I was permitted to sit down.

Everyone who spoke to me later commented on what a lovely wedding it was, and who am I to question their judgment. After the reception Christie and her husband, Lloyd, departed for Southern California on their honeymoon, leaving behind a large void. Eventually they will make their way to Big Spring, Texas, where Lloyd will learn to fly Air Force jets.

The size of the void was accentuated because the day after the wedding Pete and his wife also departed for Los Angeles. Only a day earlier he had received his diploma from the University of Denver, and now he was reporting to work in one of the nation's major banks. So in a single day we saw two of our young ones leave the city that had been their home since birth.

Now the youngsters are scattered to the four winds. Mike, in Eugene, where he is on the faculty of the University of Oregon. Pete in Los Angeles, Christie soon to be in Texas. Only Susan and her husband remain in Denver, and they live on the other side of town.

There were many times in years past when we wished fervently that the children were grown so that we would be free to do the things we wanted to do. That time has come. Perhaps it is because we have grown older, but the realization of our regained independence is not nearly so exciting as was the anticipation. We are free, and not really so very delighted with the freedom.

240

I suppose there is a lesson in all this. Enjoy your children while you can. Only too soon will they be ready and anxious to try their fledgling wings, to fly away to wherever opportunity seems to beckon, to launch their own lives as adults. We do not urge them to stay when it is their wish to go; we regret only that they must go and that it must be so soon.

By all rights this is a time of rejoicing, for now the children are on their own. The period of preparation is ended; the years of achievement and fulfillment are ahead. Now comes the testing of education and character and moral fiber, and if we have trained them well, the future is loaded with promise. And yet it must be only natural to feel a pang of loneliness, now that they are gone and for the first time the home is without children. And the income tax return is stripped of dependents.

(June 19, 1970)

15

Some Favorites

This chapter is made up of a handful of more recent columns which, for one reason or another, I liked particularly or which attracted special attention. In the column that follows, the young man in the limelight will have to serve as proxy for the other grandchildren since, unfortunately, there is not room enough to feature them all:

Mr. and Mrs. Bill Hosokawa had the pleasure of Matthew William Harveson's company for dinner at Wyatt's Cafeteria the other night. Our guest more than made up for his lack of conversational brilliance with frequent uninhibited smiles and a very charming style, although it must be admitted his table manners were deplorable.

Matthew William, as the more faithful readers of this column are aware, is grandchild Number 4 and concurrently grandson Number 3. Normally he lives in Fairfield, California, but currently he is visiting us with his folks. Since they were tied up with some social doings, Matthew had no choice but to join us for dinner.

He set the tone for the occasion by stuffing his mouth with boiled beets as soon as he sat down. But when he discovered that the flavor failed to live up to the promise of their tantalizing color, he did what any sensible person would do. He spit them out. Thereafter he went to work with a will on what apparently is his favorite vegetable, boiled green beans. He scorned the stuffed peppers and fried chicken. The first he simply dropped over the side of his highchair onto the nice carpeted floor of Wyatt's. The second, he gummed around in his mouth for a while before spitting it back out. In between he made short work of four soda crackers, demonstrating great skill in swallowing as much as he managed to scatter over the rug.

But it was on the way out that Matthew provided us with a hint as to the kind of young man he will grow up to be. First, he quickly picked up two cigarette butts, a look of triumph in his brown eyes. We could forgive this action, rationalizing that he is built very close to the ground and somewhat more likely than his adult escorts to notice discarded items. A few moments later he stopped to gape in pure astonishment at a young woman in very tight jeans and an orange sweater-blouse which was distended magnificently across the front. I admired his taste but had to remind him that it is impolite to stare, no matter how amazing the spectacle. Still, I suppose that at his age Matthew can be excused for having more than a casual interest in mammary development. In a manner of speaking, he is something of an expert on the subject.

At fourteen months, Matthew is a perceptive young man. He has become aware, for example, that grownups are inclined to hide the most interesting things out of his sight and reach. Thus he makes it a practice of probing into dark and forbidden areas, like the liquor cabinet where he found a number of large bottles filled with fluid of interesting colors. Since he has learned to walk, he has gained the ability to vanish into the most unlikely places. This led his mother to fasten a tiny metal bell to each of his shoes so that he tinkles as he moves about. One of these days soon he will realize that the bells are betraying him and he will come up with a way to dispose of them.

While Matthew is spending a few days with us, the mail brings news of his kin. His California cousin, Patrick, in Sacramento, is in the process of learning how to ride a tricycle. Up in Oregon his cousin Ashlyn is becoming a pretty fair acrobat and talks about piano lessons. And her brother Mikey is intent on learning to swim better so that it will be safe for him to go trout fishing with his father on the swift-flowing McKenzie River.

One by one the small ones are acquiring the skills that will stand them in good stead as they grope their way all too swiftly toward maturity. It won't be long before Matthew will be running instead of toddling, and Patrick, too, will be talking about going fishing with his father.

(June 15, 1973)

These grandchildren are Yonsei, meaning the fourth generation of Japanese Americans. Our own children are Sansei, the third generation, and they have made a good adjustment to the society in which they live and work. But some Sansei haven't, not yet anyway, as was indicated in this next column:

Excuse me, I was listening to some Sansei talking the other day and what I heard provoked more than a little interest and concern. The occasion was Denver's Japanese American community dinner for high school and college graduates.

The gist of the conversation was that these Sansei, who

244

in most cases were exceptionally good students, were looking forward to college with considerable anxiety. They
seemed to be painfully aware of their racial minority status.
They wondered how they would be treated by their fellow
students. They were worried about whether they would be
accepted. Some anticipated racial slights and slurs. What
it boiled down to, as I understand the situation, was that
these Sansei were terribly and frighteningly up-tight about
race.

One of the group was a college student who had been accepted for advanced studies. He, too, admitted that he had
been filled with anxieties when he left high school, and
now he reported with wonder in his voice that he had been
well accepted in college. It was as though he had half expected to be kicked in the teeth and called a dirty Jap, and
he was surprised when no one had done it.

Later, thinking about what had been voiced, I wondered
to myself whether these youngsters were "typical," whether
other Sansei in other parts of the country are experiencing
similiar anxieties. I hope not. Because if they are, they
are concerning themselves largely with ghosts that don't
exist, at least not from this viewpoint.

Let me speak like an old codger, which I have come to be.
It was exactly forty years ago this year that I was graduated
from high school. There was a goodly number of other
Nisei in Seattle, my home town, who got their high school
diplomas that year. I don't pretend to speak for all of them,
but the ones I knew were optimistic, perhaps even cocky,
about their personal prospects as they surveyed a sorry,
depression-burdened world. A good many of that bunch
went on to college, some of us because there were no jobs
and it was easier just continuing with our educations.

We knew as surely as the sun would rise that we would
face discrimination when it came to job-hunting time. The
doors of opportunity would be slammed in our faces. But

we also knew that there was equality of opportunity to learn in the classrooms, and we applied ourselves without anxiety or fear. Perhaps we were what the Japanese would call *baka-shojiki*—naive, unsophisticated, foolish. Perhaps we were kidding ourselves. But we said to hell with it and went forward unafraid.

The Sansei today faces an altogether different world. Many—although certainly not all—discriminatory barriers have fallen. The various minorities have banded together to make known their grievances, laws to guarantee equality of opportunity have been implemented, and a wide cross section of the American public has been sensitized to the need for overcoming racial discrimination. Under the circumstances it is difficult to understand the apprehension expressed by the young people I overheard.

One doesn't always gain courage by listening to a pep talk, but I hope it will encourage the shy, troubled, anxious members of the Sansei generation when I say the difficult road has been trod by their elders. Many were bruised and scarred, but most of them came through in good shape. And they helped make the road infinitely less painful for the Sansei.

(June 29, 1973)

After writing the above column, I kept wondering why some Sansei should feel so apprehensive about their futures. Had we, their elders, in our preoccupation with fighting racism and discrimination, so indoctrinated them with the idea that the great wide world was filled with fearful specters that we had distorted their perspective? Then, suddenly, the realities of life returned in the form of a bitter remark by a peripheral figure in the Watergate hearings which, of course, had nothing to do with Japanese Americans:

If the sorry drama of the Watergate hearings had drifted off into a distant and dreary realm of late for Japanese

246

American television viewers, it came back with a jolt last week when John J. Wilson, attorney for deposed White House aides H. R. Haldeman and John D. Ehrlichman, angrily referred to Senator Daniel K. Inouye as "that little Jap."

There was Wilson on national television in living color, face livid, hotly repeating a statement made earlier to a newspaperman. It was no unwitting slip of the tongue, no casual reference; it was only too obviously a racial slur flung out with calculated rancor. The questions of the television reporters crowded around Wilson with their microphones reflected the shock which reverberated around the country.

The word "Jap" carries a special bitterness which is not attached to Jew or Swede or Turk. Sometimes it is used innocently or in ignorance of its historic implications, and the JACL has been in the forefront of a campaign to educate the media and the public. At times some of us have considered JACL's campaign excessively touchy, for there is a need to distinguish between innocent usage and its use as a hate word. Wilson left no doubt and his explanation— "I consider it a description of the man—I wouldn't mind being called a little American"—was lame. Would he have called Senator Joseph Montoya, another member of the committee, a little Spik?

When Senator Inouye was asked to comment on the slur, he seemed unwilling to speak. Was he fighting down anger? On the tube he appeared overly reluctant to assert himself, perhaps too much the Quiet American when the situation seemed to call for an aggressive if statesmanlike response. "I think his statement speaks for itself," Senator Inouye said, adding a vague reference to the uncomfortable Washington climate which presumably shortens tempers and leads to indiscretions. I was disappointed.

But as it turned out the Senator knew precisely what he

247

was doing. He did not have to speak out. His colleagues on the Ervin Committee and in the Senate, and his constituents back home in Hawaii, did it for him with far more effectiveness.

As this is being written, it is too early to gauge the reaction around the country but let me tell you what happened here at the Denver *Post* where I work. I wandered down to the editorial page department to see what the reaction might be. The editor had written a brief editorial suggesting that Mr. Wilson might well be a candidate for disbarment. And our Pulitzer-winning cartoonist, Pat Oliphant, was putting the finishing touches to a powerful cartoon commentary. It showed a tiny Wilson shaking his fist in anger at the feet of a towering Inouye and saying: ". . . And you can call me a little American any time!"

It was reassuring, of course, that thirty-odd years after the Evacuation experience there should be this sort of abhorrence for a racist remark. Still, there is much of concern when an important man on a national stage callously throws a racial slur at a United States Senator.

In a great many respects the Nisei have "made it." But when the chips are down, when U.S.-Japanese relations become strained as they are likely to be in the long run, when political passions run high, when power is at stake, the old animosities can be expected to surface to our detriment.

John J. Wilson, unwittingly, has given us warning.

(August 10, 1973)

But there were other columns that related stories of selflessness and a certain nobility among people I knew. Like the one that follows:

If I have told this story in some long-forgotten column, please bear with me. It deserves re-telling. The story begins in the frigid winter of 1943, in January or maybe it was February. We were in the Heart Mountain WRA camp when we got word that my mother-in-law was suffering from some mysterious, frightening illness. Medical facilities at the camp where she was confined were limited, and there seemed to be no way to get an authoritative diagnosis. From our distance there seemed to be no way to help her. In desperation we asked that she be permitted to travel to the Mayo Clinic in Rochester, Minnesota, and we would try to get permission to meet her there.

Her permission came through much faster than we had any reason to expect. Perhaps the authorities, in their desire to shed their responsibility, were only too glad to turn the patient over to the Mayo people. When the matter first came up we had written to our bank back in Seattle to ask that the few hundred dollars on deposit be mailed to us so we could pay for transportation and take care of the medical bills. Well, the day to start the trip to Rochester arrived before the money did.

And so, with my nearly empty billfold sustained only by the optimism of youth and the desperate knowledge that something had to be done, Alice and I and our young son Mike got our pass to leave the camp, walked through the gates of snowy Heart Mountain camp, and took the bus to Billings, Montana. There we sought out a restaurant not far from the railroad tracks run by Mrs. Honkawa, whose sons had become casual acquaintances of ours when they came out to Seattle before the war to attend college. Mrs. Honkawa listened to our story and without a bit of hesitation she loaned me enough money to buy round-trip tickets to St. Paul, bus tickets from St. Paul to Rochester, and enough extra to take care of hotel and meals.

From the depot in St. Paul we telephoned some old friends, Earl Tanbara, and his wife Ruth, refugees from the San Francisco Bay Region, who had set up housekeep-

249

ing and were a sort of unofficial hostel for other Japanese Americans. Ruth had gone off to work but Earl invited us up for breakfast and a chance to bathe and rest before going on to Rochester. Over coffee, we told Earl about our financial embarrassment. He didn't have much money either, but he was glad to lend us enough to repay Mrs. Honkawa. We made our way to the Mayo Clinic where the doctors confirmed our worst fears. Then, after scouting around unsuccessfully in the Twin Cities for a job that would enable us to relocate, we made the sad trip back to Heart Mountain.

In Billings, we stopped long enough to repay Mrs. Honkawa with the money Earl Tanbara had lent us. Back in camp, we found the long-delayed check from the bank and so we were able to send Earl his money with profound appreciation.

This small chapter from the past was pulled out of the file of memory a few days ago when we got the word that Earl had died in St. Paul at age sixty-eight. He had suffered a massive stroke and never came out of it.

The tragedy of the Evacuation brought out the worst in some people, but for most of its victims it was a time when both the receiving and extending of compassion helped to ease pain and anxiety.

I have no idea how many others Earl and Ruth Tanbara helped in the way that they assisted my family, but the number must have been substantial because they were that kind of people. And so was Mrs. Honkawa, whom I met only on that one occasion. Later, I heard she had moved out to California or somewhere out West, but that was a long time ago.

What they did for me and my family in a time of need was not particularly significant to anyone except us. But it may be a measure of the importance of their kindness and faith that after thirty years Alice and I haven't forgotten. I hope Ruth will find a bit of comfort in the retelling of this story.

(January 18, 1974)

Shortly after the above column was published, Betty Yamaoka of Granada Hills, California, sent along happy news. She said Mrs. Honkawa is her sister's mother-in-law, and had been living in Los Angeles for the last twenty-five years. "I am going to read the column to her when next we meet," Betty wrote. I couldn't have been more delighted.

As you probably have noticed by now, the Japanese American world was usually earnest and sometimes grim. As an antidote, I tried to see the lighter side of things:

We were talking the other day about whether the Japanese are in fact as courteous as they are said to be. One's judgment should be based, I suppose, on the meaning of courtesy. If courtesy means respect for the social niceties, would it also mean the observance of social ritual? There's a difference. The Japanese do a lot of bowing, a heck of a lot of it. This must be considered a ritual that once expressed respect and deference, but it's quite likely that today a bow means scarcely more than the American question, "How are you?"

A European might say that the usually boorish American does express a concern for his fellow man by asking as to his health and general well-being. But "how are you" follows "hello" or "good morning" automatically these days, and the person who asks the question really doesn't expect any more of a reply than a perfunctory, "Fine, how are you?" If anyone stopped to give a detailed reply concerning his arthritis, sinus, hangnails, migraine and sundry other ailments, he would be considered an oddity and a boor.

So it is with the Japanese bow, which in most cases comes

as automatically as a chicken pecking for corn, and if I've been impolite about this, so sorry.

(July 3, 1970)

In the column for September 20, 1974, I deplored the shortage of smiles in Pacific Citizen *and announced an ethnic funny story contest with an autographed copy of Jack Matsuoka's cartoon book,* Camp II, Block 211 *as the prize. I said I would be surprised if there were more than a half-dozen entries and delighted if there were as many as a dozen. Well, I was delighted. Exactly twelve readers sent in stories. Some included several, and there were enough good ones to make judging a problem. I reported in the November 1 column:*

There were Issei stories, Nisei stories, Sansei stories, Chinese stories and even Hawaiian stories. For example, Hawaii-born Fumio Yoshida of Gardena, California, tells how his fourteen-year-old daughter Barbara Ann once asked: "Why do you Hawaiians use expressions like 'Da kine' and 'you know?' so often?" Thinking fast, Yoshida told her: "Us Hawaiians are really smart people because all we need to know is four words to express ourselves— 'da kine' and 'you know?'. Then the other party shows he knows the answer by saying, "Yeah, man." And Barbara Ann duly reported this to her teachers at school.

As a group, the Issei stories were best. Seiko Ishida of South Gate, California, tells of getting a letter from her father at Christmas time, written in Japanese, of course, saying *Suman kedo hon sukoshi mochiokure.* Seiko understood *hon sukoshi* to mean he wanted her to send him a few books and so mailed him some. Another way to read *hon sukoshi* is "just a very little" and Seiko's father had used it in that sense in asking her to send him a few New Year "mochi" cakes.

252

Tomi Hoshizaki of Los Angeles had another amusing Issei story. An Issei friend of hers kept talking about an entertainer named Shina Tora-san. Tomi thought she was referring to some Japanese singer whose name meant Chinese Tiger, but suddenly realized her friend was talking about Frank Sinatra.

Ellen Kishiyama of Santa Maria, California, recalls that her husband while on a trip to Japan wrote to her in Japanese. She could read the letter but it didn't make sense—the words were totally disconnected. She complained when he came home and he started to read it for her when suddenly he said: "You're right, something is odd. It doesn't make sense." Then it dawned on him. "You are a Nisei, an American," he said. "So I wrote the letter in Japanese but in the way Americans read, from left to right—not top to bottom and right to left."

Grace Iino of Los Angeles also relates a story in which language difficulty figures. The word *ataru* in Japanese can mean "to hit, or strike," and it can also mean to be affected by tainted food. Her uncle Ichiro once was hospitalized after eating some tainted shrimp tempura. Her brother, a youngster at the time, translated the overheard Japanese conversation and spread the news around the neighborhood in this manner: "Uncle Ichiro got hit on the head by a big tempura, bang!, and they had to take him to the hospital."

Sets Kishi of Carmichael, California, writes of her daughter Liana and her fair-skinned friend, Jennifer Wurschmidt. This past summer both girls spent much time outdoors. One day Jennifer noticed her tanned arms and cried jubilantly: "Look, Mommy, I'm beginning to look like Liana—except for my hair."

A. Miyazaki of St. Louis, Missouri, was named the winner of Jack Matsuoka's book with this story: A few weeks ago her Sansei cousin was shopping near her home in Kansas City when an Oriental clerk in one of the stores came up and spoke in a foreign language. The Sansei girl had never learned Japanese and quickly replied: "I'm sorry, but I don't speak Japanese." She was astonished when the clerk smiled and said: "Neither do I. I was speaking Chinese."

On occasion I tried to take a light approach to a serious subject, as in this imaginary conversation:

"Hey, Mac, you're the guy who knows everything. Lemme ask you a few questions. What do you think of the way *Time* wrote up our Congressman, Norman Mineta?"

"I thought it was a pretty good deal. The November 18 issue of *Time* named seven Democratic freshman congressmen as aggressive and articulate types who seem likely to be heard from in the new session and Mineta was one of them."

"Naw, that isn't what I mean. I'm talking about what they didn't say, rather than what they did say. They said Norman had a good record as mayor of San Jose and he criticized President Ford's WIN buttons as a public relations gimmick when what was really needed to control inflation was lower interest rates and strong antitrust action. What they did not say was that Norm's a Japanese American."

"Do you think they should have said that? Do you think they should have pointed out that he's the first Nisei from the mainland to be elected to Congress, that he spent his early 'teen years in a War Relocation Center?"

"Well, I don't know. That's why I'm asking you. *Time* pointed out that Congressman-elect Harold Ford of Tennessee is a Black, that Paul Tsongas of Massachusetts is of Greek descent, that a couple of Spanish-surnamed were elected governor in New Mexico and Arizona and that

254

George Ariyoshi in Hawaii became the 'first American of Japanese ancestry to reach a U.S. governor's mansion.' How come they didn't say something special about Norman Mineta?"

"Do you think that's really important? Apparently you do, or else you wouldn't be asking about it. Let's look at it this way. Maybe the editors of *Time* figured it really wasn't important any more to point out that Norman is Japanese American. After all, Dan Inouye is in the Senate, and Spark Matsunaga and Patsy Mink are House veterans. Maybe they figure that Japanese Americans are so much an integrated part of life in these United States that it isn't necessary to note Norman's ethnic background any more."

"You really believe that? I think it's still news when the first Nisei from the mainland gets elected to Congress and I think the editors of *Time* goofed when they neglected to mention it."

"Well, it's quite possible that the *Time* story in its original form did make note of Norman's race, but somehow it got cut out, along with a lot of information about a lot of different guys, because there just wasn't enough space to run it all. That sort of thing happens all the time. Most publications have a policy of mentioning a person's race or ethnic background only when that piece of information is necessary to a full understanding of the story. The only thing I can figure is that the editors of *Time* felt Norman Mineta is so much a part of the U.S. scene that his ancestry isn't pertinent. Now let me ask you a question. Suppose there was a guy named Joe Nisei, and he was involved in some horrible crime. Maybe he went berserk and shot down a bunch of people on the street and got in a battle with a whole regiment of cops before they finally flushed him out. Or let's say he pulled the swindle of the century in a plot so well-conceived that he baffled everyone before he got

255

tripped up. Do you think he ought to be identified as a Japanese American?"

"Aw, come off it, Mac. That isn't the same thing, is it?"

"Well, I don't know. It seems to be about the same thing. What you are saying, it seems to me, is that we ought to identify a Japanese American as such when he does something great, and that we should ignore the fact when he's in trouble. Right?"

"Well, I'm not sure. That's why I asked you the question in the first place. And all you did was confuse me even more."

"That's probably because I'm not sure myself."

(December 6, 1974)

And sometimes there was the ridiculous:

Among the goodies left by the U.S. mail a few weeks ago was an astonishing letter which I shall proceed to quote. It arrived first class and it began this way:
Good news for the Hosokawa family!

Did you know that the family name Hosokawa has an exclusive and particularly beautiful Coat of Arms?

I thought you might be interested, so we've had a heraldic artist recreate the Hosokawa Coat of Arms in color exactly as the heralds of medieval times did it for the knights and noblemen. Mounted on a Classic Plaque, it will add warmth and refinement to your living room, den or office. But rather than describe it, I decided to send you a photo with our own Halbert Coat of Arms on it, so you could see for yourself. (Photo enclosed.)

The Hosokawa Coat of Arms in full color will be set against the regal red flocking and mounted on a 14″ × 17″ frame. People with a flare for interior decoration recognize the plaque as a highly valued personal accessory for original wall decoration. And it's a most welcome and appreciated gift for relatives named Hosokawa.

Since we have already researched your family name and have the Hosokawa Coat of Arms on hand, we can offer it to you in full color for only $19.95. If you've shopped for similar wall plaques in department or furniture stores, you'll really appreciate this fine value. . . . Remember, you risk nothing. . . .

The letter was signed by Nancy L. Halbert of Bath, Ohio, and if I had $19.95 to spare I'd send it to good old Nancy just to see what her researchers in merrie olde medieval England have come up with in the way of a Hosokawa family coat of arms. Stalks of rice, perhaps, rampant on a rice paddy under crossed chopsticks. Anything much different from that would be a brazen forgery because the honorable ancestors were rice farmers, not knights or even samurai, as far back as anyone can determine. Chances are they were too busy trying to feed themselves and their families, and staying out of the way of samurai itching to test the sharpness of their swords, to be concerned about coats of arms even if they knew what they were.

Aristocratic and wealthy Japanese had their *mon,* a sort of family crest that they imprinted on their possessions but the Hosokawa had, and still have, so little that a *mon* is a waste of time. And as far as I know, none of them left the homeland for Europe or anywhere else until Pop Setsugo Hosokawa came to the U.S. of A. back in 1899. His father was Zenshiro H., who married Riu Shinkawa. Zenshiro's father was Yaohei H., and there the record seems to stop.

Pa married Kimiyo Omura, whose father was Yosaku O., and his father was Bunemon O. Yosaku married Uta Kunihiro whose father was Buhei K., whose father in turn was Yoshizaburo K.

I gather that the record stops along about here because,

257

until fairly recent times, Japanese common people had only one name. Then it was decreed that they could have two names, just like the rich and important folks, and so my branch of the Hosokawa clan came into being.

And if Mrs. Halbert of Bath, Ohio, can find a coat of arms out of all that, one must admit with some admiration that she has a powerfully productive imagination. It just might be worth $19.95 to find out what she'd come up with. Come to think of it, this plaque might make a nice gift for my cousin's son, Tetsuji Fukeda, who was kind enough to dig up the information about my ancestors. He'd get a kick out of learning what's important to us Americans these days.

(February 21, 1975)

In the Pacific Northwest, and Colorado as well, the Issei loved to hunt for mushrooms in the fall. They were interested only in one variety, which was hard to find. This brought out the best and the worst in them, and oddly enough many Nisei also became interested in mushrooms and displayed the same characteristics. All that made for a column:

This is being written as another wild mushroom season hurries to a close, and none too soon. For mushroom season is a time of high elation and deep deceit, of envy and greed and even an occasional display of nobility.

The mushroom is the Japanese *matsutake*. The scientific Latin name is *Armillaria ponderosa*. In some years it is found abundantly in the evergreen forests of the Northwest. It is found considerably less abundantly in the Rockies which perhaps is the reason it is sought so, shall we say, desperately.

The most popular mushroom grounds hereabouts are in Roosevelt National Forest, in the Red Feather Lakes area, a good two and a half- to three-hour drive from Denver,

depending on how violently one shatters the 55 m.p.h. highway speed limit.

Although these mushrooms are seldom up before mid-
August, the more rabid enthusiasts begin dreaming about
them any time after the Fourth of July. By the first of
August they can hardly contain themselves. And when they
finally do head for the mountains, they start out in the
middle of the night so they can be on the scene at the crack
of dawn.

Even though mushrooms, unlike wandering deer or elk,
are inanimate objects and cannot escape, the hunters feel
a need to pursue them as early in the morning as possible.
And when they see a specimen they cannot repress an urge
to leap for it as if it were a frog or squirrel that would flee.

Mushroom hunters are secretive about almost everything.
They won't tell their closest friends if they know a secret
forest glen that produces mushrooms. In fact, they are
downright deceitful, which everyone accepts, and they talk
in a kind of code which everyone understands and makes
allowances for. Let me give you a few examples.

A friend reports: "The Red Feather Lakes area is terribly dry, they haven't had any rain for months and nobody's finding any mushrooms." If you know the code, you
can translate that to mean: "It's been raining like hell up
there and mushrooms are popping up all over the place."

Or take this gem: "We found a few last Sunday, but we
had to walk two and a half miles over three ranges of
mountains." The real meaning is, "We found a half bucket
just a hundred feet off the side of the road," and the falsehood is told to discourage the listener from going mushroom hunting because of the hard hike allegedly involved.

If someone says plenty of mushrooms are to be found
by taking to the woods on the left side of the road after the
third horseshoe bend, the experienced listener makes it a
point to try the right side after the fifth or sixth bend.

One can learn to understand code, but there is no way of making sense of the directions shared by well-meaning, honest, but totally disoriented womenfolk. Their conversation might go like this:

"You know the place by the big rock and the forked tree where you can see a meadow? Well, you walk in to the left there past some red pines and an aspen grove and I heard that's a good place."

The listener takes it all in and makes a mental note, but in reality she's thinking of another place with a bigger rock and an unforked tree ten miles up the highway. She goes to the spot she thought her friend described, but it's the wrong place and there are no mushrooms there, and that's the end of a beautiful friendship.

Most folks agree the best part of mushroom hunting is finding them. That's the moment of ecstacy. Once you have them, you can gloat a while, eat some, freeze some. But mostly you give them away to the smart ones who stay at home, or airmail them at horrendous cost to friends and relatives in California. People who are habitually generous develop an all-consuming greed when they go mushrooming. They want to pick every last mushroom. They envy others who find more. But once they return home, they resume their natural generous, amiable characteristics. Do you suppose *matsutake* also have hallucinogenic properties?

(October 10, 1975)

16

To the Present

A book, like almost everything else, must have a beginning, a middle and an end. Although the Frying Pan column continues, this collection must stop somewhere. It does so with several columns that bring the story to full circle as you will discover in reading them.

Among our dearest friends in Denver was Patricia Mechau, whose husband Vaughn (better known as Bonnie) had had a special part in my life:

Pat Mechau died the other day. Her tired old heart finally gave out and she died quietly in a hospital bed. There was no funeral because she didn't want one. The remains were cremated, as she requested, but she left a world of memories for a lot of fortunate people who had known her.

A day later her daughters, Joan and Barbara, were going through her things and they found an old Gruen wristwatch. It was a man's Curvex, that is, the case was slightly curved to fit the contours of the wearer's wrist and that had made it a popular model thirty years ago.

Engraved into the 14 karat gold of the case was a little scroll, and in it was this message: THE SENTINEL. TO BONNIE MECHAU 1942–1945.

Joan and Barbara weren't quite sure what those words meant, but I knew. This is what I told them:

Bonnie Mechau was the friendly, cheerful reports officer at the Heart Mountain WRA camp in Wyoming. He had a love for people and a deep dislike of red tape and bureaucratic paper shuffling. That's what made him such a favorite with the evacuees, and sometimes the despair of the administration.

Technically, Bonnie was "adviser" to the staff of the Heart Mountain *Sentinel,* probably the best of the WRA camp newspapers. In reality he let the evacuee staff run its own show and they loved him for it.

When it came time for the camp to close, those remaining on the staff, headed by Haruo Imura, figured it would be a nice gesture to give Bonnie a remembrance in token of their appreciation and affection. They took up a collection and they wrote to former staffers who had relocated to places like Chicago and New York and even Des Moines and invite them to participate. With the money they collected they bought the Gruen watch and had it engraved.

Bonnie wore the watch with pride when postwar jobs took him to Paraguay, Brazil, and Korea. When he was based in Libya he had to fly to Germany on assignment one day and there he suffered a heart attack that killed him. Pat brought the ashes back home to Denver and the wristwatch was in her purse.

She must have put the watch in a drawer and probably had forgotten about it. And that's where Joan and Barbara found it.

Bonnie, indirectly, was the reason I and my family moved

to Denver. One day early in 1946 I dropped him a note from Des Moines after reading in *Time* about the death of his brother Frank, an outstanding artist. Bonnie wrote back asking why I didn't pull up stakes and head West. I inquired about jobs. Bonnie went down to the Denver *Post* and asked whether they were hiring. They said yes and he encouraged me to send them an application.

Six months later I was in Denver and Pat fed me a big meal to welcome me. Barbara was still in high school then. Joan was going to nursing school back east somewhere. The Mechaus were my staff and support until I learned to get around in Denver.

Now, Joan asked if I would like to have Bonnie's watch. Well, I already have a watch. And the Gruen, like a 1946 automobile, is somewhat dated.

But it is rich in memories. I accepted it with thanks as a sentimental memento. I'll put it away in a drawer, and someday somebody will find it and wonder why I was keeping an old watch with Bonnie Mechau's name engraved on it.

I guess the answer is that I accepted the watch because Bonnie and Pat were my friends.

(October 17, 1975)

In the fall of 1975 Japan's Emperor Hirohito made a precedent-shattering visit to the United States. He was welcomed warmly by President Ford and the American public greeted him with enthusiasm wherever he went. The bitter memories of World War II had been pushed aside in favor of a new era of friendly hands across the Pacific. It disturbed me that some Japanese Americans were not similarly realistic about changing times, but continued to brood and bitch about wartime injustices. I realized that many of these individuals were too young to have experienced the Evacuation personally, but had made a career of dissent. Nonetheless I was moved to write:

263

Some newspaper pundits, who are paid handsomely to explain things to the rest of us, say Emperor Hirohito's visit to the United States is considered in Japan as finally closing the book on the war.

At the White House state dinner the Emperor thanked the American people for helping to reconstruct Japan after the war which he described as "most unfortunate" and one "I deeply deplore."

In a sense it was an apology without formally being one. Equally important, the gesture put distasteful memories of World War II behind both nations, and opened the way for a new era of friendship and cooperation for world-wide peace and prosperity.

This raises an interesting point for Nisei and Sansei.

If the United States, which was attacked even as Japanese envoys were still talking peace in Washington, and Japan, which suffered grievously (including nuclear bombing) in defeat, if these two nations can put memories of that bitter war behind them and look toward closer cooperative relations in the future, is it then also time that we quit harping about the injustice of the Evacuation and concentrate instead on more constructive themes?

That's a terribly long sentence, but the meaning ought to be clear.

There are many who contend, with good reason, that the memory of the Evacuation must be kept alive so that we, the American people, will never perpetrate such an outrage again.

The same, of course, could be said of war itself, the ultimate outrage. The United States and Japan have in effect closed the book on the unpleasant past so they can focus on the present and the future. Can Japanese Americans do less?

(November 7, 1975)

Another gesture toward "closing the book" took place in the White House early in 1976. I was privileged to witness it:

Last October, Wayne K. Horiuchi, JACL's energetic young Washington representative sent out a number of letters asking for support for a campaign to get President Ford to rescind Executive Order 9066. That, as you may recall, was the document signed by President Roosevelt which provided legal authority for the Evacuation.

E.O. 9066 was a wartime measure and presumably it died with the formal proclamation ending hostilities on December 31, 1946. Still, nothing had been done to take E.O. 9066 specifically off the statute books. Horiuchi and Dave Ushio, the national executive director, figured it would be a good idea to get that done.

In response to their invitation, various citizens wrote to express astonishment that E.O. 9066 still existed and to urge President Ford to take care of that oversight. These letters were delivered to the White House with the support and encouragement of Washington's Governor Daniel J. Evans and various members of the White House staff. The target date for action was February 19, 1976, the thirty-fourth anniversary of the bill's signing.

But weeks went by and nothing happened. It appeared the anniversary date would pass without action. Then the matter was brought to the attention of Dr. Myron B. Kuropas, who had joined the White House staff less than two months earlier to look after ethnic matters. Kuropas, of Ukrainian descent, had been Midwest director of the federal ACTION program where he had come to know George Wakiji, a VISTA public information officer. Kuropas agreed to see what he could do.

On Tuesday, February 17, Horiuchi was told to stand by. President Ford might be able to sign a proclamation rescinding E.O. 9066. Ushio, in San Francisco, caught a late night plane for Washington to help with arrangements. Word that the signing was definitely scheduled came from the White House after noon on Wednesday, February 18. The ceremony would take place at 11:30 A.M. next day—less than twenty-four hours later—in the Cabinet Room.

Ushio got on the phone to round up some of the Nisei who had written in response to Horiuchi's appeal. Those in Washington were no problem. But those in California would have to fly across the continent.

Meanwhile the White House reached Senators Dan Inouye and Hiram Fong, and Spark Matsunaga, Patsy Mink and Norman Mineta from the House of Representatives. They were joined in the White House Thursday morning by perhaps twenty-five Nisei, including California state Representatives Paul Bannai and Floyd Mori and the city clerk of Carson, California, Helen Kawagoe.

Most of the West Coast delegation flew the "red-eye specials," the planes that leave San Francisco and Los Angeles late at night and reach Washington just in time to disgorge their passengers into the morning traffic jam. They assembled at Ushio's hotel room to shave (except Helen, of course) and shower and put on a fresh shirt.

But when President Ford strode into the room, fifteen minutes behind schedule, sat down and read a brief statement before the television and newspaper cameras, the effort seemed eminently worthwhile.

"We now know what we should have known then (in 1942)," the President said. "Not only was that evacuation wrong, but Japanese Americans were and are loyal Americans. . . . I call upon the American people to affirm with me this American Promise—that we have learned from the tragedy of that long-ago experience forever to treasure liberty and justice for each individual American, and resolve that this kind of action shall never again be repeated."

266

There were misty eyes among many of the Nisei who heard those words intoned. President Ford signed the proclamation, then shook hands with all the Nisei present before hurrying away to campaign in New Hampshire. As he left the room, Kuropas passed out to all witnesses souvenir pens bearing facsimiles of Gerald Ford's signature. The President had not signed the proclamation with any of these gift pens, but chances are each will be proudly displayed in years to come as The Pen that ended E.O. 9066.

(March 5, 1976)

A few months later there was another event that tied the past to the present:

Unless you were an adult member of the Evacuation Generation in 1942, it might be difficult to understand the degree of political courage it required for Colorado's Governor Ralph Carr to do what he did. He stood up in front of God and the voters to say he didn't think the Japanese Americans were guilty of anything and they were welcome to come to his state to escape the hysteria touched off by the attack on Pearl Harbor.

That simple act of decency probably ruined Carr's political career. He and a rock-ribbed conservative Democrat named Ed C. Johnson were competing for a seat in the U.S. Senate and Big Ed won. Johnson became a sort of political legend in Colorado, which he served with great diligence, but his isolationist views were a thorn in the side of a series of Presidents.

A few Saturdays ago a bust of Carr paid for with funds collected by a committee of Japanese Americans was dedicated at Denver's Sakura Square. "Those who benefited from Governor Carr's humanity," the inscription reads in part, "have built this monument in grateful memory of his

267

unflinching Americanism, and as a lasting reminder that the precious democratic ideals he espoused must forever be defended against prejudice and neglect."

The memorial was a long time in coming—more than thirty-four years after Carr stated his position, thirty years after war's end, twenty-six years after Carr's death. Yet, better late than never.

It was the deep sense of Issei *giri* and *on*—the obligation to repay a moral debt—that kept the Carr memorial project alive until Nisei of the community could be persuaded to carry the ball. So it was the Nisei who worked out the project's details. And those of the younger generations, who have demonstrated a great capacity for vicarious and rhetorical outrage at the injustice of the Evacuation despite their unfamiliarity with it, were noticeably absent on both the committee and at the dedication itself.

It would have done them good to stand in the hot sun and listen to the words of Dillon S. Myer, who as director of the War Relocation Authority had the decency and the moral fiber to stand up against the bigots and hate-mongers and the political opportunists who found a convenient target in the Japanese Americans.

The weight of the years have stooped Dillon Myer, but his mind remains sharp. He could have talked a long time to the gathered throng about the WRA, the fortitude of the evacuees that sharpened his resolve to see that justice was done, the sacrifice of Nisei who stepped out from behind barbed wire enclosures to fight and die for their country and dramatize the horror of the Evacuation, the trials he faced and the ultimate triumph. But out of deference to the length of the program and the merciless heat of the sun, he cut his speech short.

"I wish he had completed his address," said a member of the audience who had never experienced the Evacuation, and there must have been many who shared the thought.

268

The years of the WRA camps were distant, the contemporary affluence of the former evacuees apparent as they stood at the foot of the massive Tamai Towers apartment complex for the dedication. But it was easy for the mind to wander back to the misery and desolation of the camps. Denver's late summer sun, beating down from a cloudless sky, sapped the vitality of those who braved it. It was the same kind of heat that made ovens of barracks at Poston, Gila, Topaz, Granada, Heart Mountain, Minidoka, Manzanar, and Tule Lake and made the humidity nearly unbearable at Jerome and Rohwer. Occasionally there was a puff of wind, and they stirred memories of the dust clouds that rose with any movement of man or air in the camps and seeped into the barracks so that even the bedding smelled of it. This time, fortunately, everyone was able to flee into the air-conditioned gymnasium of the Buddhist church for cooling refreshments. In another time, there was no escape.

The Carr bust, despite the skill with which his likeness was fashioned into bronze, is in reality a lifeless thing unless it is made into something more than a convenient roost for pigeons. It can be brought to life only if it will inspire those who view it with the will to stand up for principle.

In this sense, perhaps the gratitude of those who contributed to the project could better have been expressed by a living memorial of some kind. But the deed has been done, the bronze cast, the granite shaped, and the inscription cut into it. What is made of all this is now up to us.

(September 10, 1976)

All across the land, one by one, the barriers that had frustrated Japanese Americans for so long continued to fall. None was more significant than the election of Dr. Samuel Ichiye Hayakawa as United States senator from California in the fall of 1976:

It must have been three years ago that a newspaper editor in San Jose, California, told me that Dr. S. I. Hayakawa was thinking seriously of running for the U.S. senate. Hayakawa had been traveling around California taking soundings, the editor said, and had been encouraged by what he heard.

That appeared far-fetched at the time. Hayakawa was still riding the crest of the popularity he gained as the no-nonsense president of San Francisco State. But could a foreign-born Japanese American—naturalized, of course—old enough to qualify for Social Security and making his first bid for political office, persuade the people of the sovereign state of California to elect him to the United States senate? It seemed to be a "mission impossible" for a "Japanese" to succeed to the California mantle once worn by the likes of James D. Phelan, U.S. Webb, and Hiram Johnson, who had enjoyed long and successful political careers based on baiting and hating Japanese Americans.

More than three million Californians demonstrated that times had changed by casting their ballots for Hayakawa last week. Hayakawa's Japanese ancestry was never a serious issue in a campaign that was marked by more than a little wackiness. The nimble Hayakawa played his maverick role to the full and seldom gave his opponent, incumbent John Tunney, a solid target.

And so Hayakawa, in the twilight of an illustrious career, goes to Washington as the Senate's oldest freshman and one of three Japanese Americans in the upper house. Hawaii's Dan Inouye is the senior member of this unlikely triumvirate. The other is Spark Matsunaga, who moved up after serving Hawaii long and well in the House.

If anything, these three Nisei will demonstrate that Japanese Americans are a diverse group with different opinions about different matters. Inouye has shown himself to be a solid mainline Democrat, hewing closely on most issues to the party line. Matsunaga, also a Democrat, has been more liberal. Both are popular with Japanese Americans.

Hayakawa, born in Vancouver, British Columbia, is a Republican. He is looked upon by many as a conservative, although they overlook the fact that he is a jazz buff who was closely associated with Black rights movements long before that became popular. And the Japanese American community is sharply divided on him. Many Sansei and younger Nisei opposed him vigorously.

The Japanese Americans, with a population of something like 0.3 per cent of the national total, will now have a 3 per cent representation in the Senate. This may make them proportionately the most heavily represented ethnic minority in the Senate, but it seems unlikely the three of them will vote together on very many issues.

It also seems somewhat unlikely that Hayakawa ever will have to plead guilty to being a politician, but he can bring honesty, integrity, humor and logic to Congress, which it can stand in generous measure.

(November 12, 1976)

For years Japanese Americans were puzzled by the performance of Earl Warren. As California's attorney general, he had taken the cheap, popular political stand against them in 1942. Yet, as Chief Justice of the Supreme Court, he had been responsible for many landmark civil rights decisions. Some believed that Warren's realization of the grievous wrong he had done the Japanese Americans caused him to search his soul, and that resulted in the enlightened view he adopted on human rights matters. Many Nisei would have liked to hear Warren say he was sorry, but he refused to speak out in public. The "apology" these Japanese Americans sought finally came out after Warren's death in his

271

memoirs, but it wasn't anything like what had been expected:

Some folks are making quite a to-do about the fact that Earl Warren, in his recently published memoirs, expressed regret that he pressed for the evacuation of Japanese Americans during World War II.

He does indeed express unequivocal remorse in the book (*The Memoirs of Chief Justice Earl Warren*, Doubleday). These are the precise words from page 149:

"I have since deeply regretted the removal order and my own testimony advocating it, because it was not in keeping with our American concept of freedom and the rights of citizens. Whenever I thought of the innocent little children who were torn from home, school friends, and congenial surroundings, I was conscience-stricken. It was wrong to react so impulsively, without positive evidence of disloyalty, even though we felt we had a good motive in the security of our state. It demonstrates the cruelty of war when fear, get-tough military psychology, propaganda, and racial antagonism combine with one's responsibility for public security to produce such acts."

Straightforward enough. Yet it all seems to be a peculiar and curious statement from the man who went on to become a distinguished Chief Justice of the United States Supreme Court.

Let us back up a moment to lay out the circumstances of which Warren speaks. He was attorney general of California in early 1942. He was charged with defending the rights of Californians and enforcing the laws of the state. He chose, instead, to demand the civil rights of Japanese Americans be violated and that the laws pertaining to those rights be suspended where the Japanese American minority was concerned.

In taking the position that Warren did in 1942, he became involved in some deep philosophical issues about Constitutional rights, issues that he had to wrestle with in later years as Supreme Court Justice. The decisions at which he arrived while on the Court did much to force Americans to recognize the rights of all minorities, particularly the Blacks.

Yet—and this is the curious part—Warren in his book makes no mention of the specific legal rights that were violated by the Evacuation. He ignores the issues that were raised by the Yasui and Hirabayashi law suits that challenged the military's selective curfew order against civilians in the absence of martial law, and the Korematsu and Endo cases that challenged the legality of the Evacuation and continued incarceration.

The Supreme Court, before Warren joined it, heard some of these cases. The Court upheld the contention that the military was justified in ordering the evacuation of Japanese Americans on a racial basis, and that precedent still stands more than three decades later. Warren chose to ignore these facts in his book. He chose, instead, to devote one paragraph of his book telling about how his conscience hurt him when he remembered that he had helped to put innocent little children behind the barbed wire of American concentration camps.

It is also peculiar that Warren devotes several pages (about the same amount of space that he gave the entire subject of Japanese Americans) to the role he had played in chasing the prostitutes out of towns near California military camps. Thus, he indicates, he helped reduce the venereal disease rate among the troops and contributed to the national defense. Were these episodes of equal importance in his life?

It is a notable footnote to history that Earl Warren, after all these years of silence, finally got around to admitting he was wrong in 1942. But it is only an awkward, mawkish admission when he could have made it so much more. It is a sorry performance, totally unworthy of an American who contributed so much to the progress of his country.

(August 15, 1977)

For the final item I go back to a portion of a column published March 12, 1971. It epitomizes the problem Japanese have had, and often continue to have, in their own country—their identity as Americans:

A large part of the Establishment in Casper, Wyoming, is of postwar vintage. As in most other Western cities the natives are scarce, and vigorous newcomers have moved into positions of influence and authority. A few Casper oldtimers remember when there was "that camp" up around Cody. When the subject comes up they cluck-cluck sympathetically, recalling what a bad thing it was. But they are vague about details because that was long ago, and besides they didn't pay much attention to the fact that American citizens were being held behind barbed wire in their state. They had been preoccupied with other matters.

Thus it is not surprising when on introduction a member of the Establishment shakes hands warmly and in his friendliest manner asks: "How long have you been in this country, Mr. Hosokawa?"

"Over fifty-five years," I tell him, and surprise creeps into his eyes. Surely his next question would have been, "How do you like our country?" but he never gets a chance to ask it because he realizes he has committed a faux pas in assuming that this stranger with the Oriental face was a foreigner. Perhaps his embarrassment will be assurance that he will not make the same mistake again. Still, it points up the necessity for Nisei to get around the country even more than they do, making themselves known.

Actually, this Establishment man knows better. There

are a few—not many—Nisei in Casper. He has had other contacts with Nisei in his business. He knows what the Nisei are. He just wasn't thinking, he just simply assumed when he saw Asiatic features that the man was a foreigner. But then, it is just this sort of careless, thoughtless assumptions that the Nisei must continue to fight against if they are to reach their goal of winning complete acceptance in their time as unhyphenated Americans.

Index

278

279

281

283